# Workshop on Unsupervised Learning in NLP 2011



**Held at EMNLP 2011**

## Edinburgh, Scotland, UK
## 30 July 2011

**ISBN: 978-1-61839-258-9**

**Printed from e-media with permission by:**

Curran Associates, Inc.
57 Morehouse Lane
Red Hook, NY 12571

**Some format issues inherent in the e-media version may also appear in this print version.**



Printed by Curran Associates, Inc. (2011)



Association for Computational Linguistics
209 N. Eighth Street
Stroudsburg, Pennsylvania 18360

Phone: 1-570-476-8006
Fax: 1-570-476-0860

acl@aclweb.org

**Additional copies of this publication are available from:**

Curran Associates, Inc.
57 Morehouse Lane
Red Hook, NY 12571 USA
Phone: 845-758-0400
Fax: 845-758-2634
Email: curran@proceedings.com
Web: www.proceedings.com

# Introduction

The rapid growth in the amount of computer-readable text in different languages, along with ever developing computational resources, raise much interest in fully automated algorithms for analyzing massive amounts of plain text without using any manually provided input. In addition to obviating the need for costly manual annotation, this line of research gives rise to exciting theoretical questions, exploring what information can be extracted purely by distributional analysis, and characterizing the theoretical significance of the output of such an automatic analysis.

Unsupervised learning is the main approach in NLP for addressing this challenge. Although this approach has grown in popularity over the past years and increasingly sophisticated methodology has been introduced, several fundamental challenges remain which need to be resolved and which cannot be effectively discussed in major conferences. This workshop aims to bridge this gap, by summarizing what has been achieved so far in unsupervised learning in NLP, by fostering discussions on these fundamental issues, and by discussing future trends.

The workshop encourages discussion on topics such as evaluation of unsupervised algorithms, comparison of different algorithmic approaches, and unsupervised learning across multiple languages. Our invited talk by Sharon Goldwater discusses the role unsupervised learning can play on shedding light on human cognition. The workshop program also includes papers that address unsupervised approaches for a broad variety of NLP tasks, ranging from syntactic parsing to lexical semantics. Finally, the workshop holds a panel discussion for exchanging ideas between leading researchers in the area, in order to gain some insight into how to best tackle the current big challenges in unsupervised NLP.

It is our hope that this workshop will provide a better understanding of this research area, and will initiate a series of workshops devoted to this important topic.

Omri Abend, Anna Korhonen, Ari Rappoport and Roi Reichart
*UNSUP 2011* Organizers

**Organizers:**

Omri Abend (Hebrew University of Jerusalem, Israel)
Anna Korhonen (University of Cambridge, UK)
Ari Rappoport (Hebrew University of Jerusalem, Israel)
Roi Reichart (MIT, USA)

**Program Committee:**

Eneko Agirre (University of the Basque Country, Spain)
Jason Baldridge (University of Texas at Austin, USA)
Tim Baldwin (University of Melbourne, Australia)
Sam Brody (Columbia University, USA)
Alexander Clark (Royal Holloway, University of London, UK)
Shay Cohen (Carnegie Mellon University, USA)
Mona Diab (Columbia University, USA)
Gregory Druck (University of Massachusetts Amherst, USA)
Jason Eisner (Johns Hopkins University, USA)
Sharon Goldwater (University of Edinburgh, UK)
Joao Graca (University of Pennsylvania, USA)
Ioannis Klapaftis (University of York, UK)
Lillian Lee (Cornell University, USA)
Percy Liang (UC Berkeley, USA)
Diana McCarthy (Lexical Computing, Ltd., UK)
Preslav Nakov (National University of Singapore, Singapore)
Roberto Navigli (University of Rome, Italy)
Vincent Ng (UT Dallas, USA)
Ted Pedersen (University of Minnesota, USA)
Andrew Rosenberg (CUNY, USA)
Valentin Spitkovsky (Stanford University, USA)
Carlo Strapparava (FBK-irst, Italy)
Ben Taskar (University of Pennsylvania, USA)
Kristina Toutanova (Microsoft Research, USA)
Andreas Vlachos (University of Wisconsin-Madison, USA)

**Invited Speaker:**

Sharon Goldwater, Institute for Language, Cognition and Computation, University of Edinburg, UK

# Table of Contents

# Conference Program

**July 30th, 2011**

**(9:00-9:15) Opening Words**

**(9:15-10:30) Invited Talk**

*Unsupervised NLP and Human Language Acquisition: Making Connections to Make Progress*
Sharon Goldwater

**(10:30-11:00) Coffee Break**

**(11:00:12:30) Morning Session**

*Structured Databases of Named Entities from Bayesian Nonparametrics*
Jacob Eisenstein, Tae Yano, William Cohen, Noah Smith and Eric Xing

*Unsupervised Cross-Lingual Lexical Substitution*
Marianna Apidianaki

*Reducing the Size of the Representation for the uDOP-Estimate*
Christoph Teichmann

**(12:30-14:00) Lunch Break**

**(14:00-14:30) Noon Session**

*Evaluating unsupervised learning for natural language processing tasks*
Andreas Vlachos

# Abstract for the Invited Talk

Unsupervised NLP and Human Language Acquisition: Making Connections to Make Progress
*Sharon Goldwater*

Natural language processing and cognitive science are two fields in which unsupervised language learning is an important area of research. Yet there is often little crosstalk between the two fields. In this talk, I will argue that considering the problem of unsupervised language learning from a cognitive perspective can lead to useful insights for the NLP researcher, while also showing how tools and methods from NLP and machine learning can shed light on human language acquisition. I will present two case examples, both of them models inspired by cognitive questions. The first is a model of word segmentation, which introduced new modeling and inference techniques into NLP while also yielding a better fit than previous models to human behavioral data on word segmentation. The second is more recent work on unsupervised grammar induction, in which prosodic cues are used to help identify syntactic boundaries. Preliminary results indicate that such cues can be helpful, but also reveal weaknesses in existing unsupervised grammar induction methods from NLP, suggesting possible directions for future research.

*Proceedings of EMNLP 2011, Conference on Empirical Methods in Natural Language Processing*, page 1,
Edinburgh, Scotland, UK, July 27–31, 2011. ©2011 Association for Computational Linguistics

# Structured Databases of Named Entities from Bayesian Nonparametrics

**Jacob Eisenstein Tae Yano William W. Cohen Noah A. Smith Eric P. Xing**
School of Computer Science
Carnegie Mellon University
Pittsburgh, PA 15213, USA
{jacobeis,taey,wcohen,nasmith,epxing}@cs.cmu.edu

## Abstract

We present a nonparametric Bayesian approach to extract a structured database of entities from text. Neither the number of entities nor the fields that characterize each entity are provided in advance; the only supervision is a set of five prototype examples. Our method jointly accomplishes three tasks: (i) identifying a set of canonical entities, (ii) inferring a schema for the fields that describe each entity, and (iii) matching entities to their references in raw text. Empirical evaluation shows that the approach learns an accurate database of entities and a sensible model of name structure.

## 1 Introduction

Consider the task of building a set of structured records from a collection of text: for example, extracting the names of people or businesses from blog posts, where each full name decomposes into fields corresponding to *first-name*, *last-name*, *title*, etc. To instruct a person to perform this task, one might begin with a few examples of the records to be obtained; assuming that the mapping from text to records is relatively straightforward, no additional instruction would be necessary. In this paper, we present a method for training information extraction software in the same way: starting from a small table of partially-complete "prototype" records (Table 1), our system learns to add new entries and fields to the table, while simultaneously aligning the records to text.

| | | | | | |
|---|---|---|---|---|---|
| John | McCain | Sen. | | | Mr. |
| George | Bush | | W. | | Mr. |
| Hillary | Clinton | | | Rodham | Mrs. |
| Barack | Obama | Sen. | | | |
| Sarah | Palin | | | | |

Table 1: A set of partially-complete prototype records, which constitutes the only supervision for the system.

We assume that the dimensionality of the database is unknown, so that neither the number of entries nor the number of fields is specified in advance. To accommodate this uncertainty, we apply a Bayesian model which is nonparametric along three dimensions: the assignment of text mentions to entities (making popular entries more likely while always allowing new entries); the alignment of individual text tokens to fields (encouraging the re-use of common fields, but permitting the creation of new fields); and the assignment of values to entries in the database itself (encouraging the reuse of values across entries in a given field). By adaptively updating the concentration parameter of stick-breaking distribution controlling the assignment of values to entries in the database, our model can learn domain-specific information about each field: for example, that titles are often repeated, while names are more varied.

Our system's input consists of a very small prototype table and a corpus of text which has been automatically segmented to identify names. Our desired output is a set of structured records in which each field contains a single string — not a distribution over strings, which would be more difficult to interpret. This requirement induces a tight probabilistic coupling between the assignment of text to cells in the table, so special care is required to ob-

*Proceedings of EMNLP 2011, Conference on Empirical Methods in Natural Language Processing*, pages 2–12,
Edinburgh, Scotland, UK, July 27–31, 2011. 

tain efficient inference. Our procedure alternates between two phases. In the first phase, we perform collapsed Gibbs sampling on the assignments of string mentions to rows and columns in the table, while marginalizing the values of the table itself. In the second phase, we apply Metropolis-Hastings to swap the values of columns in the table, while simultaneously relabeling the affected strings in the text.

Our model performs three tasks: it constructs a set of entities from raw text, matches mentions in text with the entities to which they refer, and discovers general categories of tokens that appear in names (such as titles and first names). We are aware of no existing system that performs all three of these tasks jointly. We evaluate on a dataset of political blogs, measuring our system's ability to discover a set of reference entities (recall) while maintaining a compact number of rows and columns (precision). With as few as five partially-complete prototype examples, our approach gives accurate tables that match well against a manually-annotated reference list. Our method outperforms a baseline single-link clustering approach inspired by one of the most successful entries (Elmacioglu et al., 2007) in the SEMEVAL "Web People Search" shared task (Artiles et al., 2007).

## 2 Task Definition

In this work, we assume that a bag of $M$ *mentions* in text have been identified. The $m$th mention $\boldsymbol{w}_m$ is a sequence of contiguous word tokens (its length is denoted $N_m$) understood to refer to a real-world *entity*. The entities (and the mapping of mentions to entities) are not known in advance. While our focus in this paper is names of people, the task is defined in a more generic way.

Formally, the task is to construct a table $\mathbf{x}$ where rows correspond to entities and columns to functional *fields*. The number of entities and the number of fields are not prespecified. $\boldsymbol{x}_{\cdot,j}$ denotes the $j$th column of $\mathbf{x}$, and $x_{i,j}$ is a single word type filling the cell in row $i$, column $j$. An example is Table 1, where the fields are first-name, last-name, title, middle-name, and so on. In addition to the table, we require that each mention be mapped to an entity (i.e., a row in the table). Success at this task therefore requires (i) identifying entities, (ii) discovering the internal structure of mentions (effectively canonicalizing them), and (iii) mapping mentions to entities (therefore resolving coreference relationships among mentions). Note that this task differs from previous work on knowledge base population (e.g., McNamee, 2009) because the schema is not formally defined in advance; rather, the number of fields and their meaning must be induced from just a few prototype examples.

To incorporate partial supervision, a subset of the table $\mathbf{x}$ is specified manually by an annotator. We denote this subset of "prototypes" by $\tilde{\mathbf{x}}$; for entries that are unspecified by the user, we write $\tilde{x}_{i,j} = \varnothing$. Prototypes are not assumed to provide complete information for any entity.

## 3 Model

We now craft a nonparametric generative story that explains both the latent table and the observed mentions. The model incorporates three nonparametric components, allowing an unbounded number of rows (entities) and columns (fields), as well as an unbounded number of values per column (field values). A plate diagram for the graphical model is shown in Figure 1.

A key point is that the column distributions $\phi$ range over possible values at the entity level, not over mentions in text. For example, $\phi_2$ might be the distribution over possible last names and $\phi_3$ the distribution over elected office titles. Note that $\phi_2$ would contain a low value for the last name *Obama* — which indicates that few people have this last name — even though a very high proportion of mentions in our data include the string *Obama*.

The user-generated entries ($\tilde{\mathbf{x}}$) can still be treated as the outcome of the generative process: using exchangeability, we treat these entries as the first samples drawn in each column. In this work, we treat them as fully observed, but it is possible to treat them as noisy and incorporate a stochastic dependency between $x_{i,j}$ and $\tilde{x}_{i,j}$.

## 4 Inference

We now develop sampling-based inference for the model described in the previous section. We begin with a token-based collapsed Gibbs sampler, and then add larger-scale Metropolis-Hastings moves.

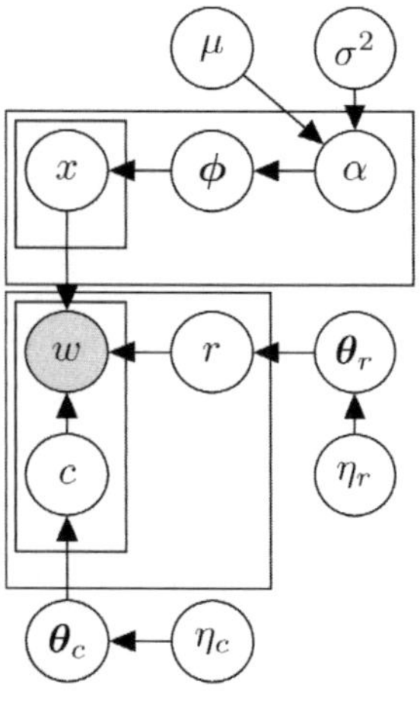


Figure 1: A plate diagram for the text-and-tables graphical model. The upper plate is the table $\boldsymbol{x}$, and the lower plate is the set of textual mentions. Notation is defined in the generative model to the right.

- **Generate the table entries**. For each column $j$,
  - Draw a concentration parameter $\alpha_j$ from a log-normal distribution, $\log \alpha_j \sim \mathcal{N}(\mu, \sigma^2)$.
  - Draw a distribution over strings from a Dirichlet process $\boldsymbol{\phi}_j \sim DP(\alpha_j, G_0)$, where the base distribution $G_0$ is a uniform distribution over strings in a fixed character alphabet, up to an arbitrary finite length.
  - For each row $i$, draw the entry $x_{i,j} \sim \boldsymbol{\phi}_j$.
- **Generate the text mentions**.
  - Draw a prior distribution over rows from a stick-breaking distribution, $\boldsymbol{\theta}_r \sim \text{Stick}(\eta_r)$.
  - Draw a prior distribution over columns from a stick-breaking distribution, $\boldsymbol{\theta}_c \sim \text{Stick}(\eta_c)$.
  - For each mention $\boldsymbol{w}_m$,
    - ∗ Draw a row in the table $r_m \sim \boldsymbol{\theta}_r$.
    - ∗ For each word token $w_{m,n}$ ($n \in \{1, \ldots, N_m\}$),
      - · Draw a column in the table $c_{m,n} \sim \boldsymbol{\theta}_c$.
      - · **Set** the text $w_{m,n} = x_{r_m, c_{m,n}}$.

### 4.1 Gibbs sampling

A key aspect of the generative process is that the word token $w_{m,n}$ is completely determined by the table $\mathbf{x}$ and the row and column indicators $r_m$ and $c_{m,n}$: given that a token was generated by row $i$ and column $j$ of the table, it must be identical to the value of $x_{i,j}$. Using Bayes' rule, we can reverse this deterministic dependence: given the values for the row and column indices, the entries in the table are restricted to exact matches with the text mentions that they generate. This allows us to marginalize the unobserved entries in the table. We can also marginalize the distributions $\boldsymbol{\theta}_r$, $\boldsymbol{\theta}_c$, and $\boldsymbol{\phi}_j$, using the standard collapsed Gibbs sampling equations for Dirichlet processes. Thus, sampling the row and column indices is all that is required to explore the entire space of model configurations.

#### 4.1.1 Conditional probability for word tokens

The conditional sampling distributions for both rows and columns will marginalize the table (besides the prototypes $\tilde{\mathbf{x}}$). To do this, we must be able to compute $P(w_{m,n} \mid r_m = i, c_{m,n} = j, \tilde{\mathbf{x}}, \boldsymbol{w}_{-(m,n)}, \boldsymbol{r}_{-m}, \boldsymbol{c}_{-(m,n)}, \alpha_j)$, which represents the probability of generating word $w_{m,n}$, given $r_m = i$ and $c_{m,n} = j$. The notation $\boldsymbol{w}_{-(m,n)}$, $\boldsymbol{r}_{-m}$, and $\boldsymbol{c}_{-m,n}$ represent the words, row indices, and column indices for all mentions besides $w_{m,n}$. For simplicity, we will elide these variables in much of the subsequent notation.

We first consider the case where we have a user-specified entry for the row and column $\langle i, j \rangle$ — that is, if $\tilde{x}_{ij} \neq \varnothing$. Then the probability is simply,

$$P(w_{m,n} \mid r_m = i, c_{m,n} = j, \tilde{\mathbf{x}}, \ldots) = \begin{cases} 1, & \text{if } \tilde{x}_{ij} = w_{m,n} \\ 0, & \text{if } \tilde{x}_{ij} \neq w_{m,n}. \end{cases} \tag{1}$$

Because the table cell $x_{ij}$ is observed, we do not marginalize over it; we have a generative probability of one if the word matches, and zero otherwise. If the table cell $x_{ij}$ is not specified by the user, then we marginalize over its possible values. For any given $x_{ij}$, the probability $P(w_{m,n} \mid x_{ij}, r_m = i, c_{m,n} = j)$ is still a delta function, so we have:

$$\int P(w_{m,n} \mid x_{r_m,c_{m,n}}) P(x_{r_m,c_{m,n}} \mid \ldots)\, dx_{r_m,c_{m,n}}$$
$$= P(x = w_{m,n} \mid \boldsymbol{w}_{-(m,n)}, \boldsymbol{r}_{-m}, \boldsymbol{c}_{-(m,n)}, \tilde{\mathbf{x}}, \ldots)$$

The integral is equal to the probability of the value of the cell $x_{r_m,c_{m,n}}$ being identical to the string $w_{m,n}$, given assignments to all other variables. To compute this probability, we again must consider two cases: if the cell $x_{i,j}$ has generated some other string $w_{m',n'}$ then its value must be identical to that string; otherwise it is unknown. More formally, for any cell $\langle i, j \rangle$, if $\exists w_{m',n'} : r_{m'} = i \wedge c_{m',n'} = j \wedge \langle m', n' \rangle \neq \langle m, n \rangle$, then $P(x_{i,j} = w_{m',n'}) = 1$; all other strings have zero probability. If $x_{i,j}$ has not generated any other entry, then its probability is conditioned on the other elements of the table $\mathbf{x}$. The known elements of this table are themselves determined by either the user entries $\tilde{\mathbf{x}}$ or the observations $\boldsymbol{w}_{-(m,n)}$. We can define these known elements as $\bar{\mathbf{x}}$, where $\bar{x}_{ij} = \varnothing$ if $\tilde{x}_{ij} = \varnothing \wedge \nexists \langle m, n \rangle : r_m = i \wedge c_{m,n} = j$. Then we can apply the standard Chinese restaurant process marginalization to obtain:

$$P(x_{ij} \mid \bar{\boldsymbol{x}}_{-(i,j)}, \alpha) = \begin{cases} \frac{\mathsf{N}(\bar{\boldsymbol{x}}_{-(i,j)} = x_{ij})}{\mathsf{N}(\bar{\boldsymbol{x}}_{-(i,j)} \neq \varnothing) + \alpha}, & \mathsf{N}(\bar{\boldsymbol{x}}_{-(i,j)} = x_{ij}) > 0 \\ \frac{\alpha}{\mathsf{N}(\bar{\boldsymbol{x}}_{-(i,j)} \neq \varnothing) + \alpha}, & \mathsf{N}(\bar{\boldsymbol{x}}_{-(i,j)} = x_{ij}) = 0 \end{cases} \tag{2}$$

In our implementation, we maintain the table $\bar{\mathbf{x}}$, updating it as we resample the row and column assignments. To construct the conditional distribution for any given entry, we first consult this table, and then compute the probability in Equation 2 for entries where $\bar{x}_{ij} = \varnothing$.

#### 4.1.2 Sampling columns

We can now derive sampling equations for the column indices $c_{m,n}$. We first apply Bayes' rule to obtain $P(c_{m,n} \mid w_{m,n}, r_m, \ldots) \propto P(c_{m,n} \mid \boldsymbol{c}_{-(m,n)}, \eta_c) \times P(w_{m,n} \mid c_{m,n}, r_m, \tilde{\mathbf{x}}, \ldots)$. The likelihood term $P(w_{m,n} \mid c_{m,n}, \ldots)$ is defined in the previous section; we can compute the first factor using the standard Dirichlet process marginalization over $\boldsymbol{\theta}_c$. Writing $\mathsf{N}(c_{-(m,n)} = j)$ for the count of occurrences of column $j$ in the set $\boldsymbol{c}_{-(m,n)}$, we obtain

$$P(c_{m,n} = j \mid c_{-(m,n)}, \eta_c) = \begin{cases} \frac{\mathsf{N}(c_{-(m,n)} = j)}{\mathsf{N}(c_{-(m,n)}) + \eta_c}, & \text{if } \mathsf{N}(c_{-(m,n)} = j) > 0 \\ \frac{\eta_c}{\mathsf{N}(c_{-(m,n)}) + \eta_c}, & \text{if } \mathsf{N}(c_{-(m,n)} = j) = 0 \end{cases} \tag{3}$$

#### 4.1.3 Sampling rows

In principle the row indicators can be sampled identically to the columns, with the caveat that the generative probability $P(\boldsymbol{w}_m \mid r_m, \ldots)$ is a product across all $N_m$ tokens in $\boldsymbol{w}_m$.[1] However, because of the tight probabilistic coupling between the row and column indicators, straightforward Gibbs sampling mixes slowly. Instead, we marginalize the column indicators while sampling $r$. Only the likelihood term is affected by this change:

$$P(\boldsymbol{w}_m \mid r_m, \boldsymbol{w}_{-m}, \boldsymbol{r}_{-m}, \ldots) = \sum_j P(c = j \mid \boldsymbol{c}_{-m}, \eta_c) P(w_{m,n} \mid c_{m,n} = j, r_m, \bar{\boldsymbol{x}}, \alpha). \tag{4}$$

The tokens are conditionally independent given the row, so we factor and then explicitly marginalize over each $c_{m,n}$. The chain rule gives the form in Equation 4, which contains terms for the prior over columns and the likelihood of the word; these are defined in Equations 2 and 3. Note that neither the inferred table $\bar{\mathbf{x}}$ nor the heldout column counts $\boldsymbol{c}_{-m}$ include counts from any of the cells in row $m$.

### 4.2 Column swaps

Suppose that during initialization, we encounter the string *Barry Obama* before encountering *Barack Obama*. We would then put *Barry* in the first-name column, and put *Barack* in some other column for nicknames. After making these initial decisions, they would be very difficult to undo using Gibbs sampling — we would have to first shift all instances of *Barry* to another column, then move an instance of *Barack* to the first-name column, and then move the instances of *Barry* to the nickname column. To rectify this issue, we perform sampling on the table itself, swapping the columns of entries in the table, while simultaneously updating the relevant column indices of the mentions.

In the proposal, we select at random a row $t$ and indices $i$ and $j$. In the table, we will swap $x_{t,i}$ with $x_{t,j}$; in the text we will swap the values of each $c_{m,n}$ whenever $r_m = t$ and $c_{m,n} = i$ or $j$. This proposal is symmetric, so no Hastings correction is required. Because we are simultaneously updating the table and the column indices, the generative likelihood of the words is unchanged; the only changes

[1] This relies on the assumption that the values of $\{c_{m,n}\}$ are mutually independent given $\boldsymbol{c}_{-m}$. Future work might apply a more structured model of the ways that fields are combined when mentioning an entity. For example, a first-order Markov model could learn that family names often follow given names, but the reverse rarely occurs (in English).

in the overall likelihood come from the column indices and the values of the cells in the table. Letting $\mathbf{x}^*, \mathbf{c}^*$ indicate the state of the table and column indices after the proposed move, we will accept with probability,

$$P_{\text{accept}}(\mathbf{x} \to \mathbf{x}^*) = \min\left(1, \frac{P(\mathbf{c}^*)P(\mathbf{x}^*)}{P(\mathbf{c})P(\mathbf{x})}\right) \quad (5)$$

We first consider the ratio of the table probabilities, $\frac{P(\mathbf{x}^*|\alpha)}{P(\mathbf{x}|\alpha)}$. Recall that each column of $\mathbf{x}$ is drawn from a Dirichlet process; appealing to exchangeability, we can treat the row $t$ as the last element drawn, and compute the probabilities $P(x_{t,i} \mid \boldsymbol{x}_{-(t,i)}, \alpha_i)$, with $\boldsymbol{x}_{-(t,i)}$ indicating the elements of the column $i$ excluding row $t$. This probability is given by Equation 2. For a swap of columns $i$ and $j$, we compute the ratio:

$$\frac{P(x_{t,i} \mid \boldsymbol{x}_{-(t,j)}, \alpha_j)P(x_{t,j} \mid \boldsymbol{x}_{-(t,i)}, \alpha_i)}{P(x_{t,i} \mid \boldsymbol{x}_{-(t,i)}, \alpha_i)P(x_{t,j} \mid \boldsymbol{x}_{-(t,j)}, \alpha_j)} \quad (6)$$

Next we consider the ratio of the column probabilities, $\frac{P(\mathbf{c}^*)}{P(\mathbf{c})}$. Again we can apply exchangeability, $P(\mathbf{c}) = P(\{\mathbf{c}_m : r_m = t\} \mid \{\mathbf{c}_{m'} : r_{m'} \neq t\})P(\{\mathbf{c}_{m'} : r_{m'} \neq t\})$. The second term $P(\{\mathbf{c}_{m'} : r_{m'} \neq t\})$ is unaffected by the move, and so is identical in both the numerator and denominator of the likelihood ratio; probabilities from columns other than $i$ and $j$ also cancel in this way. The remaining ratio can be simplified to,

$$\left(\frac{P(c = j \mid \mathbf{c}_{-t}, \eta_c)}{P(c = i \mid \mathbf{c}_{-t}, \eta_c)}\right)^{\mathsf{N}(r=t \wedge c=i) - \mathsf{N}(r=t \wedge c=j)} \quad (7)$$

where the counts $\mathsf{N}()$ are from the state of the sampler before executing the proposed move. The probability $P(c = i \mid \mathbf{c}_{-t}, \eta_c)$ is defined in Equation 3, and the overall acceptance ratio for column swaps is the product of (6) and (7).

### 4.3 Hyperparameters

The concentration parameters $\eta_r$ and $\eta_c$ help to control the number of rows and columns in the table, respectively. These parameters are updated to their maximum likelihood values using gradient-based optimization, so our overall inference procedure is a form of Monte Carlo Expectation-Maximization (Wei and Tanner, 1990).

The concentration parameters $\alpha_j$ control the diversity of each column in the table: if $\alpha_j$ is low then we expect a high degree of repetition, as with titles; if $\alpha_j$ is high then we expect a high degree of diversity. When the sampling procedure adds a new column, there is very little information for how to set its concentration parameter, as the conditional likelihood will be flat. Consequently, greater care must be taken to handle these priors appropriately.

We place a log-normal hyperprior on the column concentration parameters, $\log \alpha_j \sim \mathcal{N}(\mu, \sigma^2)$. The parameters of the log-normal are shared across columns, which provides additional information to constrain the concentration parameters of newly-created columns. We then use Metropolis-Hastings to sample the values of each $\alpha_j$, using the joint likelihood,

$$P(\alpha_j, \bar{\boldsymbol{x}}^{(j)} \mid \mu, \sigma^2) \propto \frac{\exp(-(\log \alpha_j - \mu)^2)\alpha_j^{k_j}\Gamma(\alpha_j)}{2\sigma^2\Gamma(n_j + \alpha_j)},$$

where $\bar{\boldsymbol{x}}^{(j)}$ is column $j$ of the inferred table, $n_j$ is the number of specified entries in column $j$ of the table $\bar{\boldsymbol{x}}$ and $k_j$ is the number of unique entries in the column; see Rasmussen (2000) for a derivation. After repeatedly sampling several values of $\alpha_j$ for each column in the table, we update $\mu$ and $\sigma^2$ to their maximum-likelihood estimates.

## 5 Temporal Prominence

Andy Warhol predicted, "in the future, everyone will be world-famous for fifteen minutes." A model of temporal dynamics that accounts for the fleeting and fickle nature of fame might yield better performance for transient entities, like Joe the Plumber. Among several alternatives for modeling temporal dynamics in latent variable models, we choose a simple non-parametric approach: the recurrent Chinese restaurant process (RCRP; Ahmed and Xing, 2008). The core idea of the RCRP is that time is partitioned into epochs, with a unique Chinese restaurant process in each epoch. Each CRP has a prior which takes the form of pseudo-counts computed from the counts in previous epochs. We employ the simplest version of the RCRP, a first-order Markov model in which the prior for epoch $t$ is equal to the vector of counts for epoch $t-1$:

$$P(r_m^{(t)} = i | \boldsymbol{r}_{1\ldots m-1}^{(t)}, \boldsymbol{r}^{(t-1)}, \eta_r) \propto \begin{cases} \mathsf{N}(\boldsymbol{r}_{1\ldots m-1}^{(t)} = i) + \mathsf{N}(\boldsymbol{r}^{(t-1)} = i), & \text{if} > 0; \\ \eta_r, & \text{otherwise.} \end{cases} \tag{8}$$

The count of row $i$ in epoch $t-1$ is written $\mathsf{N}(\boldsymbol{r}^{(t-1)} = i)$; the count in epoch $t$ for mentions 1 to $m-1$ is written $\mathsf{N}(\boldsymbol{r}_{1\ldots m-1}^{(t)} = i)$. As before, we can apply exchangeability to treat each mention as the last in the epoch, so during inference we can replace this with the count $\mathsf{N}(\boldsymbol{r}_{-m}^{(t)})$. Note that there is *zero probability* of drawing an entity that has no counts in epochs $t$ or $t-1$ but exists in some other epoch; the probability mass $\eta_r$ is reserved for drawing a new entity, and the chance of this matching some existing entity from another epoch is vanishingly small.

During Gibbs sampling, we also need to consider the effect of $r_m^{(t)}$ on the subsequent epoch $t+1$. While space does not permit a derivation, the resulting probability is proportional to

$$P(\boldsymbol{r}^{(t+1)} | \boldsymbol{r}_{-m}^{(t)}, r_m^{(t)} = i, \eta_r) \propto \begin{cases} 1 & \text{if } \mathsf{N}(\boldsymbol{r}^{(t+1)} = i) = 0, \\ \frac{\mathsf{N}(\boldsymbol{r}^{(t+1)} = i)}{\eta_r} & \text{if } \mathsf{N}(\boldsymbol{r}_{-m}^{(t)} = i) = 0, \\ 1 + \frac{\mathsf{N}(\boldsymbol{r}^{(t+1)} = i)}{\mathsf{N}(\boldsymbol{r}_{-m}^{(t)} = i)} & \text{if } \mathsf{N}(\boldsymbol{r}_{-m}^{(t)} = i) > 0. \end{cases} \tag{9}$$

This favors entities which are frequent in epoch $t+1$ but infrequent in epoch $t$.

The move to a recurrent Chinese restaurant process does not affect the sampling equations for the columns $c$, nor the concentration parameters of the table, $\alpha$. The only part of the inference procedure that needs to be changed is the optimization of the hyperparameter $\eta_r$; the log-likelihood is now the sum across all epochs, and each epoch makes a contribution to the gradient.

## 6 Evaluation Setup

Our model jointly performs three tasks: identifying a set of entities, discovering the set of fields, and matching mention strings with the entities and fields to which they refer. We are aware of no prior work that performs these tasks jointly, nor any dataset that is annotated for all three tasks.[2] Consequently, we focus our quantitative evaluation on what we take to be the most important subtask: identifying the entities which are mentioned in raw text. We annotate a new dataset of blog text for this purpose, and design precision and recall metrics to reward systems that recover as much of the reference set as possible, while avoiding spurious entities and fields. We also perform a qualitative analysis, noting the areas where our method outperforms string matching approaches, and where there is need for further improvement.

**Data** Evaluation was performed on a corpus of blogs describing United States politics in 2008 (Eisenstein and Xing, 2010). We ran the Stanford Named Entity Recognition system (Finkel et al., 2005) to obtain a set of 25,000 candidate mentions which the system judged to be names of people. We then pruned strings that appeared fewer than four times and eliminated strings with more than seven tokens (these were usually errors). The resulting dataset has 19,247 mentions comprising 45,466 word tokens, and 813 unique mention strings.

**Gold standard** We develop a *reference set* of 100 entities for evaluation. This set was created by sorting the unique name strings in the training set by frequency, and manually merging strings that reference the same entity. We also manually discarded strings from the reference set if they resulted from errors in the preprocessing pipeline (tokenization and named entity recognition). Each entity is represented by the set of all word tokens that appear in its references; there are a total of 231 tokens for the 100 entities. Most entities only include first and last names, though the most frequent entities have many more: for example, the entity **Barack Obama** has known names: $\{$*Barack*, *Obama*, *Sen.*, *Mr.*$\}$.

**Metrics** We evaluate the recall and precision of a system's *response* set by matching against the reference set. The first step is to create a bipartite matching between response and reference entities.[3] Using a cost function that quantifies the sim-

[2]Recent work exploiting Wikipedia disambiguation pages for evaluating cross-document coreference suggests an appealing alternative for future work (Singh et al., 2011).

[3]Bipartite matchings are typical in information extraction evaluation metrics (e.g., Doddington et al., 2004).

ilarity of response and reference entities, we optimize the matching using the Kuhn-Munkres algorithm (Kuhn, 1955). For recall, the cost function counts the number of shared word tokens, divided by the number of word tokens in the reference entities; the recall is one minus the average cost of the best matching (with a cost of one for reference entities that are not matched, and no cost for unmatched response entities). Precision is computed identically, but we normalize by the number of word tokens in the response entity. Precision assigns a penalty of one to unmatched response entities and no penalty for unmatched reference entities.

Note that this metric grossly underrates the precision of all systems: the reference set is limited to 100 entities, but it is clear that our text mentions many other people. This is harsh but fair: all systems are penalized equally for identifying entities that are not present in the reference set, and the ideal system will recover the fifty reference entities (thus maximizing recall) while keeping the table as compact as possible (thus maximizing precision). However, the raw precision values have little meaning outside the context of a direct comparison under identical experimental conditions.

**Systems** The initial seed set for our system consists of a partial annotation of five entities (Table 1) — larger seed sets did not improve performance. We run the inference procedure described in the previous section for 20,000 iterations, and then obtain a final database by taking the intersection of the inferred tables $\bar{\mathbf{x}}$ obtained at every 100 iterations, starting with iteration 15,000. To account for variance across Markov chains, we perform three different runs. We evaluate a non-temporal version of our model (as described in Sections 3 and 4), and a temporal version with 5 epochs. For the non-temporal version, a non-parallel C implementation had a wall clock sampling time of roughly 16 hours; the temporal version required 24 hours.

We compare against a baseline that incrementally clusters strings into entities using a string edit distance metric, based on the work of Elmacioglu et al. (2007). Starting from a configuration in which each unique string forms its own cluster, we incrementally merge clusters using the single-link criterion, based on the minimum Jaccard edit distance

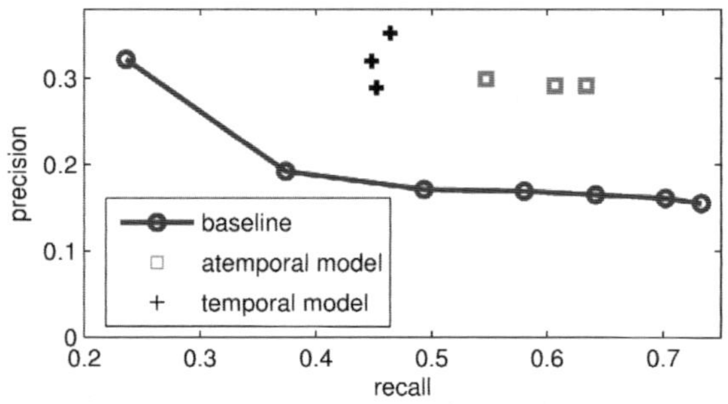


Figure 2: The precision and recall of our models, as compared to the curve defined by the incremental clustering baseline. Each point indicates a unique sampling run.

| | | | | |
|---|---|---|---|---|
| Bill | Clinton | Benazir | | Bhutto |
| Nancy | Pelosi | Speaker | | |
| John | Kerry | Sen. | | Roberts |
| Martin | King | Dr. | Jr. | Luther |
| Bill | Nelson | | | |

Table 2: A subset of the entity database discovered by our model, hand selected to show highlight interesting success and failure cases.

between each pair of clusters. This yields a series of outputs that move along the precision-recall curve, with precision increasing as the clusters encompass more strings. There is prior work on heuristics for selecting a stopping point, but we compare our results against the entire precision-recall curve (Manning et al., 2008).

## 7 Results

The results of our evaluation are shown in Figure 2. All sampling runs from our models lie well beyond the precision-recall curve defined by the baseline system, demonstrating the ability to achieve reasonable recall with a far more compact database. The baseline system can achieve nearly perfect recall by creating one entity per unique string, but as it merges strings to improve precision, its recall suffers significantly. As noted above, perfect precision is not possible on this task, because the reference set covers only a subset of the entities that appear in the data. However, the numbers do measure the ability to recover the reference entities in the most compact table possible, allowing a quantitative comparison of our models and the baseline approach.

Table 2 shows a database identified by the atemporal version of our model. The most densely-populated columns in the table correspond to well-defined name parts: columns 1 and 2 are almost exclusively populated with first and last names respectively, and column 3 is mainly populated by titles. The remaining columns are more of a grab bag. Column 4 correctly captures *Jr.* for **Martin Luther King**; column 5 correctly captures *Luther*, but mistakenly contains *Roberts* (thus merging the **John Kerry** and **John Roberts** entities), and *Bhutto* (thus helping to merge the **Bill Clinton** and **Benazir Bhutto** entities).

The model successfully distinguishes some, but not all, of the entities that share tokens. For example, the model separates **Bill Clinton** from **Bill Nelson**; it also separates **John McCain** from **John Kerry** (whom it mistakenly merges with **John Roberts**). The ability to distinguish individuals who share first names is due in part to the model attributing a low concentration parameter to first names, meaning that some repetition in the first name column is expected. The model correctly identifies several titles and alternative names, including the rare title *Speaker* for **Nancy Pelosi**; however, it misses others, such as the *Senator* title for **Bill Nelson**. This may be due in part to the sample merging procedure used to generate this table, which requires that a cell contain the same value in at least 80% of the samples.

Many errors may be attributed to slow mixing. After mistakenly merging **Bhutto** and **Clinton** at an early stage, the Gibbs sampler — which treats each mention independently — is unable to separate them. Given that several other mentions of **Bhutto** are already in the row occupied by **Clinton**, the overall likelihood would benefit little from creating a new row for a single mention, though moving all such mentions simultaneously would result in an improvement. Larger scale Metropolis-Hastings moves, such as split-merge or type-based sampling (Liang et al., 2010) may help.

## 8 Related Work

**Information Extraction** A tradition of research in information extraction focuses on processing raw text to fill in the fields of manually-defined templates, thus populating databases of events or relations (McNamee and Dang, 2009). While early approaches focused on surface-level methods such as wrapper induction (Kushmerick et al., 1997), more recent work in this area includes Bayesian nonparametrics to select the number of rows in the database (Haghighi and Klein, 2010a). However, even in such nonparametric work, the form of the template and the number of slots are fixed in advance. Our approach differs in that the number of fields and their meaning is learned from data. Recent work by Chambers and Jurafsky (2011) approaches a related problem, applying agglomerative clustering over sentences to detect *events*, and then clustering syntactic constituents to induce the relevant fields of each event entity. As described in Section 6, our method performs well against an agglomerative clustering baseline, though a more comprehensive comparison of the two approaches is an important step for future work.

**Name Segmentation and Structure** A related stream of research focuses specifically on names: identifying them in raw text, discovering their structure, and matching names that refer to the same entity. We do not undertake the problem of named entity recognition (Tjong Kim Sang, 2002), but rather apply an existing NER system as a preprocessing step (Finkel et al., 2005). Typical NER systems do not attempt to discover the internal structure of names or a database of canonical names, although they often use prefabricated "gazetteers" of names and name parts as features to improve performance (Borthwick et al., 1998; Sarawagi and Cohen, 2005).

Charniak (2001) shows that it is possible to learn a model of name structure, either by using coreference information as labeled data, or by leveraging a small set of hand-crafted constraints. Elsner et al. (2009) develop a nonparametric Bayesian model of name structure using adaptor grammars, which they use to distinguish *types* of names (e.g., people, places, and organizations). Li et al. (2004) use a set of manually-crafted "transformations" of name parts to build a model of how a name might be rendered in multiple different ways. While each of these approaches bears on one or more facets of the problem that we consider here, none provides a holistic treatment of name disambiguation and structure.

**Resolving Mentions to Entities** The problem of resolving mentions to entities has been approach from a variety of different perspectives. There is an extensive literature on probabilistic record linkage, in which database records are compared to determine if they are likely to have the same real-world referents (e.g., Felligi and Sunter, 1969; Bilenko et al., 2003). Most approaches focus on pairwise assessments of whether two records are the same, whereas our method attempts to infer a single coherent model of the underlying relational data. Some more recent work in record linkage has explicitly formulated the task of inferring a latent relational model of a set of observed datasets (e.g., Cohen et al., 2000; Pasula et al., 2002; Bhattacharya and Getoor, 2007); however, to our knowledge, these prior models have all exploited some predefined database schema (i.e., set of columns), which our model does not require. Many of these prior models have been applied to bibliographic data, where different conventions and abbreviations lead to imperfect matches in different references to the same publication. In our task, we consider name mentions in raw text; such mentions are short, and may not offer as many redundant clues for linkage as bibliographic references.

In natural language processing, *coreference resolution* is the task of grouping entity mentions (strings), in one or more documents, based on their common referents in the world. Although much of coreference resolution has on the single document setting, there has been some recent work on cross-document coreference resolution (Li et al., 2004; Haghighi and Klein, 2007; Poon and Domingos, 2008; Singh et al., 2011). The problem we consider is related to cross-document coreference, although we take on the additional challenge of providing a canonicalized name for each referent (the corresponding table row), and in inferring a structured representation of entity names (the table columns). For this reason, our evaluation focuses on the induced table of entities, rather than the clustering of mention strings. The best coreference systems depend on carefully crafted, problem-specific linguistic features (Bengtson and Roth, 2008) and external knowledge (Haghighi and Klein, 2010b). Future work might consider how to exploit such features for the more holistic information extraction setting.

## 9 Conclusion

This paper presents a Bayesian nonparametric approach to recover structured records from text. Using only a small set of prototype records, we are able to recover an accurate table that jointly identifies entities and internal name structure. In our view, the main advantage of a Bayesian approach compared to more heuristic alternatives is that it facilitates incorporation of additional information sources when available. In this paper, we have considered one such additional source, incorporating temporal context using the recurrent Chinese restaurant process.

We envision enhancing the model in several other respects. One promising direction is the incorporation of name structure, which could be captured using a first-order Markov model of the transitions between name parts. In the nonparametric setting, a transition matrix is unbounded along both dimensions, and this can be handled by a hierarchical Dirichlet process (HDP; Teh et al 2006).[4] We envision other potential applications of the HDP: for example, learning "topics" of entities which tend to appear together (i.e., given a mention of Mahmoud Abbas in the American press, a mention of Benjamin Netanyahu is likely), and handling document-specific burstiness (i.e., given that an entity is mentioned once in a document, it is much more likely to be mentioned again). Finally, we would like to incorporate lexical context from the sentences in which each entity is mentioned, which might help to distinguish, say, computer science researchers who share names with former defense secretaries or professional basketball players.

**Acknowledgments** This research was enabled by AFOSR FA95501010247, DARPA grant N10AP20042, ONR N000140910758, NSF DBI-0546594, IIS-0713379, IIS-0915187, IIS-0811562, an Alfred P. Sloan Fellowship, and Google's support of the Worldly Knowledge project at CMU. We thank the reviewers for their thoughtful feedback.

[4]One of the reviewers proposed to draw entire column sequences from a Dirichlet process. Given the relatively small number of columns and canonical name forms, this may be a straightforward and effective alternative to the HDP.

## References


Amr Ahmed and Eric P. Xing. 2008. Dynamic non-parametric mixture models and the recurrent Chinese restaurant process with applications to evolutionary clustering. In *International Conference on Data Mining*.

Javier Artiles, Julio Gonzalo, and Satoshi Sekine. 2007. The SemEval-2007 WePS evaluation: establishing a benchmark for the web people search task. In *Proceedings of the 4th International Workshop on Semantic Evaluations*, SemEval '07, pages 64–69. Association for Computational Linguistics.

Eric Bengtson and Dan Roth. 2008. Understanding the value of features for coreference resolution. In *Proceedings of the Conference on Empirical Methods in Natural Language Processing*, EMNLP '08, pages 294–303, Stroudsburg, PA, USA. Association for Computational Linguistics.

Indrajit Bhattacharya and Lise Getoor. 2007. Collective entity resolution in relational data. *ACM Trans. Knowl. Discov. Data*, 1(1), March.

Mikhail Bilenko, William W. Cohen, Stephen Fienberg, Raymond J. Mooney, and Pradeep Ravikumar. 2003. Adaptive name-matching in information integration. *IEEE Intelligent Systems*, 18(5):16–23, September/October.

A. Borthwick, J. Sterling, E. Agichtein, and R. Grishman. 1998. Exploiting diverse knowledge sources via maximum entropy in named entity recognition. In *Sixth Workshop on Very Large Corpora New Brunswick, New Jersey. Association for Computational Linguistics.*

Nathanael Chambers and Dan Jurafsky. 2011. Template-based information extraction without the templates. In *Proceedings of ACL*.

Eugene Charniak. 2001. Unsupervised learning of name structure from coreference data. In *Proceedings of the Second Meeting of the North American Chapter of the Association for Computational Linguistics*.

William W. Cohen, Henry Kautz, and David McAllester. 2000. Hardening soft information sources. In *Proceedings of the Sixth International Conference on Knowledge Discovery and Data Mining*, pages 255–259.

George Doddington, Alexis Mitchell, Mark Przybocki, Lance Ramshaw, Stephanie Strassel, and Ralph Weischedel. 2004. The automatic content extraction (ace) program: Tasks, data, and evaluation. In *4th international conference on language resources and evaluation (LREC'04)*.

Jacob Eisenstein and Eric Xing. 2010. The CMU 2008 political blog corpus. Technical report, Carnegie Mellon University.

Ergin Elmacioglu, Yee Fan Tan, Su Yan, Min-Yen Kan, and Dongwon Lee. 2007. Psnus: Web people name disambiguation by simple clustering with rich features. In *Proceedings of the Fourth International Workshop on Semantic Evaluations (SemEval-2007)*, pages 268–271, Prague, Czech Republic, June. Association for Computational Linguistics.

Micha Elsner, Eugene Charniak, and Mark Johnson. 2009. Structured generative models for unsupervised named-entity clustering. In *Proceedings of Human Language Technologies: The 2009 Annual Conference of the North American Chapter of the Association for Computational Linguistics*, pages 164–172, Boulder, Colorado, June. Association for Computational Linguistics.

I. P. Felligi and A. B. Sunter. 1969. A theory for record linkage. *Journal of the American Statistical Society*, 64:1183–1210.

Jenny R. Finkel, Trond Grenager, and Christopher Manning. 2005. Incorporating non-local information into information extraction systems by Gibbs sampling. In *Proceedings of the 43rd Annual Meeting on Association for Computational Linguistics*, ACL '05, pages 363–370, Stroudsburg, PA, USA. Association for Computational Linguistics.

Aria Haghighi and Dan Klein. 2007. Unsupervised coreference resolution in a nonparametric bayesian model. In *Proceedings of the 45th Annual Meeting of the Association of Computational Linguistics*, pages 848–855, Prague, Czech Republic, June. Association for Computational Linguistics.

Aria Haghighi and Dan Klein. 2010a. An entity-level approach to information extraction. In *Proceedings of the ACL 2010 Conference Short Papers*, ACLShort '10, pages 291–295, Stroudsburg, PA, USA. Association for Computational Linguistics.

Aria Haghighi and Dan Klein. 2010b. Coreference resolution in a modular, entity-centered model. In *Human Language Technologies: The 2010 Annual Conference of the North American Chapter of the Association for Computational Linguistics*, pages 385–393, Los Angeles, California, June. Association for Computational Linguistics.

Harold W. Kuhn. 1955. The Hungarian method for the assignment problem. *Naval Research Logistic Quarterly*, 2:83–97.

Nicholas Kushmerick, Daniel S. Weld, and Robert Doorenbos. 1997. Wrapper induction for information extraction. In *Proceedings of IJCAI*.

Xin Li, Paul Morie, and Dan Roth. 2004. Identification and tracing of ambiguous names: Discriminative and generative approaches. In *Proceedings of AAAI*, pages 419–424.

Percy Liang, Michael I. Jordan, and Dan Klein. 2010. Type-Based MCMC. In *Human Language Technologies: The 2010 Annual Conference of the North American Chapter of the Association for Computational Linguistics*, pages 573–581, Los Angeles, California, June. Association for Computational Linguistics.

Christopher D. Manning, Prabhakar Raghavan, and Hinrich Schütze. 2008. *Introduction to Information Retrieval*. Cambridge University Press, 1 edition, July.

Paul McNamee and Hoa Trang Dang. 2009. Overview of the TAC 2009 knowledge base population track. In *Proceedings of the Text Analysis Conference (TAC)*.

Hanna Pasula, Bhaskara Marthi, Brian Milch, Stuart Russell, and Ilya Shpitser. 2002. Identity uncertainty and citation matching. In *Advances in Neural Processing Systems 15*, Vancouver, British Columbia. MIT Press.

Hoifung Poon and Pedro Domingos. 2008. Joint unsupervised coreference resolution with Markov Logic. In *Proceedings of the 2008 Conference on Empirical Methods in Natural Language Processing*, pages 650–659, Honolulu, Hawaii, October. Association for Computational Linguistics.

Carl E. Rasmussen. 2000. The Infinite Gaussian Mixture Model. In *In Advances in Neural Information Processing Systems 12*, volume 12, pages 554–560.

Sunita Sarawagi and William W. Cohen. 2005. Semi-Markov conditional random fields for information extraction. In Lawrence K. Saul, Yair Weiss, and Léon Bottou, editors, *Advances in Neural Information Processing Systems 17*, pages 1185–1192. MIT Press, Cambridge, MA.

Sameer Singh, Amarnag Subramanya, Fernando Pereira, and Andrew McCallum. 2011. Large-scale cross-document coreference using distributed inference and hierarchical models. In *Association for Computational Linguistics: Human Language Technologies (ACL HLT)*.

Yee W. Teh, Michael I. Jordan, Matthew J. Beal, and David M. Blei. 2006. Hierarchical dirichlet processes. *Journal of the American Statistical Association*, 101:1566–1581, December.

Erik F. Tjong Kim Sang. 2002. Introduction to the CoNLL-2002 shared task: Language-independent named entity recognition. In *Proceedings of the Sixth Conference on Natural Language Learning*.

Greg C. G. Wei and Martin A. Tanner. 1990. A Monte Carlo Implementation of the EM Algorithm and the Poor Man's Data Augmentation Algorithms. *Journal of the American Statistical Association*, 85(411):699–704.

# Unsupervised Cross-Lingual Lexical Substitution

**Marianna Apidianaki**
Alpage, INRIA & Univ Paris Diderot
Sorbonne Paris Cité, UMRI-001
75013 Paris, France
Marianna.Apidianaki@inria.fr

## Abstract

Cross-Lingual Lexical Substitution (CLLS) is the task that aims at providing for a target word in context, several alternative substitute words in another language. The proposed sets of translations may come from external resources or be extracted from textual data. In this paper, we apply for the first time an unsupervised cross-lingual WSD method to this task. The method exploits the results of a cross-lingual word sense induction method that identifies the senses of words by clustering their translations according to their semantic similarity. We evaluate the impact of using clustering information for CLLS by applying the WSD method to the SemEval-2010 CLLS data set. Our system performs better on the 'out-of-ten' measure than the systems that participated in the SemEval task, and is ranked medium on the other measures. We analyze the results of this evaluation and discuss avenues for a better overall integration of unsupervised sense clustering in this setting.

## 1 Introduction

Lexical Substitution (LS) aims at providing alternative substitute words (or phrases) for a target word in context, a process useful for monolingual tasks such as paraphrasing and textual entailment (McCarthy and Navigli, 2009). Its multilingual counterpart, Cross-Lingual Lexical Substitution (CLLS), aims at finding for a target word in context, alternative substitute words in another language. CLLS systems may assist human translators and language learners, while their output may constitute the input to cross-language Information Retrieval and Machine Translation (MT) systems (Sinha et al., 2009; Mihalcea et al., 2010).

The multilingual context in which CLLS is performed permits to override some issues common to monolingual semantic processing tasks, such as the selection of an adequate sense inventory and the definition of the granularity of the semantic descriptions. In a multilingual context, word senses can be easily identified using their translations in other languages (Resnik and Yarowsky, 2000). Although this conception of senses presents some theoretical and practical drawbacks, it provides a standard criterion for sense delimitation which explains its wide adoption in recent works on multilingual Word Sense Disambiguation (WSD) and WSD in MT (Carpuat and Wu, 2007; Ng and Chan, 2007).

In this paper, we explain how semantic clustering may provide answers to some of the issues posed by the traditional cross-lingual sense induction approach, and how it can be efficiently exploited for CLLS. Given that existing CLLS systems rely on predefined semantic resources, we show, for the first time, that CLLS can be performed in a fully unsupervised manner. The paper is organized as follows: in the next section, we present some arguments towards unsupervised clustering for cross-lingual sense induction. The clustering method used is presented in section 3. Section 4 describes the SemEval-2010 CLLS task, and section 5 presents the cross-lingual WSD method used for CLLS. In section 6, we proceed to a detailed analysis of the obtained results, before concluding with some avenues for future work.

*Proceedings of EMNLP 2011, Conference on Empirical Methods in Natural Language Processing*, pages 13–23,
Edinburgh, Scotland, UK, July 27–31, 2011. ©2011 Association for Computational Linguistics

## 2 Cross-lingual sense induction

### 2.1 Related work

Word sense induction (WSI) methods offer an alternative to the use of predefined semantic resources for NLP. They automatically define the senses of words from textual data and may adapt the obtained descriptions to the WSD needs of specific applications. In a monolingual context, WSI is performed by exploiting more or less refined distributional information (Navigli, 2009), while in a multilingual context WSI is mostly based on translation information. In this setting, the senses of words in one language are identified by their translations in another language, usually found in a parallel corpus (Resnik and Yarowsky, 2000).

This empirical approach to sense induction offers a standard criterion for sense delimitation and, consequently, dissociates WSD from semantic theories and predefined semantic inventories. Moreover, by establishing semantic distinctions pertinent for translation between the implicated languages, it allows to tune sense induction to the needs of multilingual applications. It has thus been widely adopted in works on multilingual WSD and WSD in MT, where senses are derived from parallel data (Diab, 2003; Ide, 1999; Ide et al., 2002; Ng et al., 2003; Chan et al., 2007; Carpuat and Wu, 2007). By linking WSD and its evaluation to translation, this hypothesis also offers a solution to the problem of non-conformity of monolingual WSD methods in this setting.

Nevertheless, the assumption of biunivocal ('one-to-one') correspondences between senses and translations is rather simplistic. One word sense may be translated by different synonymous words in another language, whose relatedness should be considered during sense induction. Furthermore, this approach does not permit to account for cases of parallel ambiguities (Resnik, 2007), and cases where the senses of a word share some of their translations (Sinha et al., 2009). Additional problems arise at the practical level as the induced senses are uniform and, so, the constraints used during WSD for selecting between close and distant senses are similar. Furthermore, when WSD coincides with lexical selection in MT, the selection of a translation different from the reference is considered as wrong even if it is semantically correct. So, this conception of senses does not permit to penalize WSD errors relatively to their importance (Resnik and Yarowsky, 2000), unless semantic resources are used to identify semantic correspondences.

### 2.2 Cross-lingual sense clustering

Instead of using translations as straightforward sense indicators, it is possible to perform a more thorough semantic analysis during cross-lingual WSI by combining distributional and translation information. The sense clustering method proposed by Apidianaki (2008) identifies complex semantic relations between word senses and their translations. The method is based on the contextual hypotheses of meaning and of semantic similarity (Harris, 1954; Miller and Charles, 1991), which underlie monolingual WSI methods, and is combined to the assumption of a semantic correspondence between words and their translations in real texts (Chesterman, 1998). Following these hypotheses, information coming from the source contexts of a target word when translated with a precise translation in a parallel corpus, is used to reveal the senses carried by the translation. Furthermore, the similarity of the source contexts reveals the semantic relatedness of the translations.

This cross-lingual WSI method groups the semantically similar translations of ambiguous words into clusters that serve to describe their senses instead of the individual translations. For instance, the traditional cross-lingual WSI approach would propose three senses for the English noun *coach*, corresponding to each of its Spanish translations: *entrenador, autocar* and *autobús*.[1] However, this solution is not sound given that the translations *autocar* and *autobús* are semantically related and do not lexicalize distinct senses of the English word, as is the case with *entrenador*. Sense clustering permits to estimate the semantic similarity of the translations and to not consider synonymous translations as indicators of distinct senses. Consequently, the English word *coach* has two senses after sense clustering: one described by the cluster {*autocar, autobús*} (the "bus" sense) and one described by the cluster {*entrenador*} (the "trainer" sense). In the automat-

[1] This set of translations was extracted from the word aligned Europarl corpus (Koehn, 2005) after applying a set of filters that will be described in section 3.

ically built bilingual inventories, the senses of the words in one language are thus described by clusters of their translations in another language.

### 2.3 Applications

This type of sense clustering has proved to be useful in various application settings. When exploited in cross-lingual WSD, it permits to assign 'sense-tags' containing several semantically correct translations to new instances of words in context (Apidianaki, 2009). Moreover, the use of clustering information during evaluation allows for a differing penalization of WSD errors. In an MT evaluation setting, sense clusters have been integrated into an MT evaluation metric (METEOR) (Lavie and Agarwal, 2007) and brought about an increase of the metric's correlation with human judgments of translation quality in different languages (Apidianaki and He, 2010). The use of sense clusters in this setting permits to identify semantic correspondences between translations and hypotheses, and to circumvent the strict requirement for exact surface correspondences, one of the main critics addressed to MT evaluation metrics. The same notion of sense clusters has been adopted in the most recent SemEval Cross-Lingual WSD task (Lefever and Hoste, 2010). Instead of considering translations as indicators of distinct senses, as was the case in previous tasks, the senses of a small number of ambiguous words were described by manually created clusters of translations.

We consider that the sense cluster inventories created by the unsupervised WSI method proposed by Apidianaki (2008) would be useful in other applicative contexts as well and, especially, in CLLS. In unsupervised cross-lingual WSD, the clusters constitute the candidate senses from which one has to be selected for each new instance of the words in context. So, when an instance of a word is disambiguated, a cluster of semantically related translations is selected on the basis of the source context describing its sense. This is exactly the goal of CLLS, as described in the relevant task set up in SemEval-2010, where the systems had to provide for instances of words in context, several possible translations in another language (Sinha et al., 2009; Mihalcea et al., 2010). It seems thus that CLLS constitutes a suitable field for exploiting this sense clustering method and, in what follows, we will try to evaluate this assumption.

## 3 Unsupervised clustering for sense induction

### 3.1 Bilingual lexicons

The SemEval-2010 CLLS task concerned the pair of languages English (EN) - Spanish (SP). In order to apply our cross-lingual WSD method to the data of the SemEval-2010 CLLS task, an EN-SP sense cluster inventory had first to be built where the senses of English words would be described by clusters of their Spanish translations. The training corpus used for building the sense cluster inventory is the SP-EN part of Europarl (release v5), which contains 1,689,850 aligned sentence pairs (Koehn, 2005). Before clustering, some preprocessing steps are performed. First, the corpus is lemmatized and tagged by POS (Schmid, 1994). Then sentence pairs presenting a great difference in length (i.e cases where one sentence is three times longer than the other) are eliminated and the corpus is aligned at the level of word types using Giza++ (Och and Ney, 2003).

Two bilingual lexicons of content words are built from the alignment results, one for each translation direction (EN-SP/SP-EN). In the entries of these lexicons, source words are associated with the translations to which they are aligned. As these lexicons are automatically created, they contain some noise mainly due to spurious word alignments. In order to eliminate erroneous translation correspondences, we first apply a filter which discards translations with a probability below 0.001 (according to the scores assigned during word alignment). Then an intersection filter is applied which discards correspondences not found in lexicons of both directions. Finally, the two lexicons are filtered by POS, keeping for each *w* only its translations that pertain to the same POS category.[2] The translations of a word (*w*) used for clustering are the ones that translate *w* at least 20 times in the training corpus. This frequency threshold leaves out some translations of the source words but has a double merit: it eliminates erroneous translations

[2]For instance, for English nouns we retain their noun translations in Spanish; for verbs, we keep verbs, etc.

and reduces data sparseness issues which pose problems in distributional semantic analysis.

### 3.2 Clustering based on semantic similarity

The semantic clustering is performed in the target language by using source language feature vectors. Each translation of a word *w* is characterized by a vector built from the content words that cooccur with *w* whenever it is translated by this word in the aligned sentences of the training corpus.[3] The vector similarity is calculated using a variation of the Weighted Jaccard measure (Grefenstette, 1994) which weighs each source context feature according to its relevance for the estimation of the translations similarity.

The input of the similarity calculation consists of the frequency lists of *w*'s translations. The score assigned to a pair of translations indicates their degree of similarity. Each feature (*j*) gets a *total weight* (*tw*) relatively to a translation (*i*), which corresponds to the product of its *global* (*gw*) and its *local weight* (*lw*) with this translation. The *gw* is based on the dispersion of *j* in the contexts of *w*, and on its frequency of cooccurrence (*cooc_freq*) with *w* when translated by each *i* (cf. formula 1). So, it depends on the number of translations with which *j* is related (*nrels*) and on its probability of cooccurrence with each one of them (cf. formula 2). The *local weight* (*lw*) between *j* and *i* depends on their frequency of cooccurrence (cf. formula 3).

$$\mathrm{gw}(j) = 1 - \frac{\sum_i \mathrm{p}_{ij} \log(\mathrm{p}_{ij})}{\mathrm{nrels}} \tag{1}$$

$$\mathrm{p}_{ij} = \frac{\text{cooc\_freq of } j \text{ with } i}{|js| \text{ for } i} \tag{2}$$

$$\mathrm{lw}(j,i) = \log(\text{cooc\_freq of } j \text{ with } i) \tag{3}$$

The Weighted Jaccard (WJ) coefficient of two translations *m* and *n* is given by formula 4.

$$\mathrm{WJ}(m,n) = \frac{\sum_j \min(\mathrm{tw}(m,j)\mathrm{tw}(n,j))}{\sum_j \max(\mathrm{tw}(m,j)\mathrm{tw}(n,j))} \tag{4}$$

The pairwise similarity of the translations is thus estimated by comparing the corresponding weighted source feature vectors. A similarity score is assigned to each pair of translations and stored in a table that is being looked up by the clustering algorithm. The pertinence of the relation of each translation pair is estimated by comparing its score to a threshold defined locally for each *w* by the following iterative procedure.

1. The initial threshold (T) corresponds to the mean of the scores (above 0) of the translation pairs of *w*.
2. The set of translations is segmented into pairs whose score exceeds the threshold and pairs whose score is inferior to the threshold, creating two sets (G1, G2).
3. The average of each set is computed (*m1* = average value of G1, *m2* = average value of G2).
4. A new threshold is created that is the average of *m1* and *m2* (*T* = (m1 + m2)/2).
5. Go back to step 2, now using the new threshold computed in step 4, keep repeating until convergence has been reached.

The clustering algorithm groups the translations by exploiting the similarity calculation results. The condition for a translation to be included in a cluster is to have pertinent relations with all the elements already in the cluster. The clustering stops when all the translations of *w* are included in some cluster and all their relations have been checked. All the elements of the final clusters are linked to each other by pertinent relations. The translations not having any strong relations to other translations are included in separate one-element clusters.

### 3.3 The EN-SP sense cluster inventory

In the obtained semantic inventory, the senses of each English word are described by clusters of its semantically similar translations in Spanish.[4] Some entries from the EN-SP sense cluster inventory are presented in Table 1. We provide examples for words of different POS (nouns, verbs, adjectives and adverbs) and with varying degrees of polysemy. The

[3]We use a stoplist of English function words (conjunctions, prepositions and articles) that may be erroneously tagged as content words.

[4]The inventory contains entries for all English content words in the corpus. Here, we focus on the target words used in the CLLS task.

| POS | EN word | # SP_Ts | # occ | Sense clusters |
|---|---|---|---|---|
| Nouns | coach | 3 | 265 | {entrenador}{autocar, autobús} |
| | test | 11 | 3162 | {prueba, ensayo, examen} {experimento, análisis, examen, ensayo} {evaluación} {comprobación} {experimentación, ensayo, análisis, experimento} {inspección} {experimento, control, análisis, examen} {experimentación, control, análisis, experimento} {criterio} |
| Verbs | drop | 10 | 390 | {disminuir, reducir, bajar, caer, descender} {retirar} {dejar, abandonar} {lanzar} |
| | check | 5 | 1343 | {examinar} {revisar} {controlar, verificar, comprobar} |
| Adjs | heavy | 7 | 448 | {elevado, fuerte, grave, grande}{elevado, enorme}{grave, duro, fuerte, grande} {grave, alto, elevado} |
| | open | 6 | 6286 | {público, libre, transparente} {público, franco, transparente} {abierto} {sincero, franco} |
| Advs | around | 5 | 742 | {alrededores}{casi, aproximadamente, cerca}{menos} |
| | now | 9 | 33662 | {aquí, actualmente, hoy, ahora bien} {actualmente, ahora, hoy} {entretanto, aquí, ahora bien} {de momento}, {adelante}, {por ahora, entretanto} |

Table 1: *Entries from the EN-SP sense cluster inventory.*

third column of the table gives the number of Spanish words (SP_Ts) translating more than 20 occurrences of the English words in the corpus and retained for clustering. This threshold ensures that the words being clustered are good translations of the English words. The fourth column of the table shows the number of English word occurrences translated by the retained translations.

As is shown in these examples, the translations of the English words are not considered as straightforward indicators of their senses but are grouped into clusters describing senses. For instance, the word *drop*, which is translated by ten different words into Spanish (*disminuir, reducir, bajar, caer, descender, retirar, dejar, abandonar, lanzar*) is not considered as having ten distinct senses but four, described by each cluster of translations: {disminuir, reducir, bajar, caer, descender}: "decrease, reduce", {retirar}: "remove, withdraw", {dejar, abandonar}: "leave, abandon" and {lanzar}: "launch". The obtained clusters group semantically similar words which would be erroneously considered as indicators of distinct senses by the traditional cross-lingual sense induction method.

Another important point is that this algorithm performs a soft clustering, highly adequate in this setting. Given that the generated clusters describe senses, their overlaps describe the relations between the corresponding senses. For instance, the two senses of the word *test* described by the clusters {experimentación, control, análisis, experimento} and {experimento, control, análisis, examen} share three elements and are closer than those described by {experimentación, control, análisis, experimento} and {evaluación}, which have no element in common. The first two senses could also be considered as nuances of a coarser sense ("examination / analysis") that could be obtained by merging the overlapping clusters. Capturing inter-sense relations is important in lexical semantics and numerous works have been criticized for just enumerating word senses without describing their relations. Discovering these links automatically, as is done with this sense clustering method, permits to account for differences in the status of senses during WSD and its evaluation. It also offers the possibility to automatically modify the granularity of the obtained senses according to the WSD needs of the applications. Moreover, when the sense cluster inventory is used for cross-lingual WSD, it allows to capture subtle relations between word usages in cases where the senses of a word share some of their translations but not all of them, an issue highlighted in the SemEval CLLS task (Sinha et al., 2009) which will be presented in the next section.

## 4 The SemEval-2010 CLLS task

In the SemEval-2010 Cross-Lingual Lexical Substitution task, annotators and systems had to provide several alternative correct translations in Spanish for English target words in context. Given a paragraph containing an instance of an English target word, the annotators had to find as many good substitute translations as possible for that word in Spanish. Unlike a full-blown MT task, CLLS targets one word at a time rather than an entire sentence. So, annotators were asked to translate the target word and not entire sentences. Moreover, they were asked to supply, for each instance, as many translations as they felt were valid and not just one translation, which would be the case in MT.

The task of the participating systems was then to predict the translations provided by the annotators for each target word instance. By analyzing the context of the English target word instances, the systems had to provide for each instance, several correct Spanish translations which should fit the given source language context. The set of target words in the SemEval CLLS task is composed of Nouns, Verbs, Adjectives and Adverbs exhibiting a wide variety of substitutes. The annotators were allowed to use any resources they wanted to in order to supply substitutes for instances of the English target words. So, instances of the target words in context were tagged by sets of Spanish translations.[5] The inter-annotator agreement for this task was calculated as pairwise agreement between sets of substitutes from annotators and corresponds to 0.2777.

The sets of translations provided for different instances of a target word could overlap in different degrees, depending on the meaning of the instances. These overlaps reveal subtle relations between word usages in cases where they share some of their translations but not all of them (Sinha et al., 2009). This also shows the absence of clear divisions between usages and senses: usages overlap to different extents without having identical translations. Although no clustering of translations from a specific resource into senses was performed for this task, the interest of examining the possibility of clustering the translations provided by the annotators is highlighted (Mihalcea et al., 2010).

## 5 Cross-lingual WSD

The source language features that revealed the similarity of the translations and served to their clustering (cf. section 3) can be exploited by an unsupervised WSD classifier (Apidianaki, 2009). In order to disambiguate a new instance of an English word *w*, cooccurrence information coming from its context is compared to these feature sets and the cluster that has the highest similarity with the new context is selected. We adopt this WSD method in order to exploit the sense clustering results and perform CLLS in an unsupervised manner. Instead of comparing the new contexts to the features that are common to all the translations in a cluster (i.e. the intersection of their source language features), as is done in the initial method, we compare them to the features shared by each pair of translations. This increases the coverage of the method, given that these source features sets are larger than the ones containing the intersection of the features of all the clustered translations. As the training corpus was lemmatized and POS-tagged prior to building the feature vectors (only content word cooccurrences were retained), the new contexts have to be lemmatized and POS-tagged as well.

If common features (CFs) are found between the new context and a translation pair, a score is assigned to this 'context-pair' association which corresponds to the mean of the weights of the CFs relatively to each translation of the pair. The weights used here are the total weights (*tw*s) that were assigned to the context features relatively to the translations during the semantic similarity calculation (cf. section 3.2). In formula 5, $i$ is equal to 2 (i.e. the number of translations in the pair) and $j$ is the number of CFs between the translation pair and the new context.

If the highest-ranked translation pair is found in just one sense cluster, this cluster is selected as describing the sense of the new instance. Otherwise, if the translation pair is found in different clusters, it is checked whether the CFs characterize the other translations in these clusters (or some of them). If this is the case, a score is assigned to each cluster

[5] The average numbers of substitutes provided by the annotators for words of different POS are: 4.47 for nouns, 5.2 for verbs, 4.99 for adjectives and 4.77 for adverbs.

| Test instance | WSD suggestion | Gold annotation |
|---|---|---|
| test.n 1698 | prueba;ensayo;examen; | examen 4;prueba 4;test 1; |
| board.n 1781 | consejo;bordo;junta;comité;cuenta; administración; | junta directiva 2;consejo 2;mesa directiva 1;junta 1;junta de ayuda 1;directiva 1;comite 1;comision 1; |
| drop.v 1288 | bajar;disminuir;reducir;caer;descender | dejar caer 2;tirar 1;arrojar 1;lanzar 1;soltar 1;dejar 1;bajar 1; |
| check.v 851 | comprobar;controlar;verificar; | verificar 3;checar 2;confirmar 1;anotar 1;rectificar 1;revisar 1;comprobar 1; |
| yet.r 1766 | todavía;aún;sin embargo; | sin embargo 2;pero 2;no obstante 1;aun 1;todavia 1; |
| now.r 1019 | hoy;aquí;actualmente;ahora bien; | hoy 2;ahora 2;este momento 2;a partir 1;el presente 1;de aqui 1; |

Table 2: *Clusters suggested by the WSD method.*

depending on the weights of the features with the other translations, and the cluster with the highest score is selected as describing the sense of the new instance. The score is again calculated by formula 5 but this time *i* is equal to the number of translations in the cluster having CFs with the new context.

$$\text{score} = \frac{\sum_i \sum_j tw(i,j)}{i * j} \qquad (5)$$

If no CFs are found using the translation pairs, the WSD algorithm considers each translation's feature set separately (which is naturally larger than the feature sets of the translation pairs). If CFs exist, the translation with the highest score is selected as well as the cluster containing it. If the translation is found in the intersection of different clusters, it is checked whether the CFs characterize some of the other translations found in the clusters. If this is the case, a score is assigned to the clusters depending on the weights of the features with the translations and the cluster with the highest score is selected. The cluster containing the translation pair with the highest similarity to the new context is retained as the sense of the new instance. If no CFs are found in this way neither, a most frequent sense heuristic is used which selects the most frequent cluster (i.e. the one assigned to most of the new instances of *w*).

For the 1000 test instances in the SemEval CLLS task, the WSD method proposes 625 clusters with more than one element and 118 one element clusters.[6] The most frequent translation is suggested in 210 cases while the most frequent cluster is chosen in 43 cases. A cluster is chosen randomly only in 3 cases. In Table 2, we present some suggestions made by the WSD method for target words of different POS (n: nouns, v: verbs, a: adjectives, r: adverbs) and the corresponding gold standard (GS) annotations. For instance, the following occurrence of the English noun *test*:

> Entries typically identify the age or school grade levels for which the **test** is appropriate, as well as any subtests.

is tagged by the Spanish cluster {*prueba, examen, ensayo*} during WSD, which is close to the GS annotation {*examen, prueba, test*} and correctly describes its sense.

The first translation provided in the results is the word of the cluster that translates most of the English target word instances in the corpus (and which is duplicated in order to be reinforced during the 'out-of-ten' evaluation, as we will explain in the next section). We observe that this most frequent word, although it is a correct translation (i.e. found in the GS annotations), does not coincide with the annotators' first choice. This explains the evaluation results that we present in the next section.

It is also important to note that the system suggests not only translations that have been proposed by the annotators, but also other semantically pertinent translations that were found in the training corpus and which do not exist in the GS annotations. This is the case, for instance, with the translation

[6] 262 clusters with two elements; 157 clusters with three; 73 with four; 64 with five; 69 clusters with more than five and less than ten elements; 23 clusters with ten elements and 22 clusters with more than ten elements.

"controlar" of the verb *check* and the translation "ensayo" proposed for the noun *test*. This shows that the suggestions made by the WSD method greatly depend on the corpus used for training.

## 6 Evaluation

### 6.1 The setting

We evaluate our method on the SemEval-2010 CLLS task test set. The metrics used for evaluation are the *best* and *out-of-ten* (oot) precision (P) and recall (R) scores. In the SemEval task, the systems were allowed to supply as many translations as they felt fit the context. These suggestions were then given credit depending on the number of annotators that had picked each translation. The credit was divided by the number of annotator responses for the item. For the *best* score, the credit for the system answers for an item was also divided by the number of answers provided by the system, which allows more credit to be given to instances with less variation.

The *oot* scorer allows up to ten system responses and does not divide the credit attributed to each answer by the number of system responses. This scorer allows duplicates which means that systems can get inflated scores (i.e. $> 100$), as the credit for each item is not divided by the number of substitutes and the frequency of each annotator response is used. Allowing duplicates permits that the systems boost their scores with duplicates on translations with higher probability.[7]

Two baselines are used for evaluation: a dictionary-based one (DICT), which contains the Spanish translations of all target words provided by an SP-EN dictionary, and a dictionary and corpus-based one (DICTCORP), where the translations provided by the dictionary for a given target word are ranked according to their frequencies in the Spanish Wikipedia. In DICT, the *best* baseline is produced by taking the first translation provided by the dictionary while the *oot* baseline considers the first ten translations.

### 6.2 Results

In order to evaluate our WSD method, we proceed as follows. If the cluster selected by the WSD method contains ten translations (or more), all the translations are given in the *oot* results. Otherwise, the translations found in the cluster are proposed and the most frequent translation is duplicated till reaching ten elements. For *best*, we always retain the most frequent translation of the selected cluster.

Our intuition was that the WSD method, which assigns sense clusters (i.e. sets of semantically similar and, more or less, substitutable translations), would fit and perform well on the *oot* subtask of the SemEval CLLS task. This is confirmed by the results presented in Table 3.[8] Our method (denoted by 'WSD' in the table) outperforms the 14 systems that participated in the CLLS task as well as the recall (R) and precision (P) baselines. It is important to note that, contrary to our method which is totally unsupervised, all the systems that participated in the SemEval-2010 task used predefined resources. The second ranked system (SWAT-E), for instance, performs lexical substitution in English and then translates each substitute into Spanish using two predefined bilingual dictionaries, while SWAT-S does the inverse, performing lexical substitution in the translated text (Wicentowski et al., 2010).

| Systems | R | P | Mode R | Mode P |
|---|---|---|---|---|
| **WSD** | **180.10** | **186.25** | **56.52** | **58.44** |
| SWAT-E | 174.59 | 174.59 | 66.94 | 66.94 |
| SWAT-S | 97.98 | 97.98 | 79.01 | 79.01 |
| UvT-v | 58.91 | 58.91 | 62.96 | 62.96 |
| UvT-g | 55.29 | 55.29 | 73.94 | 73.94 |
| DICT | 44.04 | 44.04 | 73.53 | 73.53 |
| DICTCORP | 42.65 | 42.65 | 71.60 | 71.60 |

Table 3: **oot** results (%)

Another interesting point is that the sense cluster inventory used by the cross-lingual WSD method is derived from Europarl, which is the European Parliament Proceedings parallel corpus (Koehn, 2005). Despite this fact, the WSD method that exploits this inventory performs particularly well on this task which concerns the semantic analysis and translation of words of general language. We would thus expect the results to be even better if the sense induc-

[7]The metrics used for evaluation are defined in Mihalcea et al. (2010).

[8]We report the results obtained by the highest-ranked systems in the SemEval-2010 CLLS task. The full table of results can be found in Mihalcea et al. (2010).

tion and the WSD method were trained on a bigger, or more general, parallel corpus.

The mode recall and precision (Mode R and Mode P) metrics evaluate the performance of the systems in predicting the translation that was most frequently selected by the annotators, provided that such a translation extists. To identify the most frequent response, we order the system responses according to their frequency as translations of the target words in the training corpus. The relatively low scores obtained for the Mode R and Mode P metrics (compared to R and P) are explained by the fact that the most frequent translation in the training corpus does not always correspond to the translation that was most frequently selected by the annotators, although it may be a good translation for the target word.

The same reason explains the weaker performance of the method in the *best* evaluation subtask (cf. Table 4), where our system is ranked eighth compared to the 14 systems that participated in the task.[9] Here too, the *best* translation according to the annotators does not correspond to the most frequent translation in the corpus. This highlights the impact that the relevance of the training corpus to the domains of the processed texts has on unsupervised CLLS.

| Systems | R | P | Mode R | Mode P |
|---|---|---|---|---|
| UBA-T | 27.15 | 27.15 | 57.20 | 57.20 |
| USPWLV | 26.81 | 26.81 | 58.85 | 58.85 |
| WLVUSP | 25.27 | 25.27 | 52.81 | 52.81 |
| **WSD** | **19.73** | **19.93** | **41.29** | **41.75** |
| UBA-W | 19.68 | 19.68 | 39.09 | 39.09 |
| SWAT-S | 18.87 | 18.87 | 36.63 | 36.63 |
| IRST-1 | 15.38 | 22.16 | 33.47 | 45.95 |
| TYO | 8.39 | 8.62 | 14.95 | 15.31 |
| DICT | 24.34 | 24.34 | 50.34 | 50.34 |
| DICTCORP | 15.09 | 15.09 | 29.22 | 29.22 |

Table 4: **best** results (%)

Another important factor that has to be taken into account is that the WSD method that we use is oriented towards multilingual applications (more precisely MT). In these applications, it is possible to filter the proposed sense clusters by reference to the target language context (for instance, by using a language model) in order to retain the most adequate translation. It is interesting to note that the systems that perform better in the *best* subtask get relatively low results in the *oot* subtask, and the inverse. This is the case, for instance, for UBA-T (Basile and Semeraro, 2010), while Aziz and Specia (2010) clearly specify that their main goal is to maximize the accuracy of their system (USPwlv) in choosing the *best* translation. A conclusion that can be drawn is that each subtask has different requirements, which may be satisfied by different types of methods.

In order to investigate other possible reasons behind the different behavior of the WSD method in the two evaluation subtasks, we performed the evaluation separately for each POS. The results are presented in Tables 5 and 6.

| POS | R | P | Mode R | Mode P |
|---|---|---|---|---|
| **Adjs** | **287.94** | **296.41** | **72.44** | **74.43** |
| **Nouns** | 127.01 | 141.65 | 37.78 | 42.29 |
| **Verbs** | 115.94 | 121.43 | 53.17 | 55.90 |
| **Advs** | 111.46 | 111.46 | 65.15 | 65.15 |

Table 5: **oot** results for different POS (%)

| POS | R | P | Mode R | Mode P |
|---|---|---|---|---|
| **Adjs** | **30.77** | **31.00** | **63.56** | **64.13** |
| **Nouns** | 14.61 | 16.29 | 25.78 | 28.86 |
| **Verbs** | 14.98 | 14.98 | 29.76 | 29.76 |
| **Advs** | 13.07 | 13.07 | 37.88 | 37.88 |

Table 6: **best** results for different POS (%)

In both the *oot* and *best* evaluation subtasks, the best scores are obtained for adjectives. Especially in the *best* subtask, where the method seemed to perform worse than the other systems, the recall and precision scores obtained for adjectives (with and without mode) are higher than those obtained by the highest-ranked system (cf. Table 4) and much higher than the baselines. A more detailed look at the obtained results proved that the most frequent translation of the English adjectives in our training corpus – proposed in the *best* evaluation subtask and emphasized in the *oot* subtask – is often the most frequent translation proposed by the annotators. This is not the case for the other POS, where the most frequent

[9]We report some indicative results from the *best* subtask. The full table of results can be found in Mihalcea et al. (2010).

translation in the corpus often does not correspond to the annotators' first choice. Furthermore, the translation proposed by the system is not the same as the most frequent translation of the word in the general dictionary and the Spanish Wikipedia which were used, respectively, for the DICT and DICT-CORP baselines. Consequently, this issue could probably be resolved if a more balanced corpus was used for training the WSI and WSD methods.

## 7 Conclusions and future work

We have shown that Cross-Lingual Lexical Substitution can be performed in a totally unsupervised manner, if a parallel corpus is available. We applied an unsupervised cross-lingual WSD method based on semantic clustering to the SemEval-2010 CLLS task. The method performs well compared to the systems that participated in the task, which exploit predefined lexico-semantic resources. It is ranked first on the *out-of-ten* measure and medium on measures that concern the choice of the *best* translation. We wish to pursue this work and explore other ways for selecting *best* translations than solely relying on frequency information. As unsupervised methods heavily rely on the training data, it would also be interesting to experiment with different corpora in order to evaluate the impact of the type and the size of the corpus on CLLS.

The sense clusters assigned to target word instances during CLLS contain semantically similar translations of these words, more or less substitutable in the target language context. We consider that it would be interesting to integrate target language information in the CLLS decision process for selecting *best* translations. Given that MT is one of the envisaged applications for this type of task, but the use of a full-blown MT system would probably mask system capabilities at a lexical level, a possibility would be to exploit the CLLS system suggestions in a simplified MT task such as *word translation* (Vickrey et al., 2005) or *lexical selection* (Apidianaki, 2009), or in an MT evaluation context. This would permit to estimate the usefulness of the system suggestions in a specific application setting.

## References


Marianna Apidianaki and Yifan He. 2010. An algorithm for cross-lingual sense clustering tested in a MT evaluation setting. In *Proceedings of the 7th International Workshop on Spoken Language Translation (IWSLT-10)*, pages 219–226, Paris, France.

Marianna Apidianaki. 2008. Translation-oriented sense induction based on parallel corpora. In *Proceedings of the 6th International Conference on Language Resources and Evaluation (LREC-08)*, pages 3269–3275, Marrakech, Morocco.

Marianna Apidianaki. 2009. Data-driven Semantic Analysis for Multilingual WSD and Lexical Selection in Translation. In *Proceedings of the 12th Conference of the European Chapter of the Association for Computational Linguistics (EACL-09)*, pages 77–85, Athens, Greece.

Wilker Aziz and Lucia Specia. 2010. USP*wlv* and WLV*usp*: Combining Dictionaries and Contextual Information for Cross-Lingual Lexical Substitution. In *Proceedings of the 5th International Workshop on Semantic Evaluations (SemEval-2), ACL 2010*, pages 117–122, Uppsala, Sweden.

Pierpaolo Basile and Giovanni Semeraro. 2010. UBA: Using Automatic Translation and Wikipedia for Cross-Lingual Lexical Substitution. In *Proceedings of the 5th International Workshop on Semantic Evaluations (SemEval-2), ACL 2010*, pages 242–247, Uppsala, Sweden.

Marine Carpuat and Dekai Wu. 2007. Improving Statistical Machine Translation using Word Sense Disambiguation. In *Proceedings of the Joint EMNLP-CoNLL Conference*, pages 61–72, Prague, Czech Republic.

Yee Seng Chan, Hwee Tou Ng, and David Chiang. 2007. Word Sense Disambiguation Improves Statistical Machine Translation. In *Proceedings of the 45th Annual Meeting of the Association for Computational Linguistics (ACL-07)*, pages 33–40, Prague, Czech Republic.

Andrew Chesterman. 1998. *Contrastive Functional Analysis*. John Benjamins Publishing Company, Amsterdam/Philadelphia.

Mona Diab. 2003. *Word sense disambiguation within a multilingual framework*. Ph.D. dissertation, University of Maryland.

Gregory Grefenstette. 1994. *Explorations in Automatic Thesaurus Discovery*. Kluwer Academic Publishers, Norwell, MA.

Zelig Harris. 1954. Distributional structure. *Word*, 10:146–162.

Nancy Ide, Tomaz Erjavec, and Dan Tufis. 2002. Sense discrimination with parallel corpora. In *Proceedings of the ACL Workshop on Word Sense Disambiguation:*

*Recent Successes and Future Directions*, pages 54–60, Philadelphia.

Nancy Ide. 1999. Cross-lingual sense determination: Can it work? *Computers and the Humanities*, 34(1-2):223–234.

Philip Koehn. 2005. Europarl: A Parallel Corpus for Statistical Machine Translation. In *Proceedings of MT Summit X*, pages 79–86, Phuket, Thailand.

Alon Lavie and Abhaya Agarwal. 2007. METEOR: An Automatic Metric for MT Evaluation with High Levels of Correlation with Human Judgments. In *Proceedings of the ACL-2007 Workshop on Statistical Machine Translation*, pages 228–231, Prague, Czech Republic.

Els Lefever and Veronique Hoste. 2010. SemEval-2010 Task 3: Cross-lingual Word Sense Disambiguation. In *Proceedings of the 5th International Workshop on Semantic Evaluations (SemEval-2), ACL 2010*, pages 15–20, Uppsala, Sweden.

Diana McCarthy and Roberto Navigli. 2009. The English lexical substitution task. *Language Resources and Evaluation Special Issue on Computational Semantic Analysis of Language: SemEval-2007 and Beyond*, 43(2):139–159.

Rada Mihalcea, Ravi Sinha, and Diana McCarthy. 2010. SemEval-2010 Task 2: Cross-Lingual Lexical Substitution. In *Proceedings of the 5th International Workshop on Semantic Evaluations (SemEval-2), ACL 2010*, pages 9–14, Uppsala, Sweden.

George A. Miller and Walter G. Charles. 1991. Contextual correlates of semantic similarity. *Language and Cognitive Processes*, 6(1):1–28.

Roberto Navigli. 2009. Word Sense Disambiguation: a Survey. *ACM Computing Surveys*, 41(2):1–69.

Hwee Tou Ng and Yee Seng Chan. 2007. SemEval-2007 Task 11: English lexical sample task via English-Chinese parallel text. In *Proceedings of the 4th International Workshop on Semantic Evaluations (SemEval-2007)*, pages 54–58, Prague, Czech Republic.

Hwee Tou Ng, Bin Wang, and Yee Seng Chan. 2003. Exploiting Parallel Texts for Word Sense Disambiguation: An Empirical Study. In *Proceedings of the 41st Annual Meeting of the Association for Computational Linguistics*, pages 455–462, Sapporo, Japan.

Franz Josef Och and Hermann Ney. 2003. A Systematic Comparison of Various Statistical Alignment Models. *Computational Linguistics*, 29(1):19–51.

Philip Resnik and David Yarowsky. 2000. Distinguishing Systems and Distinguishing Senses: New Evaluation Methods for Word Sense Disambiguation. *Natural Language Engineering*, 5(3):113–133.

Philip Resnik. 2007. WSD in NLP applications. In Eneko Agirre and Philip Edmonds, editors, *Word Sense Disambiguation: Algorithms and Applications*, pages 299–337, Dordrecht. Springer.

Helmut Schmid. 1994. Probabilistic Part-of-Speech Tagging Using Decision Trees. In *Proceedings of the International Conference on New Methods in Language Processing*, pages 44–49, Manchester, UK.

Ravi Sinha, Diana McCarthy, and Rada Mihalcea. 2009. SemEval-2010 Task 2: Cross-Lingual Lexical Substitution. In *Proceedings of the NAACL-HLT Workshop SEW-2009 - Semantic Evaluations: Recent Achievements and Future Directions*, pages 76–81, Boulder, Colorado.

David Vickrey, Luke Biewald, Marc Teyssier, and Daphne Koller. 2005. Word-Sense Disambiguation for Machine Translation. In *Proceedings of the Joint Conference on Human Language Technology / Empirical Methods in Natural Language Processing (HLT-EMNLP)*, pages 771–778, Vancouver, Canada.

Richard Wicentowski, Maria Kelly, and Rachel Lee. 2010. SWAT: Cross-Lingual Lexical Substitution using Local Context Matching, Bilingual Dictionaries and Machine Translation. In *Proceedings of the 5th International Workshop on Semantic Evaluations (SemEval-2), ACL*, pages 123–128, Uppsala, Sweden.

# Reducing the Size of the Representation for the uDOP-Estimate

**Christoph Teichmann**
Abteilung Automatische Sprachverarbeitung
Institute of Computerscience
University of Leipzig
Max Planck Institute for Human Cognitive and Brain Sciences
Leipzig
teichmann@informatik.uni-leipzig.de

## Abstract

The unsupervised Data Oriented Parsing (uDOP) approach has been repeatedly reported to achieve state of the art performance in experiments on parsing of different corpora. At the same time the approach is demanding both in computation time and memory. This paper describes an approach which decreases these demands. First the problem is translated into the generation of probabilistic bottom up tree automata (pBTA). Then it is explained how solving two standard problems for these automata results in a reduction in the size of the grammar. The reduction of the grammar size by using efficient algorithms for pBTAs is the main contribution of this paper. Experiments suggest that this leads to a reduction in grammar size by a factor of 2. This paper also suggests some extensions of the original uDOP algorithm that are made possible or aided by the use of tree automata.

## 1 Introduction

The approaches to unsupervised parsing given by Bod (2006a,2006b,2007) are all based on using all possible subtrees over a training corpus. This means that a great number of subtrees has to be represented. For every sentence the number of binary trees that can be proposed for that sentence[1] is given by the Catalan number of the length of the sentence. The number of subtrees for a tree in this set is exponential with respect to the length of the sentence.

In Bod (2007) a packed representation for all subtrees was proposed that is based on a technique for supervised Data Oriented Parsing (*DOP*) given in Goodman (2003). This paper aims to relate the problem of representing an estimate for all subtrees over a corpus to the field of tree automata (Fülöp and Vogler, 2009). With this step it will be possible to reduce the size of the packed representation of the subtrees even further. This newly formulated approach will also consider working with partially bracketed corpora.

The next step in this paper will be a short discussion of uDOP. Then the necessary terminology is introduced. The reduction approach of this paper is given in section 4. In the final section it will be discussed how the step to tree automata creates additional possibilities to influence the final estimate produced by the uDOP estimator. In section 5 some evaluation results will be given for the decrease in grammar size that can be achieved by the techniques presented here.

## 2 A Short Discussion of uDOP

The unsupervised Data Oriented Parsing (uDOP) approach (Bod 2006a,2006b,2007) is defined by two steps. The first step is proposing every binary parse tree for each sentence in the corpus. This is followed by adding any subtree that occurs in the trees to the grammar as a possible derivation step. Since binary trees have more subtrees than nonbinary trees, the binary

**Acknowledgments:** The author would like to thank Amit Kirschbaum, Robert Remus, Anna Janska and the anonymus reviewers for their remarks.

[1] Only a single nonterminal X is used

*Proceedings of EMNLP 2011, Conference on Empirical Methods in Natural Language Processing*, pages 24–34,
Edinburgh, Scotland, UK, July 27–31, 2011. ©2011 Association for Computational Linguistics

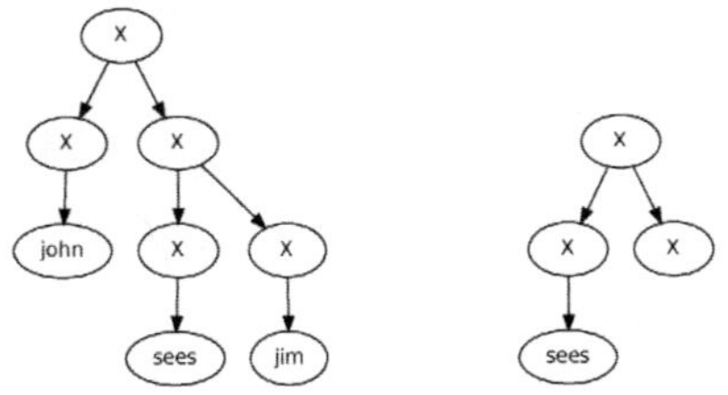


(a) A possible tree proposed over a corpus sentence

(b) another possible subtree

Figure 1: an example for the uDOP approach

ones would always be the parses the approach prefers. Therefore the uDOP approach only uses the binary trees. The only nonterminal used is a new symbol usually refered to as 'X'.

The second step is estimation. For each subtree the number of occurrences in the proposed trees is counted. This number is divided by the sum of all occurrences of subtrees starting with the same nonterminal, which allows to derive a probability distribution over all trees.

If one takes the sentence 'john sees jim', one tree that can be proposed is shown in Figure 1(a). Then one possible subtree is shown in Figure 1(b). The subtree in Figure 1(b) would occur twice among the parses for the sentence 'jim sees the french guest', since there are two possible binary parses with the nonterminal 'X' for the substring 'the french guest'. One is given by

$$X(X(X(the)X(french))X(guest)) \quad (1)$$

the other is given by:

$$X(X(the)X(X(french)X(guest))) \quad (2)$$

In this paper a small extension of the original uDOP algorithm is considered. The idea is well known from Pereira and Schabes (1992). The extension is assuming that the corpus may consist of partial parses. The algorithm is changed so that for every partial tree all binary trees that are completions of the partial tree are proposed. Labels for the constituents in the partial tree are kept. Only a single nonterminal is used for the completions.

Take for example the sentence 'john sees the reporter'. If one is confident that 'the reporter' is a constituent of the type $NP$ then the corpus entry would be:

$$X(X(john)X(sees)NP(X(the)X(reporter))) \quad (3)$$

This entry has two completions, the first one is given by:

$$X(X(X(john)X(sees))NP(X(the)X(reporter))) \quad (4)$$

The second one is given by:

$$X(X(john)X(X(sees)NP(X(the)X(reporter)))) \quad (5)$$

So making a parse complete means introducing additional brackets until the tree is binary. One may also consider not introducing brackets inside of existing brackets in order to allow for nonbinary branching.

These two parses contain subtrees starting and terminating with the nonterminal $NP$. This shows that such partial brackets and their class labels can create recursion on the introduced labels. These partial parses could come from other algorithms and reduce the final grammar size.

Approaches like the ones in Hänig (2010), Santamaria and Araujo (2010) and Ponvert et al. (2011) could be combined with the uDOP approach using this simple extension. All three approaches do not necessarily produce binary parse trees. This could be used to extend uDOP to nonbinary trees. Using the low level bracketings from the algorithms would reduce the size of an uDOP grammar estimated from them. Partial bracketing could also be approximated by using HTML annotation, punctuation and semantical annotation (Spitkovsky et al., 2010; Spitkovsky et al., 2011; Naseem and Barzilay, 2011).

## 3 Terminology

This section introduces stochastic tree substitution grammars. It will also introduce a version of probabilistic bottom up tree automata suited for representation of large stochastic tree substitution grammars. Furthermore it gives a more formal definition of the uDOP-estimate. Some definitions are not standard.[2]

The first definition necessary is the concept of trees.

**Definition 1** (Trees)**.** *The set of trees over leaf nodes $L$ and internal nodes $I$ is denoted by $T(L, I)$ and is defined as the smallest set conforming to:*

$$\forall \alpha \in (T(L, I) \cup L)^* : \forall y \in I : y(\alpha) \in T(L, I) \tag{6}$$

*Where $X^*$ denotes all tuples over the set $X$.*[3]

*If a tree has the form $y(\alpha)$ then $y \in I$ is called the root node. The leftmost node of an element $t \in (L \cup T(L, I))$ is denoted by $lm(t)$ and given by:*

$$lm(t) = \begin{cases} t \text{ if } t \in L \\ lm(x_1) \text{ if } t = y(x_1, \ldots, x_n) \end{cases} \tag{7}$$

This definition basically states that trees are bracketed structures. Annotation gives the type of the bracket. Note that the definition of trees excludes trees that consist of only a single leaf node. This is a restriction that is common for STSGs.

The next element that needs to be defined is the concept of *extending a tree*. If a node in a tree has more than two daughters, then the tree can be extended. This is done by replacing two of the daughter nodes by a new node $N$ labeled with any nonterminal and making the two removed daughter nodes the daughter nodes of the new node $N$. A *complete tree* is a tree that has no extensions. In other words, a complete tree has only nodes with less than two daughters. A tree $t$ is a completion of the tree $t'$ if $t$ is complete and can be generated from $t'$ by any number of completions. Next it is necessary to define subtrees.

**Definition 2** (Subtrees)**.** *Let*

$$t = L(\ldots M(N_1(\ldots), \ldots, N_i(\alpha), \ldots, N_k(\ldots)) \ldots)$$

*be a tree then*

$$t' = M(N_1(\ldots), \ldots, N_i(\alpha), \ldots, N_k(\ldots))$$

*is a direct subtree of $t$ and if the root of $\alpha$ is in $I$ then*

$$t'' = L(\ldots M(N_1(\ldots), \ldots, N_i(), \ldots, N_k(\ldots)) \ldots)$$

*is also a direct subtree of $t$. The set of subtrees for a tree $t$ is denoted by $ST(t)$ and contains $t$ and all direct subtrees of trees in $ST(t)$.*

The first important fact about subtrees is that each node has either all or none of its daughters included in a subtree. The second important fact is that subtrees of less than two nodes are not allowed.

**Definition 3** (Stochastic Tree Substitution Grammar)**.** *A stochastic tree substitution grammar (STSG) is a tuple $\langle \Sigma, N, \tau, N_0, \omega \rangle$ where $\Sigma$ is a finite alphabet of terminals, $N$ is a finite set of nonterminals, $N_0 \in N$ is the start nonterminal, $\tau \subseteq T((\Sigma \cup N), N)$ is the set of trees*[4] *and $\omega : \tau \to \mathbb{R}^+$ is the weight function, where $\mathbb{R}^+$ is the set of positive real numbers.*

For space reasons it will not be discussed how a STSG defines a distribution over strings and trees. Note that since a CFG can be found that defines the same distribution over strings for every STSG (Goodman, 2003) similar constraints hold for STSGs and CFGs when it comes to defining proper distributions. In order to ensure that all string weights sum up to 1 the trees in

[2] No rank is assumed for the labels of trees, to give an example.

[3] The empty tuple is included.

[4] This set may be finite or infinite. The uDOP Estimate results in a finite set if the corpus is finite.

$T$ for each possible root nonterminal must sum to one.[5]

**Definition 4** (Probabilistic Bottom Up Tree Automaton). *A probabilistic bottom up tree automaton (pBTA) is a tuple* $\langle Q, \Sigma, \delta, q_0, \omega, \lambda \rangle$ *where* $Q$ *is a finite set of states,* $\Sigma$ *is the finite alphabet,* $\delta \subseteq Q^+ \times \Sigma \times Q$ *is the finite set of transitions where* $Q^+$ *denotes all nonempty tuples over the states,* $q_0$ *is the start state,* $\omega : \delta \rightarrow \mathbb{R}^+$ *is the transition weight function and* $\lambda : \delta \rightarrow \mathbb{R}^+$ *is the final weight function.*

**Definition 5** (Weight of a Tree in a pBTA). *The weight of an element* $t \in T(\Sigma, Q \times \Sigma \cup \{q_0\} \cup \Sigma)$ *given an automaton* $A = \langle Q, \Sigma, \delta, q_0, \omega, \lambda \rangle$ *is denoted by* $\Omega(t, A)$ *and is defined by:*

$$\Omega(q_0, A) = 1 \tag{8}$$

$$\Omega(q, l(\alpha), A) = \sum_{\beta \in Q^n} \omega(\langle \langle \beta \rangle, l, q \rangle) \cdot \prod_{l_m(t_m) \in \alpha} \Omega(q_m, l_m(t_m), A) \tag{9}$$

*Where* $\alpha = l_1(t_1), \ldots, l_n(t_n)$ *and* $\beta = q_1, \ldots, q_n$. *Where these formulas do not define a weight, it is assumed to be* 0.

*The final weight of the tree* $t = l(l_1(t_1), \ldots, l_n(t_n))$ *for the automaton* $A$ *is denoted by* $\Lambda(l(l_1(t_1), \ldots, l_n(t_n)), A)$ *and is defined as:*

$$\Lambda(l(\alpha), A) = \sum_{q \in Q} \sum_{\beta \in Q^n} \lambda(\langle \langle \beta \rangle, l, q \rangle) \cdot \prod_{t_m \in \alpha} \Omega(q_m, l_m(t_1), A) \tag{10}$$

*Where again* $\alpha = l_1(t_1), \ldots, l_n(t_n)$ *and* $\beta = q_1, \ldots, q_n$.

The definitions for pBTAs basically specify a bottom up parsing proceedure in which finished trees are combined. The intermediate trees are labeled with states that guide the derivation process.

[5] Ensuring that the weight of the finite strings sums to one is more difficult. See Nederhof and Satta (2006).

**Definition 6** (Language). *The Language of a pBTA* $A$ *denoted* $L(A)$ *is the set:*

$$L(A) = \{t | \Lambda(t, A) \neq 0\} \tag{11}$$

The penultimate set of definitions is concerned with the language weight of a pBTA, inside and outside weights.

**Definition 7** (Language Weight). *The language weight for a pBTA* $A = \langle Q, \Sigma, \delta, q_0, \omega, \lambda \rangle$ *is denoted by* $wl(A)$ *and defined by:*

$$wl(A) = \sum_{t \in T(\Sigma, \Sigma)} \Lambda(t, A) \tag{12}$$

The *inside weight* for a state $q \in Q$ for an automaton $A = \langle Q, \Sigma, \delta, q_0, \omega, \lambda \rangle$ is denoted by inside$(q, A)$. It is the language weight of $A'$. Here $A'$ is $A$ changed so that it only has one final transition from $\langle q \rangle$ to some state with weight 1.

The *outside weight* for a state $q \in Q$ needs a recursive definition. The weight is made up of two summands. The first summand is the outside weight of the right hand side of all transitions $q$ occurs in.[6] This is multiplied with the inside weight of all states other than $q$ in the left hand side of the transition. Finally this value is taken times the number of occurrences of $q$ in the left hand side. The second summand is the same as the first only with the outside weight replaced by the final weight of the transitions.

Now only the uDOP estimate and the connection between STSGs and pBTAs are still missing.

**Definition 8** (uDOP Estimate). *For a STSG* $G = \langle \Sigma, \{X\}, T, N_0, \omega \rangle$ *and a corpus* $c = \langle c_1, \ldots, c_m \rangle$ *such that each* $c_l$ *is a tree of the form* $L(L_1(x_1), \ldots, L_n(x_n))$ *or an extension of such a tree. Let* $c'$ *be derived from* $c$ *by replacing each* $c_l$ *by all the complete trees in* $Ext(c_l)$. *Then the uDOP estimate uDOP*$(t, c)$ *is given by:*

$$\omega(t) = \frac{\sum_{c_1 \in c'} num(t, c_1)}{\sum_{t' \in T(N, N \cup \Sigma)} \sum_{c_1 \in c'} num(t', c_1)} \tag{13}$$

*where* $num(t, x)$ *is the number of times subtree* $t$ *occurs in the tree* $x$.

[6] In a transition $\langle \alpha, l, q \rangle$ $\alpha$ is the left hand side and $q$ the right hand side.

Here $c'$ is a corpus that contains each completion $t'$ once for every tree $t$ in the original corpus, such that $t'$ is a completion of $t$. This corpus is of course never generated explictly and only used in the definition.

**Definition 9** (STSG Given by a pBTA). *Let* $G = \langle \Sigma, N, \tau, N_0, \omega \rangle$ *be a STSG. The grammar is given by a pBTA A if* $t \in T \leftrightarrow L(A)$ *and* $\omega(x) = \Omega(x, A)$.

This definition states that the set of trees is the language of the automaton and the weight of each tree is the weight the automaton assigns to it.

The goal of this paper can now be described in the following way: given a corpus of trees $\langle c_1, \ldots, c_n \rangle$ find a pBTA $A$ that gives the uDOP estimate and is as small as possible. The relevant measure here is the number of transitions. The number of states that are useful, the number of labels that are used and the number of entries for the weight function are all dependent on the number of transitions. This measure is also independent of any specific implementation details. From the connection between STSGs and pBTAs some extensions to the uDOP algorithm are possible that will be discussed at the end of the paper in section 6.

Only completion with the nonterminal $X$ is used. All algorithms given in this paper can be adapted to more brackets by creating a transition for the additional labels whenever one for $X$ is created.

## 4 Reducing the Size of the Estimate

The generation process for the uDOP estimate that this paper proposes is as follows. First generate a pBTA representing all the complete parse trees for the corpus. Every tree $t$ in the corpus will have as its weight in the automaton the number of times it occurs in the completed corpus. The completed corpus is again the corpus with each tree replaced by all the trees completions.

As a second step manipulate the automaton for the set of completions in such a way that the set of subtrees is given and they are associated with the intended relative weights. Then apply normalization similar to the one employed by Maletti and Satta (2009). The normalization algorithm has to be slightly changed to account for the fact that the trees are not supposed to stand on their own, but rather be used in an STSG. A sketch will be given. For all final transition with label $l$ sum up the final weight of the transition times the inside weight of all states on the left hand side of the transition. Then multiply the weight of final transitions with label $l$ with the multiplication of the inside weights of their left hand side states and divide the weight by the sum for the label $l$. All other weights are normalized as described in Maletti and Satta (2009).

The reduction that will be proposed here is based on reducing the size of the representation of all trees. Once this is achieved, a simple algorithm can be applied that gives the uDOP estimate and only increases the size of the representation by a maximum factor of $2 \cdot |I| + |I|^2 + 1$ plus one transition for every nonterminal label.[7]

To understand the mapping to subtrees consider the following: If an automaton gives the set of all trees, then the outside weight of any state will be the number of trees this state is embedded in. The inside weight will be the number of trees embedded at this position. This is the case because inside and outside weights sum over the possible derivations.

For each nonterminal label $l$ a state $q_l$ is created only to represent the introduction of $l$. A transition of the form $\langle\langle q_0\rangle, l, q_l\rangle$ is added to the representation of all trees.[8] This transition is weighted by 1.

Denote the automaton representing all trees by $AT$. Let $r = \langle\langle q_1, q_2\rangle, X, q\rangle$ be a transition in $AT$. For each label $l$:

$$\text{inlab}(q_x, l) = \sum_{\langle \alpha, l, q_x \rangle \in \delta} \omega(r) \cdot \prod_{q_y \in \alpha} \text{inside}(q_x, AT) \tag{14}$$

[7] $I$ is the set of labels that occur on internal nodes or - in other words - the nonterminal labels. The factor is explained further into the section. Note that for the standard uDOP approach $|I| = 1$.

[8] $q_0$ is assumed to be the start state.

For each nonterminal label $l$ create the rules[9]:

$$r1 = \langle\langle q_l, q_2\rangle, X, q\rangle \quad (15)$$
$$r2 = \langle\langle q_1, q_l\rangle, X, q\rangle \quad (16)$$

For each pair of nonterminal labels $l_1, l_2$ create a rule[10]:

$$r3 = \langle\langle q_{l_1}, q_{l_2}\rangle, X, q\rangle \quad (17)$$

Let $w$ be the weight of the original transition. Set $\omega(r1) = in(q_2, l) \cdot w$,$\omega(r2) = in(q_1, l) \cdot w$ and $\omega(r3) = in(q_1, l_1) \cdot in(q_2, l_2) \cdot w$ respectively. Add final weight $out(q)$ to each transition.[11] This assigns to each subtree the number of counts. After the transformation each transition can be a point at which a derivation ends. Outside weight is assigned according to the number of trees the subtree is embedded in. The derivation can also start with any node. Therefore inside weight is added according to the number of embedded trees.

Normalizing the automaton afterwards gives the weights according to the uDOP estimator.

Bansal and Klein (2010) give a transformation from parse trees to subtrees that reduces the size of the representation even further. Since a version of the transformation from their paper can be applied to any representation of the full parse trees, it is complementary to the approach used here. For this reason it will not be discussed here and it should suffice to say that using this transformation would improve the results in this paper even further.

Before it is discussed how the size of the representation of all trees can be reduced further, the first step will be to present the approach by Goodman (2003).

### 4.1 The Goodman Reduction

The approach from Goodman (2003) was intended for use with the supervised version of Data Oriented Parsing. We will discuss a version of the algorithm that is based on tree automata and the considerations made so far.

The original approach works by creating a state for every node in the corpus. Each group of daughter nodes is then connected to its mother node by a weighted transition with weight 1. The transition from the daughters of the root node of a sentence is assigned a final weight of 1. Finally, the projection to the subtrees is applied.

The version for unsupervised parsing is similar to and based on parse forests and parse items. The states correspond to parsing items as in the CYK algorithm.[12]

The reduction can be described as follows: create a state/parse item $\langle i, j, k\rangle$ for every sentence $k$ and every range from $i$ to $j$ in the sentence. Also create one state for every type of terminal node. This is illustrated in Figures 2(a) and 2(b). Rules are introduced from the start state for each possible terminal to the terminal type nodes with weight 1. If terminal $x$ occurs in sentence $k$ from $i$ to $i+1$, create a transition from the terminal state for $x$ to the state $\langle i, i+1, k\rangle$ with weight 1. Label those transitions with $X$ or with the appropriate preterminal nonterminal if there is one in the partial corpus tree. All states with a difference greater than 1 between the start and the end point are connected to all state pairs $\langle i, m, k\rangle, \langle m, j, k\rangle$. Here $m$ is a point between $i$ and $j$. These transitions are again labeled by $X$ unless there is a bracket labeled by $L$ from $i$ to $j$ in this case the transition is labeled by $L$. The weight for each such transition is 1.

If $i$ is 0 and $j$ is the length of the sentence number $k$ then the final weight for transitions to the state $\langle i, j, k\rangle$ is 1.

In order to comply with the requirement that we only use completions of the given trees, one adjustment is necessary. When a bracket $a, b$ is present, no state $i, j, k$ is proposed such that $a < i < b < j \vee i < a < j < b$. Thereby all crossing brackets are ruled out.

[9]This accounts for the factor $2 \cdot |I|$.

[10]This accounts for the factor $|I|^2$.

[11]An actual implementation would not create a rule if all weights are 0.

[12]See for example (Younger, 1967).

## 4.2 Making the Representation of All Trees Deterministic

A possible step in size reduction is making the representation deterministic. Generally determinization does not lead to a reduction in size of a finite state automaton. Here however, determinization means simply that states representing equivalent subtrees are merged. This is similar to the graph packing idea used in Bansal and Klein (2010).

Assume a partial tree is given in the string form that was used in section 3, i.e. , as a string of brackets and symbols. Then two identical strings represent identical trees which have identical completions. Let the bracketing for sequence from $i$ to $j$ in sentence $k$ be identical to the bracketing for the sequence from $l$ to $m$ in sentence $n$. Assume also that the sequences represent the same string. Then the state $\langle i, j, k \rangle$ may be replaced in every transition by the state $\langle l, m, n \rangle$. The only thing that has to be kept track of is how many times a certain string corresponded to a full corpus entry. In the Goodman approach a final weight of 1 is used, since new states are created for every sentence. In the deterministic case the final weight for all transitions reaching a state that represents a bracketed sequence $x$ must be increased by 1 for each time $x$ occurs in the corpus. An illustration of the idea[13] is given in Figures 2(c) and 2(d).

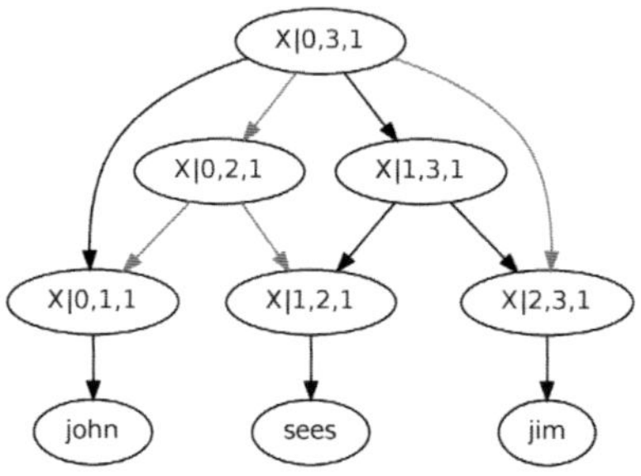


(a) Goodman reduction states

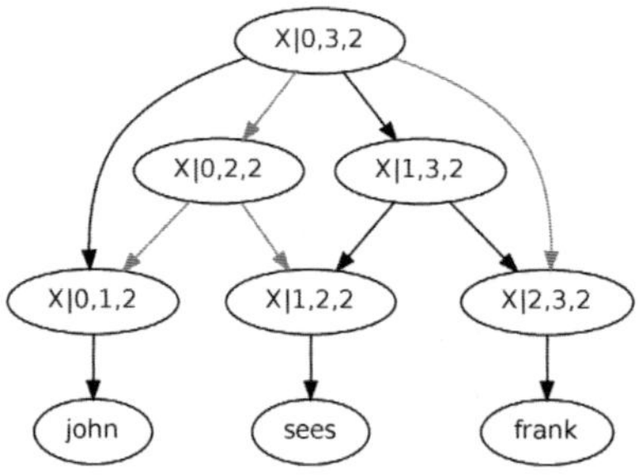


(b) Goodman reduction states

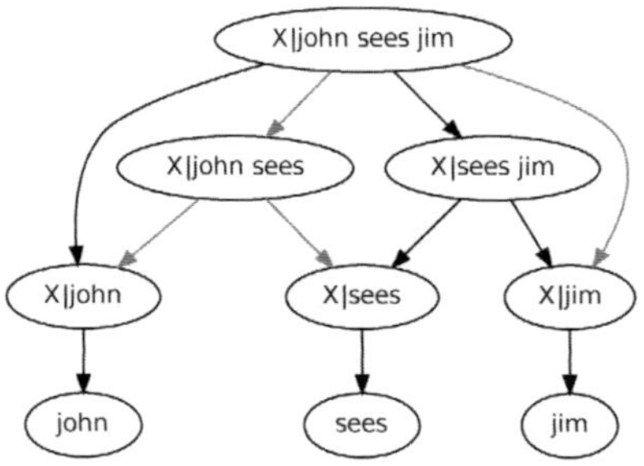


(c) Deterministic reduction states

## 4.3 Using Minimization

Finally one can try finding the minimal deterministic weighted tree automaton for the distribution. This is a well defined notion.

**Definition 10** (Minimal deterministic pBTA). *The minimal deterministic pBTA* $A' = \langle Q', \Sigma', \delta', q'_0, \omega', \lambda' \rangle$ *for a given pBTA* $A = \langle Q, \Sigma, \delta, q_0, \omega, \lambda \rangle$ *fulfills* $\Omega(x, p) = \Omega(x, A')$ *and there is no automaton* $A'' = \langle Q'', \Sigma'', \delta'', q''_0, \omega'', \lambda'' \rangle$ *fulfilling this criterion with* $|Q''| < |Q'|$.

A minimal deterministic pBTA is unique for the distribution it represents up to renaming the states.

[13]Here shown without any bracketing data

Note that this means that after the minimization the automaton is as small as possible for a deterministic pBTA. The only way to improve on this while staying in the pBTA framework would be to find a minimal nondeterministic automaton. That this is possible is shown in Bozapalidis (1991). It is however not clear that this problem could be solved in reasonable time for an automaton with hundreds of thousands of states.

In order to generate a minimal automaton, an efficiently verifiable criterion for two states

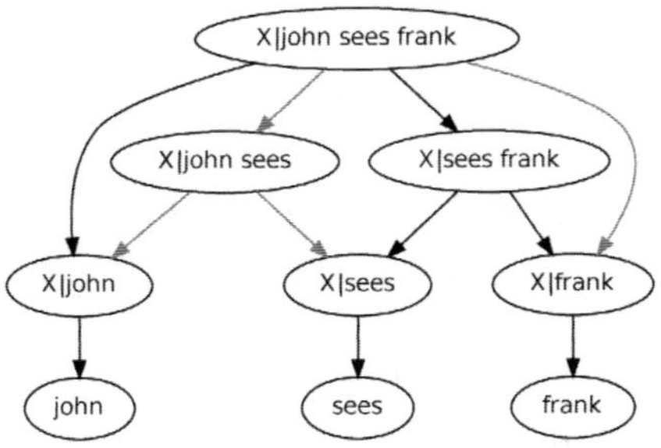


(d) Deterministic reduction states

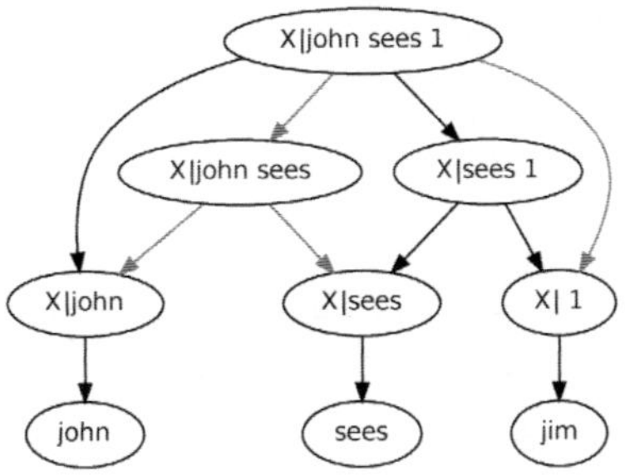


(e) Minimization reduction states

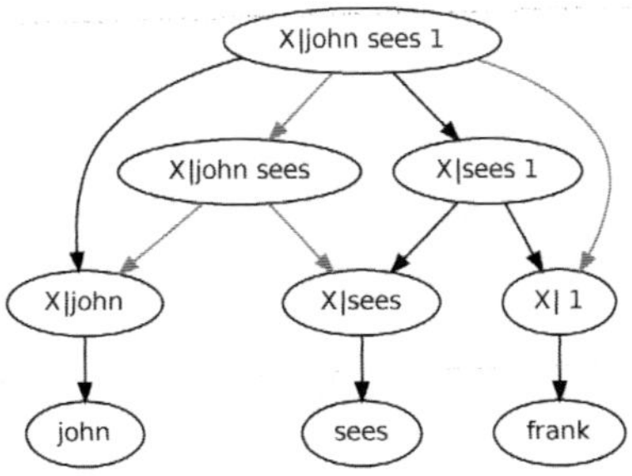


(f) Minimization reduction states

Figure 2: the different reduction approaches illustrated, different edge colors correspond to different parses. The Figures 2(b) and 2(a) are for the Goodman approach. Every span of words has its own state proposed. Figures 2(c) and 2(d) show how equals spans of words will lead to the repetition of the same state in the deterministic approach. Figures 2(e) and 2(f) show how two states that have equal contexts are merged into one state called '1'. This is an illustration of the minimization approach.

to be equivalent is necessary. For deterministic pBTA this is given by Maletti (2009). Since the automaton for all trees is nonrecursive after the deterministic construction, normalization allows minimizing the automaton in linear time, depending on the number of transitions.[14] For the algorithms to work, the fact that a deterministic pBTA is constructed is a necessary precondition.

Figures 2(e) and 2(f) illustrate this approach. The tree $X(jim)$ is distributed equally to the tree $X(frank)$. Since this is the case, a merged state for both trees is introduced. This state is labeled as 1.

## 5 Experimental Results

The algorithm was tested in two domains. The first one was the Negra Corpus (Skut et al., 1997). The second one was the Brown Corpus (Francis, 1964). The standard approach in unsupervised parsing is to use sequences of tags with certain punctuation removed (Klein and Manning, 2002). This is supposed to simulate spoken language. Once the punctuation is removed all sequences of length 10 or less are used for most approaches in unsupervised parsing. This ensures that the hypothesis space is relatively small for the sentences left in the corpus. The same approach is chosen for this paper, as this is the context in which uDOP grammars are most likely to be evaluated. A slightly different definition of punctuation is used. Note that no bracketing structure is used. This means that for every string in the corpus, a number of transitions has to be created that is limited by $n^3$ in the worst case, were $n$ is the length of the string.

Note that the removal of more punctuation marks will lead to a sample that is harder to reduce in size by determinization and minimization. Punctuation occurs frequently and can therefore easily net a great number of reductions by merging states.

For the Negra Corpus all tags matching

$/\backslash\$ \backslash S^*/$

are removed.[15] This leads to a corpus of 7248

[14]The normalization can also be implemented in linear time for nonrecursive pBTA.

[15]Here

$/\backslash\$ \backslash S^*/$

is an regular expression according to the ruby regular expression specifications (Flanagan and Matsumoto,

| | negra | brown5000 |
|---|---|---|
| Goodman Based | 1528256 | 1238717 |
| Deterministic | 857150 | 785427 |
| Minimized | 633907 | 602491 |
| | brown10000 | brown15000 |
| Goodman Based | 2389442 | 3603050 |
| Deterministic | 1402536 | 2030252 |
| Minimized | 1029786 | 1457499 |

Table 1: The results from the experimental evaluation. The numbers given reflect the number of transitions after the transformation to subtrees.

tag sequences of length 10 or less.

For the Brown Corpus the tags that are removed are specified by the regular expression

$/\backslash W^{+}/$

Not the whole sample from the Brown Corpus is used. Instead samples of 5000,10000 and 15000 sequences of tags are used.

The results of the algorithms can be seen in Table 5. In order to make the comparison implementation independent, the number of transitions after the transformation to subtrees, as explained in section 4, is given.

The results show that the minimization algorithm tends to cut the number of transitions in half for all corpora. This means these reductions in the number of transitions could be used to double the size of the corpus used in uDOP.[16] Note that if one was to extend the corpus with more strings of limited size the benefit of the new approaches should become more pronounced. This is the case since the determinstic construction only introduces one state per observed substring. The set of possible tag sequences of length 10 or less is limited. This holds especially true if one considers linguistic constraints. This tendency can be seen from the statistics for 15000 sentences from the Brown corpus.

2008).

[16]This is the case, since the number of states grows linearly with corpus size for fixed sentence length.

## 6 Possible Extensions

Note that tree automata are closed under intersection (Fülöp and Vogler, 2009). Bansal and Klein (2010) propose improving a DOP estimate by changing the weights of the subtrees. This is done by using a weighting scheme that distributes along the packed representation. This can be extended with the techniques in this paper in the following way: Assume one wants to give the weight of the subtree as the joint probability of a tree automaton model that has previously been given and the uDOP estimate. All that is necessary to achieve this would be to represent the uDOP estimate as a tree automaton, intersect it with the previously given automaton and apply a normalization as discussed above.[17].

The algorithm allows another generalization in addition to the one proposed. This is the case since the mapping to subtrees can be implemented by application of a tree transducer (Knight and Graehl, 2005). Therefore, the final estimation can be made more complex. Simply replace the mapping step by the application of a transducer.

## 7 Conclusion

In this paper it was discussed how the size of the unsupervised Data Oriented Parsing estimate for STSGs can be reduced. By translating the problem into the domain of finite tree automata, the problem of reducing the grammar size could be handled by solving standard problems in that domain.

The code used for the experiments in this paper can be found at `http://code.google.com/p/gragra/`.

## References

Mohit Bansal and Dan Klein. 2010. Simple, accurate parsing with an all-fragments grammar. In *ACL 2010, Proceedings of the 48th Annual Meeting of the Association for Computational Linguistics, Uppsala, Sweden*, pages 1098–1107. The Association for Computer Linguistics.

[17]the last step is necessary for the subtree probabilities to sum to 1

Rens Bod. 2006a. An all-subtrees approach to unsupervised parsing. In *ACL-44: Proceedings of the 21st International Conference on Computational Linguistics and the 44th annual meeting of the Association for Computational Linguistics*, pages 865–872. The Association for Computational Linguistics.

Rens Bod. 2006b. Unsupervised parsing with u-dop. In *CoNLL-X '06: Proceedings of the Tenth Conference on Computational Natural Language Learning*, pages 85–92. Association for Computational Linguistics.

Rens Bod. 2007. Is the end of supervised parsing in sight? In *Proceedings of the 45th Annual Meeting of the Association for Computational Linguistics*, pages 400–407. The Association for Computer Linguistics.

Symeon Bozapalidis. 1991. Effective construction of the syntactic algebra of a recognizable series on trees. *Acta Informatica*, 28(4):351–363.

David Flanagan and Yukihiro Matsumoto. 2008. *The ruby programming language.* O'Reilly, first edition.

W. Nelson Francis. 1964. A standard sample of present-day english for use with digital computers. Technical report, Brown University.

Zoltan Fülöp and Heiko Vogler, 2009. *Weighted Tree Automata and Tree Transducers*, chapter 9, pages 313–394. Springer Publishing Company, Incorporated, 1st edition.

Joshua Goodman. 1998. *Parsing Inside-Out.* Ph.D. thesis, Harvard University.

Joshua Goodman. 2003. Efficient algorithms for the dop model. In *Data Oriented Parsing.* Center for the Study of Language and Information, Stanford, California.

Christian Hänig. 2010. Improvements in unsupervised co-occurrence based parsing. In *Proceedings of the Fourteenth Conference on Computational Natural Language Learning*, pages 1–8. Association for Computational Linguistics.

Dan Klein and Christopher D. Manning. 2002. A generative constituent-context model for improved grammar induction. In *Proceedings of the Association for Computational Linguistics*, pages 128–135. Association for Computational Linguistics.

Kevin Knight and Jonathan Graehl. 2005. An overview of probabilistic tree transducers for natural language processing. In *CICLing*, volume volume 3406 of Lecture Notes in Computer Science, pages 1–24.

Andreas Maletti and Giorgio Satta. 2009. Parsing algorithms based on tree automata. In *IWPT '09: Proceedings of the 11th International Conference on Parsing Technologies*, pages 1–12. Association for Computational Linguistics.

Andreas Maletti. 2009. Minimizing deterministic weighted tree automata. *Information and Computation*, 207(11):1284–1299.

Tahira Naseem and Regina Barzilay. 2011. Using semantic cues to learn syntax. In *AAAI 2011: Twenty-Fifth Conference on Artificial Intelligence.*

Mark-Jan Nederhof and Giorgio Satta. 2006. Estimation of consistent probabilistic context-free grammars. In *Proceedings of the main conference on Human Language Technology Conference of the North American Chapter of the Association of Computational Linguistics*, pages 343–350, Morristown, NJ, USA. Association for Computational Linguistics.

Fernando Pereira and Yves Schabes. 1992. Inside-outside reestimation from partially bracketed corpora. In *Proceedings of the 30th annual meeting on Association for Computational Linguistics*, ACL '92, pages 128–135, Stroudsburg, PA, USA. Association for Computational Linguistics.

Elias Ponvert, Jason Baldridge, and Katrin Erk. 2011. Simple unsupervised grammar induction from raw text with cascaded finite state models. In *Proceedings of the 49th Annual Meeting of the Association for Computational Linguistics: Human Language Technologies.*

Jesus Santamaria and Lourdes Araujo. 2010. Identifying patterns for unsupervised grammar induction. In *Proceedings of the Fourteenth Conference on Computational Natural Language Learning (CoNLL).* Association for Computational Linguistics.

Wojciech Skut, Brigitte Krenn, Thorsten Brants, and Hans Uszkoreit. 1997. An annotation scheme for free word order languages. In *Proceedings of the fifth conference on Applied natural language processing*, ANLC '97, pages 88–95. Association for Computational Linguistics.

Valentin I. Spitkovsky, Daniel Jurafsky, and Hiyan Alshawi. 2010. Profiting from mark-up: hypertext annotations for guided parsing. In *Proceedings of the 48th Annual Meeting of the Association for Computational Linguistics*, ACL '10, pages 1278–1287, Stroudsburg, PA, USA. Association for Computational Linguistics.

Valentin I. Spitkovsky, Hiyan Alshawi, and Daniel Jurafsky. 2011. Punctuation: Making a point in unsupervised dependency parsing. In *In Proceedings of the Fifteenth Conference on Computational Natural Language Learning (CoNLL-2011).*

Daniel H. Younger. 1967. Recognition and parsing of context-free languages in time $n^3$. *Information and Control*, 10:189–208.

# Evaluating unsupervised learning for natural language processing tasks

**Andreas Vlachos**
Department of Biostatistics and Medical Informatics
University of Wisconsin-Madison
vlachos@biostat.wisc.edu

## Abstract

The development of unsupervised learning methods for natural language processing tasks has become an important and popular area of research. The primary advantage of these methods is that they do not require annotated data to learn a model. However, this advantage makes them difficult to evaluate against a manually labeled gold standard. Using unsupervised part-of-speech tagging as our case study, we discuss the reasons that render this evaluation paradigm unsuitable for the evaluation of unsupervised learning methods. Instead, we argue that the rarely used *in-context* evaluation is more appropriate and more informative, as it takes into account the way these methods are likely to be applied. Finally, bearing the issue of evaluation in mind, we propose directions for future work in unsupervised natural language processing.

## 1 Introduction

The development of unsupervised learning methods for natural language processing (NLP) tasks has become an important and popular area of research. The main attraction of these methods is that they can learn a model using only unlabeled data. This is an important advantage, as unlabeled text in digital form is in abundance, while labeled datasets are usually expensive to construct. While methods such as crowdsourcing (Snow et al., 2008) can help reduce this cost, in tasks for which specialist knowledge is required, such as part-of-speech (PoS) tagging or syntactic parsing, labeling datasets in this fashion can be substantially harder.

Nevertheless, the advantage of requiring only unlabeled data to learn a model renders the evaluation of unsupervised learning methods to be more challenging than that of their supervised counterparts. This is primarily because the output of unsupervised methods does not contain labels that would be found in a manually constructed gold standard. Simplistically expressed, no labels for model learning means that there are no labels in the output. As a result, the standard evaluation paradigm of comparing against a gold standard using a performance measure such as accuracy or F-score cannot be used, at least not in the way it would be used in evaluating supervised methods. Since methods are proposed or rejected by researchers, and papers describing these methods are assessed by their peers partly on the basis of such results, the issue of evaluation is an important one.

Before we proceed, it is important to characterize the unsupervised learning methods we are considering, as the term unsupervised is used in multiple ways in the literature. In this work we focus on methods that use only unlabeled data to learn a model and do not involve any form of supervision at any stage. Thus we exclude methods that use seeds such as the dictionaries of PoS tags used by Ravi and Knight (2009) and rules for producing labeled output, e.g. those proposed by Teichert and Daumé III (2009). We also exclude methods for which the data used to learn a model does not contain any of the labels we are learning to predict, but it does contain other information that we use in the learning process. For example, the multilingual PoS induction approach of Das and Petrov (2011) assumes no supervision for the language whose PoS tags are being

*Proceedings of EMNLP 2011, Conference on Empirical Methods in Natural Language Processing*, pages 35–42,
Edinburgh, Scotland, UK, July 27–31, 2011. 

induced, but it assumes access to a labeled dataset of a different language.

We begin by surveying recent work on unsupervised PoS tagging, focusing on the issue of evaluation (Section 2). While PoS tagging is not the only task for which unsupervised learning methods are popular, its relative simplicity and the variety of evaluation paradigms employed make it a useful case study. Based on this survey, we show that evaluation against a PoS tagging gold standard is not only difficult, but it can be misleading as well. The reason for this is that the unsupervised learning methods used, while they produce output that correlates with PoS tags, perform a different task, namely clustering-based word representation induction (Turian et al., 2010). Instead, we argue that *in-context* evaluation is more appropriate and more informative, as it takes into account the application context in which these methods are intended to be used (Section 3). Finally, bearing the issue of evaluation in mind, we propose some directions for future work in unsupervised learning for NLP (Section 4).

## 2 The case of unsupervised part-of-speech tagging

PoS tagging is the task of assigning lexical categories such as noun or verb to tokens in a sentence. It is commonly used either as an end-goal or as intermediate processing stage for a downstream task such as syntactic parsing. For languages with substantial amounts of labeled data available such as English, the performance of supervised approaches has reached very high levels.[1] Thus, the research focus has shifted to semisupervised and unsupervised approaches which would allow the processing of languages which do not have similar resources available.

At an abstract level, the unsupervised learning methods applied to PoS tagging take as input tokenized unlabeled sentences, from which they learn a model. These models are either hidden Markov models (HMMs) (Clark, 2003; Goldwater and Griffiths, 2007) or clustering models (Biemann, 2006; Abend et al., 2010). During model learning, state identifiers are assigned to the tokens (Figure 1a). Independently of the learning method and the model, these identifiers are semantically void, i.e. they have no linguistic meaning. Nevertheless, all the studies conclude that there is a strong correlation between the state identifiers assigned and the PoS tags in a labeled gold standard (Figure 1b).

The most common way of assessing the level of correlation achieved is the use clustering evaluation measures. The latter operate on a confusion matrix (Figure 1c), which is constructed by assuming that each cluster consists of all the tokens assigned the same state identifier. Intuitively, all clustering evaluation measures provide definitions for the two desirable properties that a good clustering should possess with respect to a gold standard, homogeneity and completeness. Homogeneity represents the degree to which each cluster contains instances from a single gold standard class, while completeness the degree to which each gold standard class is contained in a single cluster. Note that there tends to be a trade-off between these two properties since, increasing the number of clusters is likely to improve homogeneity but worsen completeness and vice-versa. Therefore, clustering evaluation measures need to balance appropriately between them.

Some authors proposed clustering evaluation techniques that first induce the mapping from state identifiers to gold standard tags automatically and then use supervised measures to compare the mapped output to the gold standard. For example, Gao and Johnson (2008) proposed to induce a many-to-one mapping of state identifiers to PoS tags from one half of the corpus and evaluate on the second half, which is referred to as cross-validation accuracy. However, such techniques evaluate the clustering together with the induced mapping, thus the quality of the latter influences the results obtained. This can be misleading as unsupervised learning methods for PoS tagging induce the clustering, but not the mapping on which they are eventually evaluated.

In order to avoid the mapping induction step, the use of information theoretic measures was proposed instead. These include Variation of Information (VI) (Meilă, 2007), V-measure (Rosenberg and Hirschberg, 2007), and their respective variants NVI (Reichart and Rappoport, 2009) and V-beta (Vlachos et al., 2009). Each of these measures exhibits

[1] According to the ACL wiki, state-of-the-art performance in English is more than 97% per token accuracy.

| *1* | *2* | *3* | *4* | *1* | *5* |
|---|---|---|---|---|---|
| There | are | 70 | children | there | . |

(a) Unsupervised PoS tagger output

| *EX* | *VBP* | *CD* | *NNS* | *RB* | . |
|---|---|---|---|---|---|
| There | are | 70 | children | there | . |

(b) Gold standard

| | 1 | 2 | 3 | 4 | 5 |
|---|---|---|---|---|---|
| *EX* | 1 | 0 | 0 | 0 | 0 |
| *VBP* | 0 | 1 | 0 | 0 | 0 |
| *CD* | 0 | 0 | 0 | 1 | 0 |
| *NNS* | 0 | 0 | 1 | 0 | 0 |
| *RB* | 1 | 0 | 0 | 0 | 0 |
| . | 0 | 0 | 0 | 0 | 1 |

(c) Confusion matrix

Figure 1: Unsupervised PoS tagging evaluation pipeline.

some kind of bias towards certain solutions though, e.g. V-measure favors clusterings with large number of clusters, while VI exhibits the opposite behavior. While these biases might follow some reasonable intuitions, unsurprisingly none is universally accepted as the most appropriate.

In order to avoid these problems, Biemann et al. (2007) proposed to evaluate unsupervised PoS tagging as a source of features for supervised learning approaches to NLP tasks, such as named entity recognition and shallow parsing. The intuition behind this extrinsic evaluation is that if a task relies on discriminating between PoS labels rather than the PoS labels semantics themselves, then the state identifiers obtained by an unsupervised method can be used in the same way as PoS tags obtained from a gold standard or a supervised system. In their experiments they showed that the features obtained from the unsupervised PoS tagger improve the performance in all tasks, and in particular when little training data is available.

Van Gael et al. (2009) evaluated the output of different configurations of their unsupervised PoS tagging approach both by comparing it against a gold standard via clustering evaluation measures and by using it as a source of features for shallow parsing. Table 1 summarizes the results of their experiments. In agreement with Biemann et al. (2007), they found that the features provided by the unsupervised PoS tagger improved shallow parsing performance. However, they observed that the clustering evaluation scores did not correlate with the results of this extrinsic evaluation. In other words, better clustering evaluation scores did not always result in better features for shallow parsing. Van Gael et al. noted that homogeneity correlated better with shallow parsing performance, hypothesizing it is probably worse to assign the same state identifier to tokens that belong to different PoS tags, e.g. verb and adverbs, rather than to generate more than one state identifier for the same PoS. In the same spirit, Christodoulopoulos et al. (2010) used the output of a number of unsupervised PoS tagging methods to extract seeds for the prototype-driven model of Haghighi and Klein (2006). Like Van Gael et al., they also found that better clustering evaluation scores did not result in better seeds.

Given these results, as well as remembering that unsupervised learning methods do not use any label information in model learning, one is entitled to question whether it is reasonable to expect their output to match a particular labeled gold standard. Why not assume that the state identifiers obtained correlate with named entity recognition tags or categorial grammar tags instead of PoS tags, tasks for which sequential models are very common? Even if the state identifiers induced correlate better with PoS tags than with other kinds of annotation, evaluating them using a PoS tagging gold standard and even naming the task unsupervised PoS tagging or induction is probably misleading. We argue that the task performed by the unsupervised PoS tagging methods proposed is more accurately described as clustering-based word representation induction

| | homogeneity | completeness | VI | V-measure | V-beta | F-score | accuracy |
|---|---|---|---|---|---|---|---|
| DP-learned | 69.39 | 51.21 | 4.19 | 58.93 | 55.37 | 90.98 | 94.48 |
| DP-fixed | 51.80 | 54.84 | 3.94 | 53.27 | 52.88 | 89.99 | 93.89 |
| PY-fixed | 62.02 | 56.25 | 3.74 | 59.00 | 58.79 | 90.31 | 94.15 |
| no PoS | - | - | - | - | - | 93.81 | 96.07 |
| supervised PoS | - | - | - | - | - | 88.58 | 93.25 |

Table 1: Summary the results reported for the three configurations (DP-learned, DP-fixed, PY-fixed) of the unsupervised PoS tagger of Van Gael et al. (2009) and the two baselines (no PoS tags, supervised PoS tags). Except for VI, higher scores mean better performance. The clustering evaluation scores (VI, V-measure, V-beta) are obtained by comparing against a PoS gold standard, while F-score and accuracy scores are obtained by extrinsinc evaluation using shallow parsing.

(Turian et al., 2010), and that this should be taken into account in the evaluation. As further evidence of the relation between the two tasks, note that some of the unsupervised PoS tagging methods applied by Christodoulopoulos et al. (2010) were also used by Turian et al. (2010) for clustering-based word representation induction.

## 3 *In-context* evaluation

All the papers on unsupervised PoS tagging mentioned in the previous section agree on the fact that its evaluation, at least using clustering evaluation measures, is difficult. This is an important problem for other NLP tasks (e.g. anaphora resolution, word sense induction) in which systems produce clusters that need to be mapped to gold standard classes. In their recent position paper, Guyon et al. (2009) argue that the problem lies in ignoring the *context* in which clustering is performed. They distinguish between two such contexts. The first one is the use of clustering as a *pre-processing* step for a downstream task, in which the evaluation of the latter is used to evaluate the former. The second context is that of data *exploration* in order to assist a human to analyze a large dataset. In this case, performance might not be as straightforward to assess, since it relies on many external factors among which the human computer interaction interface used is likely to be crucial. We cumulatively refer to these evaluation paradigms as *in-context* evaluation.

Returning to unsupervised PoS tagging and NLP, the extrinsic evaluation of Biemann et al. (2007) and Van Gael et al. (2009) falls under the pre-processing paradigm. The approach of Christodoulopoulos et al. (2010) falls between pre-processing and data exploration, as the clusters of tokens produced are semi-automatically processed in order to produce seeds which were then used by the prototype-driven model of Haghighi and Klein (2006).[2] In-context evaluation can be used to assess the performance of unsupervised learning methods for tasks other than clustering-based word representation approaches. For example, topic modeling (Blei et al., 2003) has recently been used and evaluated in approaches to learning models of selectional preferences (Ritter et al., 2010; Ó Séaghdha, 2010).

The issues affecting the evaluation of unsupervised learning methods are not restricted to PoS tagging. Schwartz et al. (2011) discussed similar issues in the context of unsupervised dependency parsing. Note that some of them arise due to the fact unsupervised dependency parsing produces unlabeled directed edges which are interpreted as denoting head-dependent relations. However, there are linguistic phenomena where unless the edges are labeled with a specific interpretation, both directions could be considered correct, e.g. the relation between modal verb and main verb. Even though evaluation against a syntactic parsing gold standard is useful, we argue that in-context evaluation of the output of unsupervised dependency parsers is likely to be more informative and more appropriate.

Despite the criticism against clustering evaluation measures as well as other methods for comparing the

[2]Note that while evaluating in-context, these authors still refer to the task performed as PoS tagging or induction and some of their conclusions are drawn via comparisons against a PoS tagging gold standard.

output of unsupervised learning methods against a gold standard, we argue that they are still useful. The various measures proposed, along with their inherent biases and definitions of clustering quality, provide quantitative analysis of the behavior of unsupervised learning methods by assessing correlations between their output and a gold standard. This can be very useful when developing such methods, as their use is admittedly simpler than the in-context evaluation paradigms discussed. However, they are not as informative as in-context evaluation and they should not be used to draw strong conclusions about the usefulness of a method.

Acknowledging that the evaluation of unsupervised learning for NLP is better performed in-context instead of against a labeled gold standard leads to the use of more appropriate experimental setups. Sometimes unsupervised learning methods are restricted to learning models using the unlabeled gold standard against which they are evaluated subsequently. Thus, they neither take full advantage of nor they demonstrate their main strength, which is that they can use as much data as possible. Using the pre-processing paradigm, clustering-based word representations induced from a large unlabeled dataset would be evaluated according to whether they improve the performance of the downstream task they are evaluated with, whose evaluation is likely to be on a different dataset. This use of clustering-based word representation is sometimes referred to as semi-supervised learning and has been shown to be effective in a variety of tasks, including named entity recognition, shallow parsing and syntactic dependency parsing (Koo et al., 2008; Turian et al., 2010).

The use of large datasets would also help assess the scalability of the unsupervised methods proposed, as the amount of data that can be handled efficiently by an unsupervised method can be as important as the range of linguistic intuitions it can capture. To examine this trade-off, it would be informative to show performance curves with different amounts of data, which should be straightforward to produce under the pre-processing evaluation paradigm. An added benefit is that, as discussed by Ben-Hur et al. (2002), assessing clustering stability using multiple runs and sub-samples of a dataset can help establish whether a particular combination of clustering algorithm and user-defined parameters (including the number of clusters to be discovered) is able to discover an appropriate clustering of the dataset considered.

Avoiding comparisons against a labeled gold standard would also remove the temptation of adapting it to the output of the unsupervised learning method. For example, in unsupervised PoS tagging authors sometimes simplify the gold standard by collapsing the original 45 PoS tags of the Penn treebank to 17, e.g. by removing the distinctions between different noun tags. While such simplifications are linguistically plausible, they substitute one problem for another, as methods are no longer penalized for missing some of the finer distinctions, but they are penalized for making them. Perhaps more importantly, they result in fitting the gold standard to the output of the method being evaluated, which is unlikely to be informative.

Another related issue is that since unsupervised learning methods do not need labeled data, it is a tempting and common practice to learn a model and report results on the same dataset, which usually consists of all the labeled data available and which is used to tune the parameters of the method evaluated. This is equivalent to reporting results for supervised learning methods on the development set, while it is generally accepted that results on a separate test set on which no parameter tuning is allowed provide better performance estimates. The use of the pre-processing evaluation paradigm with a supervised learning approach for the downstream task is likely to result in use the standard distinction between training, development and test set for the evaluation of unsupervised learning methods.

## 4 Directions for future work

While the previous sections have focused on why unsupervised learning for NLP tasks is hard to evaluate, our intention is not to discourage further research, but to encourage it. Unsupervised learning can help exploit the large amounts of unlabeled text that are available. For this purpose though we need appropriate evaluation, and we argue that in-context evaluation is likely to be more informative than the evaluation against a gold standard.

A potential problem is that in-context evaluation

adds an extra layer in the experimental setup, either in the form of a downstream task or of a human-computer interaction study. This can make comparisons between methods harder as there are more experimental conditions to control for and discourage researchers from adopting it. Therefore, it would be useful to have a shared task that would provide an experimental setup that can be re-used. Shared tasks have been beneficial in cases where the existence of multiple datasets and task definitions hindered progress and we would expect them to have a similar effect on unsupervised learning methods.

As different application contexts are likely to benefit from different solutions, this naturally leads to the development of modeling approaches that are adaptable, preferably in ways that enable experts to incorporate their knowledge. This research direction has already been pursued in clustering (Wagstaff and Cardie, 2000; Basu et al., 2006) and more recently in topic modeling (Blei and Mcauliffe, 2008; Andrzejewski et al., 2011). We argue though that the wider adoption of in-context evaluation will help assess their performance and merits in a more informative way. An alternative approach to accommodate for the needs of different application contexts is to induce multiple clusterings simultaneously for the same dataset as proposed by Dasgupta and Ng (2010) in the context of text classification. Such considerations are particularly relevant to NLP applications as language exhibits ambiguity and polysemy, which are rather difficult to capture in a context-independent labeled gold standard.

If in-context evaluation must be avoided, it is advisable to focus on tasks for which most application contexts would agree on the clustering or latent structure that must be discovered, such as the Web People Search (Artiles et al., 2010) task on clustering webpages about persons who share the same name. Even in this case though, in-context evaluation as pre-processing for an information extraction system or as a visualization component in an interface for exploring web pages is still likely to be informative.

Finally, in this paper we considered methods whose output consists of state identifiers which are semantically void. However, obtaining meaningful labels such as those found in a gold standard is a useful and important goal in many NLP tasks. However, this purpose is better served by injecting appropriate supervision to the model, instead of trying to achieve it as an afterthought. Such approaches include the use of PoS dictionaries by sequential tagging models (Haghighi and Klein, 2006; Ravi and Knight, 2009), the use of labeled data from different languages (Snyder et al., 2008; Das and Petrov, 2011) or the (possibly indirect) assignment of labels to topics (Ramage et al., 2009; Zhu et al., 2009). Research in unsupervised learning methods is likely to benefit these partially supervised ones, as they both seek to take advantage of unlabeled data. As the output of such methods uses the same labels as those found in the gold standard, they can be evaluated against a labeled gold standard.

## 5 Conclusions

In this position paper, we discussed the issue of evaluation of unsupervised learning methods for NLP tasks. Using PoS tagging as our case study, we examined recent attempts of evaluating unsupervised approaches and showed that a lot of confusion is caused due to evaluating their output against a labeled gold standard. Instead, we argue that it is more appropriate to evaluate unsupervised methods in context, either as a pre-processing step for a downstream task or as a tool for data exploration. Following this, we proposed that future work should focus on adapting to and evaluating unsupervised learning methods in the context in which they are intended to be used and that a shared task would facilitate research in this direction. Finally, we hope that the adoption of in-context evaluation will result in the development of improved unsupervised learning methods for NLP tasks, so that researchers and practitioners can exploit the large amounts of textual data available.

## Acknowledgments

The author would like thank Mark Craven and Diarmuid Ó Séaghdha for helpful comments and discussions. The author was funded by NIH/NLM grant R01 / LM07050.

## References

Omri Abend, Roi Reichart, and Ari Rappoport. 2010. Improved unsupervised POS induction through prototype discovery. In *Proceedings of the 48th Annual Meeting of the Association for Computational Linguistics*, pages 1298–1307.

David Andrzejewski, Xiaojin Zhu, Mark Craven, and Benjamin Recht. 2011. A framework for incorporating general domain knowledge into latent Dirichlet allocation using first-order logic. In *Proceedings of the 22nd International Joint Conferences on Artificial Intelligence*.

Javier Artiles, Andrew Borthwick, Julio Gonzalo, Satoshi Sekine, and Enrique Amigó. 2010. WePS-3 evaluation campaign: Overview of the web people search clustering and attribute extraction tasks. In *Proceedings of the Conference on Multilingual and Multimodal Information Access Evaluation*.

Sugato Basu, Mikhail Bilenko, Arindam Banerjee, and Raymond J. Mooney. 2006. Probabilistic semi-supervised clustering with constraints. In O. Chapelle, B. Schoelkopf, and A. Zien, editors, *Semi-Supervised Learning*, pages 73–102. MIT Press.

Asa Ben-Hur, André Elisseeff, and Isabelle Guyon. 2002. A stability based method for discovering structure in clustered data. In *Proceedings of the Pacific Symposium on Biocomputing*, pages 6–17.

Chris Biemann, Claudio Giuliano, and Alfio Gliozzo. 2007. Unsupervised part-of-speech tagging supporting supervised methods. In *Proceedings of the International Conference in Recent Advances in Natural Language Processing*.

Chris Biemann. 2006. Unsupervised part-of-speech tagging employing efficient graph clustering. In *Proceedings of the 21st International Conference on Computational Linguistics and 44th Annual Meeting of the Association for Computational Linguistics: Student Research Workshop*, pages 7–12.

David Blei and Jon Mcauliffe. 2008. Supervised topic models. In *Proceedings of the 22nd Annual Conference on Neural Information Processing Systems*.

David M. Blei, Andrew Y. Ng, and Michael I. Jordan. 2003. Latent Dirichlet Allocation. *Journal of Machine Learning Research*, 3:993–1022, January.

Christos Christodoulopoulos, Sharon Goldwater, and Mark Steedman. 2010. Two decades of unsupervised POS induction: how far have we come? In *Proceedings of the 2010 Conference on Empirical Methods in Natural Language Processing*, pages 575–584.

Alexander Clark. 2003. Combining distributional and morphological information for part of speech induction. In *Proceedings of the 10th Conference of the European Chapter of the Association for Computational Linguistics*, pages 59–66.

Dipanjan Das and Slav Petrov. 2011. Unsupervised part-of-speech tagging with bilingual graph-based projections. In *Proceedings of the 49th Annual Meeting of the Association for Computational Linguistics: Human Language Technologies*.

Sajib Dasgupta and Vincent Ng. 2010. Mining clustering dimensions. In *Proceedings of the 27th International Conference on Machine Learning*, pages 263–270.

Jianfeng Gao and Mark Johnson. 2008. A comparison of Bayesian estimators for unsupervised hidden Markov model POS taggers. In *Proceedings of the 2008 Conference on Empirical Methods in Natural Language Processing*, pages 344–352.

Sharon Goldwater and Tom Griffiths. 2007. A fully Bayesian approach to unsupervised part-of-speech tagging. In *Proceedings of the 45th Annual Meeting of the Association of Computational Linguistics*, pages 744–751.

Isabelle Guyon, Ulrike Von Luxburg, and Robert C. Williamson. 2009. Clustering: Science or art. In *NIPS 2009 Workshop on Clustering Theory*.

Aria Haghighi and Dan Klein. 2006. Prototype-driven learning for sequence models. In *Proceedings of Human Language Technology Conference of the North American Chapter of the Association of Computational Linguistics*, pages 320–327.

Terry Koo, Xavier Carreras, and Michael Collins. 2008. Simple semi-supervised dependency parsing. In *Proceedings of the 46th Annual Meeting of the Association of Computational Linguistics: Human Language Technologies*, pages 595–603.

Marina Meilă. 2007. Comparing clusterings—an information based distance. *Journal of Multivariate Analysis*, 98(5):873–895.

Diarmuid Ó Séaghdha. 2010. Latent variable models of selectional preference. In *Proceedings of the 48th Annual Meeting of the Association for Computational Linguistics*, pages 435–444.

Daniel Ramage, David Hall, Ramesh Nallapati, and Christopher D. Manning. 2009. Labeled LDA: a supervised topic model for credit attribution in multi-labeled corpora. In *Proceedings of the 2009 Conference on Empirical Methods in Natural Language Processing*, pages 248–256.

Sujith Ravi and Kevin Knight. 2009. Minimized models for unsupervised part-of-speech tagging. In *Proceedings of the Joint Conference of the 47th Annual Meeting of the ACL and the 4th International Joint Conference on Natural Language Processing of the AFNLP*, pages 504–512.

Roi Reichart and Ari Rappoport. 2009. The NVI clustering evaluation measure. In *Proceedings of the 13th Conference on Computational Natural Language Learning*, pages 165–173.

Alan Ritter, Mausam, and Oren Etzioni. 2010. A latent Dirichlet allocation method for selectional preferences. In *Proceedings of the 48th Annual Meeting of the Association for Computational Linguistics*, pages 424–434.

Andrew Rosenberg and Julia Hirschberg. 2007. V-measure: A conditional entropy-based external cluster evaluation measure. In *Proceedings of the 2007 Joint Conference on Empirical Methods in Natural Language Processing and Computational Natural Language Learning*, pages 410–420.

Roy Schwartz, Omri Abend, Roi Reichart, and Ari Rappoport. 2011. Neutralizing linguistically problematic annotations in unsupervised dependency parsing evaluation. In *Proceedings of the 49th Annual Meeting of the Association of Computational Linguistics*.

Rion Snow, Brendan O'Connor, Daniel Jurafsky, and Andrew Ng. 2008. Cheap and Fast – But is it Good? Evaluating Non-Expert Annotations for Natural Language Tasks. In *Proceedings of the 2008 Conference on Empirical Methods in Natural Language Processing*, pages 254–263.

Benjamin Snyder, Tahira Naseem, Jacob Eisenstein, and Regina Barzilay. 2008. Unsupervised multilingual learning for pos tagging. In *Proceedings of the 2008 Conference on Empirical Methods in Natural Language Processing*, pages 1041–1050.

Adam R. Teichert and Hal Daumé III. 2009. Unsupervised part of speech tagging without a lexicon. In *NIPS Workshop on Grammar Induction, Representation of Language and Language Learning*.

Joseph Turian, Lev Ratinov, and Yoshua Bengio. 2010. Word representations: a simple and general method for semi-supervised learning. In *Proceedings of the 48th Annual Meeting of the Association for Computational Linguistics*, pages 384–394.

Jurgen Van Gael, Andreas Vlachos, and Zoubin Ghahramani. 2009. The infinite HMM for unsupervised PoS tagging. In *Proceedings of 2009 Conference on Empirical Methods in Natural Language Processing*, pages 678–687.

Andreas Vlachos, Anna Korhonen, and Zoubin Ghahramani. 2009. Unsupervised and Constrained Dirichlet Process Mixture Models for Verb Clustering. In *Proceedings of the EACL workshop on GEometrical Models of Natural Language Semantics*.

Kiri Wagstaff and Claire Cardie. 2000. Clustering with instance-level constraints. In *Proceedings of the 17th International Conference on Machine Learning*, pages 1103–1110.

Jun Zhu, Amr Ahmed, and Eric P. Xing. 2009. MedLDA: maximum margin supervised topic models for regression and classification. In *Proceedings of the 26th Annual International Conference on Machine Learning*, pages 1257–1264.

# Unsupervised Language-Independent Name Translation Mining from Wikipedia Infoboxes

**Wen-Pin Lin, Matthew Snover, Heng Ji**
Computer Science Department
Queens College and Graduate Center
City University of New York
New York, NY 11367, USA
danniellin@gmail.com, msnover@qc.cuny.edu, hengji@cs.qc.cuny.edu

## Abstract

The automatic generation of entity profiles from unstructured text, such as Knowledge Base Population, if applied in a multi-lingual setting, generates the need to align such profiles from multiple languages in an unsupervised manner. This paper describes an unsupervised and language-independent approach to mine name translation pairs from entity profiles, using Wikipedia Infoboxes as a stand-in for high quality entity profile extraction. Pairs are initially found using expressions that are written in language-independent forms (such as dates and numbers), and new translations are then mined from these pairs. The algorithm then iteratively bootstraps from these translations to learn more pairs and more translations. The algorithm maintains a high precision, over 95%, for the majority of its iterations, with a slightly lower precision of 85.9% and an f-score of 76%. A side effect of the name mining algorithm is the unsupervised creation of a translation lexicon between the two languages, with an accuracy of 64%. We also duplicate three state-of-the-art name translation mining methods and use two existing name translation gazetteers to compare with our approach. Comparisons show our approach can effectively augment the results from each of these alternative methods and resources.

## 1 Introduction

A shrinking fraction of the world's web pages are written in English, while about 3,000 languages are endangered (Krauss, 2007). Therefore the ability to access information across a range of languages, especially low-density languages, is becoming increasingly important for many applications. In this paper we hypothesize that in order to extend cross-lingual information access to all the language pairs on the earth, or at least to some low-density languages which are lacking fundamental linguistic resources, we can start from the much more scalable task of "information" translation, or more specifically, new name translation.

Wikipedia, as a remarkable and rich online encyclopedia with a wealth of general knowledge about varied concepts, entities, events and facts in the world, may be utilized to address this need. As of March 2011 Wikipedia contains pages from 275 languages[1], but statistical machine translation (MT) techniques can only process a small portion of them (e.g. Google translate can only translate between 59 languages). Wikipedia infoboxes are a highly structured form of data and are composed of a set of subject-attribute-value triples that summarize or highlight the key features of the concept or subject of each article. A large number of instance-centered knowledge-bases that have harvested this structured data are available. The most well-known are probably DBpedia (Auer et al., 2007), Freebase (Bollacker et al., 2007) and YAGO (Suchanek et al., 2007). However, almost all of these existing knowledge bases contain only one language. Even for high-density languages, more than 70% of Wikipedia pages and their infobox entries do not contain cross-lingual links.

[1] http://meta.wikimedia.org/wiki/List_of_Wikipedias

*Proceedings of EMNLP 2011, Conference on Empirical Methods in Natural Language Processing*, pages 43–52,
Edinburgh, Scotland, UK, July 27–31, 2011. ©2011 Association for Computational Linguistics

Recent research into Knowledge Base Population, the automatic generation of profiles for named entities from unstructured text has raised the possibility of automatic infobox generation in many languages. Cross-lingual links between entities in this setting would require either expensive multilingual human annotation or automatic name pairing. We hypothesize that overlaps in information across languages might allow automatic pairing of profiles, without any preexisting translational capabilities. Wikipedia infoboxes provide a proxy for these high quality cross lingual automatically generated profiles upon which we can explore this hypothesis.

In this paper we propose a simple and general unsupervised approach to discover name translations from knowledge bases in any language pair, using Wikipedia infoboxes as a case study. Although different languages have different writing systems, a vast majority of the world's countries and languages use similar forms for representing information such as time/calendar date, number, website URL and currency (IBM, 2010). In fact most languages commonly follow the ISO 8601 standard[2] so the formats of time/date are the same or very similar. Therefore, we take advantage of this language-independent formatting to design a new and simple bootstrapping based name pair mining approach. We start from language-independent expressions in any two languages, and then extract those infobox entries which share the same slot values. The algorithm iteratively mines more name pairs by utilizing these pairs and comparing other slot values. In this unsupervised manner we don't need to start from any name transliteration module or document-wise temporal distributions as in previous work.

We conduct experiments on English and Chinese as we have bi-lingual annotators available for evaluating results. However, our approach does not require any language-specific knowledge so it's generally applicable to any other language pairs. We also compare our approach to state-of-the-art name translation mining approaches.

### 1.1 Wikipedia Statistics

A standard Wikipedia entry includes a title, a document describing the entry, and an "infobox" which is a fixed-format table designed to be added to the top right-hand corner of the article to consistently present a summary of some unifying attributes (or "slots") about the entry. For example, in the Wikipedia entry about the singer *"Beyonce Knowles"*, the infobox includes information about her birth date, origin, song genres, occupation, etc. As of November 2010, there were 10,355,225 English Wikipedia entries, and 772,826 entries. Only 27.2% of English Wikipedia entries have cross-lingual hyperlinks referring to their corresponding Chinese entries.

Wikipedia entries are created and updated exponentially (Almeida et al., 2007) because of the increasing number of contributors, many of whom are not multi-lingual speakers. Therefore it is valuable to align the cross-lingual entries by effective name mining.

### 1.2 Motivating Example

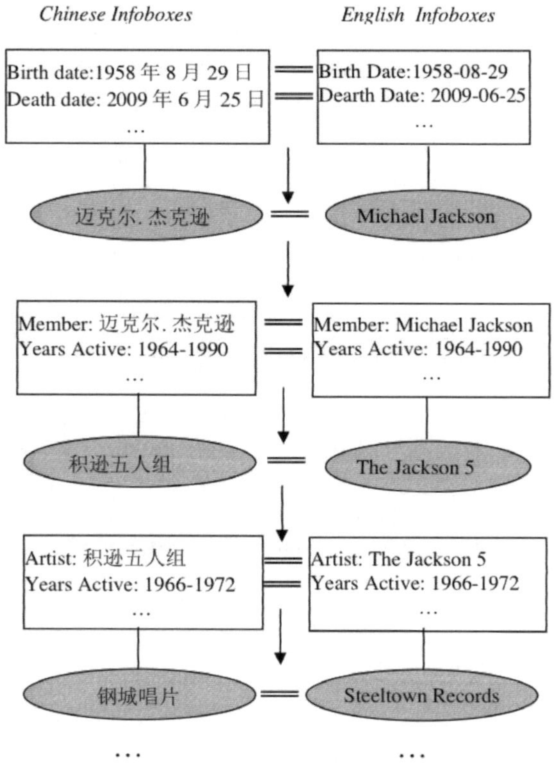


Figure 1: A Motivating Example

Figure 1 depicts a motivating example for our approach. Based on the assumption that if two person entries had the same birth date and death date,

[2] http://en.wikipedia.org/wiki/ISO_8601

they are likely to be the same person, we can find the entity pair of (*Michael Jackson* / 迈克尔.杰克逊). We can get many name pairs using similar language-independent clues. Then starting from these name pairs, we can iteratively get new pairs with a large portion of overlapped slots. For example, since "积逊五人组" and "*The Jackson 5*" share many slot values such as '*member*' and '*years active*', they are likely to be a translation pair. Next we can use the new pair of (*The Jackson 5* / 积逊五人组) to mine more pairs such as "钢城唱片" and "*Steeltown Records.*"

## 2 Data and Pre-Processing

Because not all Wikipedia contributors follow the standard naming conventions and date/number formats for all languages, infoboxes include some noisy instances. Fortunately the NIST TAC Knowledge Base Population (KBP) task (Ji et al., 2010) defined mapping tables which can be directly used to normalize different forms of slot types[3]. For example, we can group '*birthdate*', '*date of birth*', '*datebirth*' and '*born*' to '*birth_date.*' In addition, we also normalized all date slot values into one standard format as "YYYY MM DD." For example, both "1461-8-5" and "5 August, 1461" are normalized as "1461 08 05." Only those Wikipedia entries that have at least one slot corresponding to the Knowledge Base Population task are used for name mining. Entries with multiple infoboxes are also discarded as these are typically "List of ___" entries and do not correspond to a particular named entity. The number of entries in the resulting data set are shown in Table 1. The set of slots were finally augmented to include the entry's name as a new slot. The cross-lingual links between Chinese and English Wikipedia pages were used as the gold standard that the unsupervised algorithm attempted to learn.

| Language | Entries | Slot Values | E-Z Pairs |
|---|---|---|---|
| English (E) | 634,340 | 2,783,882 | 11,109 |
| Chinese (Z) | 21,152 | 110,466 | |

Table 1: Processed Data Statistics

[3]It is important to note that the vast majority of Chinese Wikipedia pages store slot types in English in the underlying wiki source, removing the problem of aligning slot types between languages.

## 3 Unsupervised Name Pair Mining

The name pair mining algorithm takes as input a set of English infoboxes $E$ and Chinese infoboxes $Z$. Each infobox consists of a set of slot-value pairs, where each slot or value may occur multiple times in a single infobox. The output of the algorithm is a set of pairs of English and Chinese infoboxes, matching an infobox in one language to the corresponding infobox in the other language. There is nothing inherently designed in the algorithm for English and Chinese, and this method could be applied to any language pair.

Because the algorithm is unsupervised, it begins with no initial pairs, nor is there any initial translation lexicon between the two languages. As the new pairs are learned, both the entries titles and the values of their infoboxes are used to generate new translations which can be used to learn more cross-lingual name pairs.

### 3.1 Search Algorithm

The name pair mining algorithm considers all pairs of English and Chinese infoboxes[4], assigns a score, described in Section 3.2, to each pair and then greedily selects the highest scoring pairs, with the following constraints:

1. Each infobox can only be paired to a single infobox in the other language, with the highest scoring infobox being selected. While there are some instances of two entries in one language for one entity which both have translation links to the same page in another language, these are rare occurrences and did not occur for the KBP mapped data used in these experiments.

2. An pair $(e, z)$ can only be added if the score for the pair is at least $95\%$[5] percent higher than the score for the second best pair for both $e$ and $z$. This eliminates the problem of ties in the data, and follows the intuition that if there are

[4]The algorithm does not need to compare all pairs of infoboxes as the vast majority will have a score of 0. Only those pairs with some equivalent slot-value pairs need to be scored. The set of non-zero scoring pairs can thus be quickly found by indexing the slot-value pairs.

[5]The value of 95% was arbitrarily chosen; variations in this threshold produce only small changes in performance.

multiple pairs with very similar scores it is beneficial to postpone the decision until more evidence becomes available.

To improve the speed of the algorithm, the top 500 scoring pairs, that do not violate these constraints, are added at each iteration. The translation lexicon is then updated. The translation lexicon is updated each iteration from the total set of pairs learned using the following procedure. For each pair $(e, z)$ in the learned pairs, new translations are added for each of the following conditions:

1. A translation of the name of $e$ to the name $z$ is added.
2. If a slot $s$ in $e$ has one value, $v_e$, and that slot in $z$ has one value, $v_z$, a translation $v_e \rightarrow v_z$ is added.
3. If a slot $s$ has multiple values in $e$ and $z$, but all but one of these values, for both $e$ and $z$, have translations to values in the other entry, then a translation is learned for the resulting untranslated value.

These new translations are all given equal weight and are added to the translation lexicon even if the evidence for this translation occurs in only a single name pair[6]. These translations can be used to align more name pairs in subsequent iterations by providing more evidence that a given pair should be aligned. After a translation is learned, we consider the English side to be equivalent to the Chinese side when scoring future infobox pairs.

The algorithm halts when there are no longer any new name pairs with non-zero score which also satisfy the search constraints described above.

### 3.2 Scoring Function

A score can be calculated for the pairing of an English infobox, $e$ and a Chinese infobox, $z$ according to the following formula:

$$\sum_{s \in \text{slots}} \begin{cases} I_Z(s) + I_E(s) & \exists v_1, v_2 : z.s.v_1 \approx e.s.v_2 \\ 0 & \text{otherwise} \end{cases} \tag{1}$$

[6]Assigning a probability to each translation learned based upon the number of entries providing evidence for the translation could be used to further refine the predictions of the model, but was not explored in this work.

A slot-value pair in Chinese, $z.s.v_1$, is considered equivalent to a slot-value pair in English, $e.s.v_2$, if the values are the same (typically only the case with numerical values) or if there is a known translation from $v_1$ to $v_2$. These translations are automatically learned during the name-mining process. Initially there are no known translations between the two languages.

The term $I_L(s)$ in equation 1 reflects how informative the slot $s$ is in either English ($E$) or Chinese ($Z$), and is calculated as the number of unique values for that slot for that language divided by the total number of slot-value pairs for that language, as shown in equation 2.

$$I_L(\text{slot } s) = \frac{|\{v | i \in L \wedge \exists i.s.v\}|}{|\{i.s.v | i \in L\}|} \tag{2}$$

If a slot $s$ contains unique values such that a slot and value pair is never repeated then $I_L(s)$ is 1.0 and indicates that the slot distinguishes entities very well. Slots such as '*date_of_birth*' are less informative since many individuals share the same birthdate, and slots such as '*origin*' are the least informative since so many people are from the same countries. A sampling of the $I_L(s)$ scores is shown in Table 2. The slots '*origin*' and '*religion*' are the two lowest scoring slots in both languages, while '*infobox_name*' (the name of wikipedia page in question), '*website*', '*founded*' are the highest scoring slot types.

| Slot | $I_Z$ | $I_E$ |
|---|---|---|
| origin | 0.21 | 0.03 |
| religion | 0.24 | 0.08 |
| parents | 0.57 | 0.60 |
| date_of_birth | 0.84 | 0.33 |
| spouse | 0.97 | 0.86 |
| founded_by | 0.97 | 0.94 |
| website | 0.99 | 0.96 |
| infobox_name | 1.00 | 1.00 |

Table 2: Sample $I(s)$ Values

## 4 Evaluation

In this section we present the evaluation results of our approach.

### 4.1 Evaluation Method

Human evaluation of mined name pairs can be difficult as a human assessor may frequently need to consult the infoboxes of the entries along with contextual documents to determine if a Chinese entry and an English entry correspond to the same entity. This is especially true when the translations are based on meanings instead of pronunciations. An alternative way of mining name pairs from Wikipedia is to extract titles from a Chinese Wikipedia page and its corresponding linked English page if the link exists (Ji et al., 2009). This method results in a very high precision but can miss pairs if no such link between the pages exists. We utilized these cross-lingual page links as an answer key and then only performed manual evaluation, using a bilingual speaker, on those pairs generated by our algorithm that were not in the answer key.

### 4.2 Results

Figure 2 shows the precision, recall and f-score of the algorithm as it learns more pairs. The final output of the mining learned 8799 name pairs, of which 7562 were correct according to the cross-lingual Wikipedia links. This results in a precision of 85.94%, a recall of 68.07% and a F1 score of 75.9%. The precision remains above 95% for the first 7,000 name pairs learned. If highly precise answers are desired, at the expense of recall, the algorithm could be halted earlier. The translation lexicon contained 18,941 entries, not including translations learned from the entry names themselves.

| Assessment | Number | |
|---|---|---|
| Link Missing From Wikipedia | 35 | 2.8% |
| Same Name, Different Entity | 17 | 1.4% |
| Partially Correct | 98 | 7.9% |
| Incorrect | 1,087 | 87.9% |

Table 3: Human Assessment of Errors

Because the answer key for name mining is automatically extracted from the cross-lingual links in Wikipedia, it is possible that correct name pairs could be missing from the answer key if no cross-lingual link exists. To examine if any such pairs were learned, a manual assessment of the name pairs that were not in the answer key was performed, as shown in Table 4.2. This assessment was performed by bilingual speakers with an inter-annotator agreement rate of 93.75%.

The vast majority, 87.9%, of the presumably erroneous name pairs assessed that were missing from the answer-key were actually incorrect pairs. However, 35, or 2.8%, of the name pairs were actually correct with their corresponding Wikipedia pages lacking cross-lingual links (these corrections are not reflected in the previous results reported above, which were based solely on the pairs in the answer key). For a small portion, 1.4%, of the errors, the name translation is correct but the entries actually refer to different entities with the same name. One such example is (*Martin Rowlands* / 羅能士). The English entity, *"Martin Rowlands"* is an athlete (an English football player), while the Chinese entity is a former Hong Kong government official, whose name translates to English as *"Martin Rowlands"*, as revealed on his Wikipedia page. Neither entity has an entry in the other language. The final category are partially correct answers, such as the pair (*Harrow, London* / 哈羅區), where the English entry refers to an area within the London Borough of Harrow, while the Chinese entry refers to the London Borough of Harrow as a whole. The English entry *"Harrow, London"* does not have a corresponding entry in Chinese, although there is an entry in both language for the larger Borough itself. All of these cases represent less 15% of the learned name pairs though as 85.94% of the name pairs were already determined to be correct based on cross-lingual Wikipedia links.

| Judgement | Percent |
|---|---|
| Correct | 64.4% |
| Partial | 18.4% |
| Incorrect | 15.1% |
| Not Translations | 2.1% |

Table 4: Slot Value Translation Assessment from Random Sample of 1000

The name mining algorithm bootstraps many name pairs by using possible translations between the slot values in previously learned pairs. The final translation lexicon learned had 18,941 entries. A random sample of 1,000 entries from the trans-

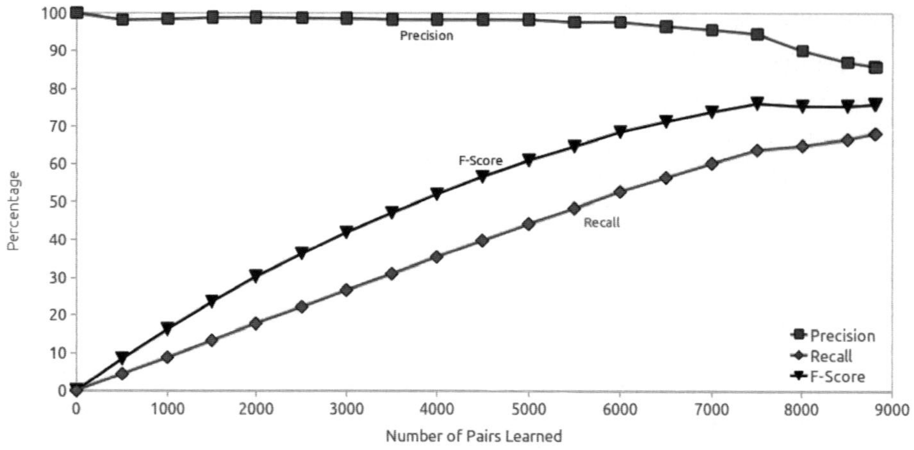


Figure 2: Performance of Unsupervised Name Mining

lation lexicon was assessed by a human annotator, and judged as correct, partial, incorrect or not translations, as shown in Table 4.2. Partial translations were usually cases where a city was written with its country name in language and as just the city name in the other languages, such as *"Taipei Taiwan Republic of China"* and "臺北市" (*Taipei*). Cases are marked as "not translations" if both sides are in the same language, typically English, such as *"Eric Heiden"* in English being considered a translation of *"Eric Arthur Heiden"* from a Chinese entry (not in Chinese characters though). This normally occurs if the Chinese page contained English words that were not translated or transliterated.

An example[7] of the name mining is shown in Figure 3, where the correct name pair for (*George W. Bush* / 乔治· 沃克· 布什) is learned in iteration $i$, is mined for additional translations and then provides evidence in iteration $i+1$ for the correct name pair (*Laura Bush* / 劳拉· 威尔士· 布什). When learning the name pair for *"George W. Bush"*, evidence is first found from the slots marked as equivalent ($approx$). Translations for *"Harvard Business School"* and *" Republican Party"* were learned in previous iterations from other name pairs and now provide evidence, along with the identical values in the *'date_of_birth'* slot for the pair (*George W. Bush* / 乔治· 沃克· 布什). After learning this pair, new translations are extracted from the pair for *"George W. Bush"*, *"George Walker Bush"*, *"President of the United States"*, *"Laura Bush"*, and *"Yale University"*. The translations for *"Laura Bush"* and *"George W. Bush"* provide crucial information in the next iteration that the pair (*Laura Bush* / 劳拉· 威尔士· 布什) is correct. From this, more translations are learned, although not all of these translations are fully correct, such as *"Author Teacher Librarian First Lady"* which is now postulated to be a translation of 图书管理员 *(Librarian)*, which is only partially true, as the other professions are not represented in the translation. While such translations may not be fully correct, they still could prove useful for learning future name pairs (although this is unlikely in this case since there are very few entries with *"first lady"* as part of their title.

[7]Many slot value pairs that were not relevant for the calculation are not shown to save space. Otherwise, this example is as learned in the unsupervised name mining.

## 5 Discussion

Besides retaining high accuracy, the final list of name pairs revealed several advantages of our approach.

Most previous name translation methods are limited to names which are phonetically transliterated (e.g. translate Chinese name "尤申科 (*You shen ke*)" to "*Yushchenko*" in English). But many other types of names such as organizations are often rendered semantically, for example, the Chinese name "解放之虎 (*jie fang zhi hu*)" is translated into *"Liberation Tiger"* in English. Some other names in-

Iteration $i$

| George W. Bush | | | 乔治· 沃克· 布什 *(George Walker Bush)* | |
|---|---|---|---|---|
| alt_names | George Walker Bush | | alt_names | 乔治· · 布什 *(George Bush)* |
| title | President of the United States | | title | 美國總統 *(President of the USA)* |
| date_of_birth | 1946-7-6 | ≈ | date_of_birth | 1946-7-6 |
| member_of | Republican Party | ≈ | member_of | 共和黨 *(Republican Party)* |
| spouse | Laura Bush | | spouse | 劳拉· 威尔士· 布什 *(Laura Welch Bush)* |
| schools_attended | Yale University | | schools_attended | 耶魯大學 *(Yale University)* |
| schools_attended | Harvard Business School | ≈ | schools_attended | 哈佛商学院 *(Harvard Business School)* |

Iteration $i+1$

| Laura Bush | | | 劳拉· 威尔士· 布什 *(Laura Welch Bush)* | |
|---|---|---|---|---|
| alt_names | Laura Bush | ≈ | alt_names | 劳拉· 威尔士· 布什 *(Laura Welch Bush)* |
| | | | alt_names | 劳拉· 莲恩· 威尔士 *(Laura Lane Welch)* |
| date_of_birth | 1946-11-4 | ≈ | date_of_birth | 1946-11-4 |
| place_of_birth | Midland Texas | | place_of_birth | 得克萨斯州米德兰 *(Texas Midland)* |
| title | Author Teacher Librarian First Lady | | title | 图书管理员 *(Librarian)* |
| title | First Lady of the United States | ≈ | title | 美國第一夫人*(First Lady of USA)* |
| spouse | George W. Bush | ≈ | spouse | 乔治· 沃克· 布什 *(George Walker Bush)* |

Figure 3: Example of Learned Name Pairs with Gloss Translations in Parentheses

volve both semantic and phonetic translations, or none of them. Our approach is able to discover all these different types, regardless of their translation sources. For example, our approach successfully mined a pair (*Tarrytown* / 柏油村) where *"Tarrytown"* is translated into "柏油村" neither by its pronunciation *"bai you cun"* nor its meaning *"tar village."*

Name abbreviations are very challenging to translate because they need expansions based on contexts. However our approach mined many abbreviations using slot value comparison. For example, the pair of (*Yctc* / 业强科技) was successfully mined although its English full name *"Yeh-Chiang Technology Corp."* did not appear in the infoboxes.

Huang (2005) also pointed out that name translation benefited from origin-specific features. In contrast, our approach is able to discover name pairs from any origins. For example, we discovered the person name pair (*Seishi Yokomizo* / 横溝正史) in which *"Seishi Yokomizo"* was transliterated based on Japanese pronunciation.

Furthermore, many name translations are context dependent. For example, a person name in Chinese "亚西尔•阿拉法特" could be translated into *"Yasser Arafat" (PLO Chairman)* or *"Yasir Arafat" (Cricketer)* based on different contexts. Our method can naturally disambiguate such entities based on slot comparison at the same time as translation mining.

More importantly, our final list includes a large portion of uncommon names, which can be valuable to address the out-of-vocabulary problem in both MT and cross-lingual information processing. Especially we found many of them are not in the name pairs mined from the cross-lingual Wikipedia title links, such as (*Axis Communications* / 安讯士), (*Rowan Atkinson* / 路雲· 雅堅遜), (*ELSA Technology* / 艾爾莎科技) and (*Nelson Ikon Wu* / 吳訥孫).

## 6 Comparison with Previous Methods and Resources

There have been some previous methods focusing on mining name translations using weakly-supervised learning. In addition there are some existing name translation gazetteers which were manually constructed. We duplicated a variety of alternative state-of-the-art name translation mining methods and mined some corresponding name pair sets for comparison. In fact we were able to implement the techniques in previous approaches but could not duplicate the same number of results because we could not access the same data sets. Therefore the main purpose of this experiment is not to claim our approach outperforms these existing methods, rather to investigate whether we can mine any new information on top of these methods from reasonable amounts of data.

1. **Name Pair Mining from Bitexts**
   Within each sentence pair in a parallel corpus, we ran an HMM based bilingual name tagger (references omitted for anonymous review). If the types of the name tags on both sides are identical, we extract the name pairs from this sentence. Then at the corpus-wide level, we count the frequency for each name pair, and only keep the name pairs that are frequent enough. The corpora used for this approach were all DARPA GALE MT training corpora.

2. **Comparable Corpora**
   We implemented an information extraction driven approach as described in Ji (2009) to extract name pairs from comparable corpora. This approach is based on extracting information graphs from each language and align names by a graph traverse algorithm. The corpora used for this approach were 2000 English documents and 2000 Chinese documents from the Gigaword corpora.

3. **Using patterns for Web mining**
   We constructed heuristic patterns such as parenthetical structure "Chinese name (English name)" (Lin et al., 2008) to extract name pairs from web data with mixed Chinese and English. We used about 1,000 web pages for this experiment.

4. **Bilingual Gazetteer**
   We exploited an LDC bilingual name dictionary (LDC2005T34) and a Japanese-English person name dictionary including 20126 Japanese names written in Chinese characters (Kurohashi et al., 1994).

5. **ACE2007 Entity Translation Training Data**
   We also used ACE 2007 entity translation training corpus which includes 119 Chinese-English document pairs.

Table 5 shows the number of correct and unique pairs mined pairs from each of the above approaches, as well as how these name mining methods can be augmented using the infobox name mining described in this paper. The names mined from our approach greatly extend the total number of correct translations with only a small number of conflicting name translations.

## 7 Related Work

Most of the previous name translation work combined supervised transliteration approaches with Language Model based re-scoring (Al-Onaizan and Knight, 2002; Huang et al., 2004; Huang, 2005). Our goal of addressing name translation for a large number of languages is similar to the panlingual lexical translation project (Etzioni et al., 2007). Some recent research used comparable corpora to re-score name transliterations (Sproat et al., 2006; Klementiev and Roth, 2006) or mine new word translations (Udupa et al., 2009; Ji, 2009; Fung and Yee, 1998; Rapp, 1999; Shao and Ng, 2004; Hassan et al., 2007). However, most of these approaches needed large amount of seeds and suffered from information extraction errors, and thus relied on phonetic similarity or document similarity to re-score candidate name translation pairs.

Some recent cross-lingual information access work explored attribute mining from Wikipedia pages. For example, Bouma et al. (2009) aligned attributes in Wikipedia infoboxes based on cross-page links. Navigli and Ponzetto (2010) built a multilingual semantic network by integrating the cross-lingual Wikipedia page links and WordNet. Ji et

| Method | | # Name Pairs | Infobox Mining | |
|---|---|---|---|---|
| | | | # New | # Conflicting |
| Automatic | (1) Bitexts | 2,451 | 8,673 | 78 |
| | (2) Comparable Corpora | 288 | 8,780 | 13 |
| | (3) Patterns for Web Mining | 194 | 8799 | 0 |
| Manual | (4) Bilingual Gazetteer | 59,886 | 8,689 | 74 |
| | (5) ACE2007 Training Data | 1,541 | 8,718 | 52 |

Table 5: Name Pairs Mined Using Previous Methods

al. (2009) described various approaches to automatically mine name translation pairs from aligned phrases (e.g. cross-lingual Wikipedia title links) or aligned sentences (bi-texts). G et al. (2009) mined candidate words from Wikipedia and validated translations based on parallecl corpora. Some other work mined name translations from monolingual documents that include foreign language texts. For example, Lin et al. (2008) described a parenthesis translation mining method; You et al. (2010) applied graph alignment algorithm to obtain name translation pairs based on co-occurrence statistics. This kind of data does not commonly exist for low-density languages. Sorg and Cimiano (2008) discovered cross-lingual links between English and German using supervised classification based on support vector machines. Adar et al. (2009) aligned cross-lingual infoboxes using a boolean classifier based on self-supervised training with various linguistic features. In contrast, our approach described in this paper is entirely based on unsupervised learning without using any linguistic features. de Melo and Weikum (2010) described an approach to detect imprecise or wrong cross-lingual Wikipedia links based on graph repair operations. Our algorithm can help recover those missing cross-lingual links.

## 8 Conclusion and Future Work

In this paper we described a simple, cheap and effective self-boosting approach to mine name translation pairs from Wikipedia infoboxes. This method is implemented in a completely unsupervised fashion, without using any manually created seed set, training data, transliteration or pre-knowledge about the language pair. The underlying motivation is that some certain expressions, such as numbers and dates, are written in language-independent forms among a large majority of languages. Therefore our approach can be applied to any language pairs including low-density languages as long as they share a small set of such expressions. Experiments on English-Chinese pair showed that this approach is able to mine thousands of name pairs with more than 85% accuracy. In addition the resulting name pairs can be used to significantly augment the results from existing approaches. The mined name pairs are made publicly available.

In the future we will apply our method to mine other entity types from more language pairs. We will also extend our name discovery method to all infobox pairs, not just those that can be mapped into KBP-like slots. As a bi-product, our method can be used for automatic cross-lingual Wikipedia page linking, as well as unsupervised translation lexicon extraction, although this might require confidence estimates on the translations learned. Once our approach is applied to a panlingual setting (most languages on the Wikipedia), we can also utilize the voting results across multiple languages to automatically validate information or correct potential errors in Wikipedia infoboxes. Finally, as automatic name profile generation systems are generated cross-lingually, our method could be attempted to automatic cross-lingual mappings between entities.

## Acknowledgement

This work was supported by the U.S. Army Research Laboratory under Cooperative Agreement Number W911NF-09-2-0053, the U.S. NSF CAREER Award under Grant IIS-0953149 and PSC-CUNY Research Program. The views and conclusions contained in this document are those of the authors and should not be interpreted as representing the official policies, either expressed or implied, of the Army Research Laboratory or the U.S. Government. The U.S. Government is authorized to reproduce and distribute reprints for Government purposes notwithstanding any copyright notation hereon.

## References

Eytan Adar, Michael Skinner, and Daniel S. Weld. 2009. Information arbitrage across multi-lingual wikipedia. In *Second ACM International Conference on Web Search and Data Mining (WSDM'09), Barcelona, Spain, February 2009*, February.

Yaser Al-Onaizan and Kevin Knight. 2002. Translating named entities using monolingual and bilingual resources. In *ACL 2002*.

Rodrigo B. Almeida, Barzan Mosafari, and Junghoo Cho. 2007. On the evolution of wikipedia. In *Int. Conf. on Weblogs and Social Media*.

Sören Auer, Christian Bizer, Georgi Kobilarov, Jens Lehmann, Richard Cyganiak, and Zachary Ives. 2007. Dbpedia: A nucleus for a web of open data. In *The 6th International Semantic Web Conference*.

Kurt Bollacker, Robert Cook, and Patrick Tufts. 2007. Freebase: A shared database of structured general human knowledge. In *The National Conference on Artificial Intelligence (Volume 2)*.

Gosse Bouma, Sergio Duarte, and Zahurul Islam. 2009. Cross-lingual alignment and complettion of wikipedia templates. In *The Third International Workshop on Cross Lingual Information Access: Addressing the Information Need of Multilingual Societies*.

Gerard de Melo and Gerhard Weikum. 2010. Untangling the cross-lingual link structure of wikipedia. In *48th Annual Meeting of the Association for Computational Linguistics (ACL 2010), Uppsala, Sweden*.

Pascale Fung and Lo Yuen Yee. 1998. An ir approach for translating new words from nonparallel and comparable texts. In *COLING-ACL*.

Rohit Bharadwaj G, Niket Tandon, and Vasudeva Varma. 2009. An iterative approach to extract dictionaries from wikipedia for under-resourced languages. In *Proc. ICON2010*, February.

Ahmed Hassan, Haytham Fahmy, and Hany Hassan. 2007. Improving named entity translation by exploiting comparable and parallel corpora. In *RANLP*.

Fei Huang, Stephan Vogel, and Alex Waibel. 2004. Improving named entity translation combining phonetic and semantic similarities. In *HLT/NAACL2004*.

Fei Huang. 2005. Cluster-specific name transliteration. In *HLT-EMNLP 2005*.

IBM. 2010. Ibm globalization library.

Heng Ji, Ralph Grishman, Dayne Freitag, Matthias Blume, John Wang, Shahram Khadivi, Richard Zens, and Hermann Ney. 2009. Name translation for distillation. Handbook of Natural Language Processing and Machine Translation: DARPA Global Autonomous Language Exploitation.

Heng Ji, Ralph Grishman, Hoa Trang Dang, and Kira Griffitt. 2010. An overview of the tac2010 knowledge base population track. In *Text Analytics Conference (TAC2010)*.

Heng Ji. 2009. Mining name translations from comparable corpora by creating bilingual information networks. In *ACL-IJCNLP 2009 workshop on Building and Using Comparable Corpora (BUCC 2009): from Parallel to Non-parallel Corpora*.

Michael E. Krauss. 2007. *Keynote-mass Language Extinction and Documentation: The Race Over Time. The Vanishing Languages of the Pacific Rim.* Oxford University Press.

Sadao Kurohashi, Toshihisa Nakamura, Yuji Matsumoto, and Makoto Nagao. 1994. Improvements of japanese morphological analyzer juman. In *The International Workshop on Sharable Natural Language Resources and pp.22-28*.

Dekang Lin, Shaojun Zhao, Benjamin Van Durme, and Marius Pasca. 2008. Mining parenthetical translations from the web by word alignment. In *ACL2008*.

Roberto Navigli and Simone Paolo Ponzetto. 2010. Babelnet: Building a very large multilingual semantic network. In *48th Annual Meeting of the Association for Computational Linguistics (ACL 2010), Uppsala, Sweden*.

Reinhard Rapp. 1999. Automatic identification of word translations from unrelated english and german corpora. In *ACL 1999*.

Li Shao and Hwee Tou Ng. 2004. Mining new word translations from comparable corpora. In *COLING2004*.

Philipp Sorg and Philipp Cimiano. 2008. Enriching the crosslingual link structure of wikipedia - a classification-based approach. In *AAAI 2008 Workshop on Wikipedia and Artifical Intelligence*, June.

Fabian M. Suchanek, Gjergji Kasneci, and Gerhard Weikum. 2007. Yago: A core of semantic knowledge. In *The 16th International World Wide Web conference*.

Raghavendra Udupa, K. Saravanan, A. Kumaran, and Jagadeesh Jagarlamudi. 2009. Mint: A method for effective and scalable mining of named entity transliterations from large comparable corpora. In *EACL2009*.

Gae-won You, Seung won Hwang, Young-In Song, Long Jiang, and Zaiqing Nie. 2010. Mining name translations from entity graph mapping. In *EMNLP2010*.

# Twitter Polarity Classification with Label Propagation over Lexical Links and the Follower Graph

**Michael Speriosu**
University of Texas at Austin
speriosu@mail.utexas.edu

**Nikita Sudan**
University of Texas at Austin
nsudan@utexas.edu

**Sid Upadhyay**
University of Texas at Austin
sid.upadhyay@utexas.edu

**Jason Baldridge**
University of Texas at Austin
jbaldrid@mail.utexas.edu

## Abstract

There is high demand for automated tools that assign polarity to microblog content such as tweets (Twitter posts), but this is challenging due to the terseness and informality of tweets in addition to the wide variety and rapid evolution of language in Twitter. It is thus impractical to use standard supervised machine learning techniques dependent on annotated training examples. We do without such annotations by using label propagation to incorporate labels from a maximum entropy classifier trained on noisy labels and knowledge about word types encoded in a lexicon, in combination with the Twitter follower graph. Results on polarity classification for several datasets show that our label propagation approach rivals a model supervised with in-domain annotated tweets, and it outperforms the noisily supervised classifier it exploits as well as a lexicon-based polarity ratio classifier.

## 1 Introduction

Twitter is a microblogging service where users post messages ("tweets") of no more than 140 characters. With around 200 million users generating 140 million tweets per day, Twitter represents one of the largest and most dynamic datasets of user generated content. Along with other social networking websites such as Facebook, the content on Twitter is real time: tweets about everything from a friend's birthday to a devastating earthquake can be found posted during and immediately after an event in question.

This vast stream of real time data has major implications for any entity interested in public opinion and even acting on what is learned and engaging with the public directly. Companies have the opportunity to examine what customers and potential customers are saying about their products and services without costly and time-consuming surveys or explicit requests for feedback. Political organizations and candidates might be able to determine what issues the public is most interested in, as well as where they stand on those issues. Manual inspection of tweets can be useful for many such analyses, but many applications and questions require real-time analysis of massive amounts of social media content. Computational tools that automatically extract and analyze relevant information about opinion expressed on Twitter and other social media sources are thus in high demand.

Full sentiment analysis for a given question or topic requires many stages, including but not limited to: (1) extraction of tweets based on an initial query, (2) filtering out spam and irrelevant items from those tweets, (3) identifying subjective tweets, and (4) identifying the polarity of those tweets. Like most work in sentiment analysis, we focus on the last stage, polarity classification. The simplest approaches are based on the presence of words or emoticons that are indicators of positive or negative polarity (e.g. Twitter's own API, O'Connor et al. (2010)), or calculating a ratio of positive to negative terms (Choi and Cardie, 2009). Though these are a useful first pass, the nuance of language often defeats them (Pang and Lee, 2008). Tweets provide additional challenges compared to edited text; e.g. they are short and include informal/colloquial/abbreviated language.

*Proceedings of EMNLP 2011, Conference on Empirical Methods in Natural Language Processing*, pages 53–63,
Edinburgh, Scotland, UK, July 27–31, 2011. 

Standard supervised classification methods improve the situation somewhat (Pang et al., 2002), but these require texts labeled with polarity as input and they do not adapt to changes in language use. One way around this is to use noisy labels (also referred to as "distant supervision"), e.g. by taking emoticons like ':)' as positive and ':(' as negative, and train a standard classifier (Read, 2005; Go et al., 2009).[1] Semi-supervised methods can also reduce dependence on labeled texts: for example, Sindhwani and Melville (2008) use a polarity lexicon combined with label propagation. Several have used label propagation starting with a small number of hand-labeled words to induce a lexicon for use in polarity classification (Blair-Goldensohn et al., 2008; Rao and Ravichandran, 2009; Brody and Elhadad, 2010).

In this paper, we bring together several of the above approaches via label propagation using modified adsorption (Talukdar and Crammer, 2009). This also allows us to explore the possibility of exploiting the Twitter follower graph to improve polarity classification, under the assumption that people influence one another or have shared affinities about topics. We construct a graph that has users, tweets, word unigrams, word bigrams, hashtags, and emoticons as its nodes; users are connected based on the Twitter follower graph, users are connected to the tweets they created, and tweets are connected to the unigrams, bigrams, hashtags and emoticons they contain. We seed the graph using the polarity values in the OpinionFinder lexicon (Wilson et al., 2005), the known polarity of emoticons, and a maximum entropy classifier trained on 1.8 million tweets with automatically assigned labels based on the presence of positive and negative emoticons, like Read (2005) and Go et al. (2009).

We compare the label propagation approach to the noisily supervised classifier itself and to a standard lexicon-based method using positive/negative ratios. Evaluation is performed on several datasets of tweets that have been annotated for polarity: the Stanford Twitter Sentiment set (Go et al., 2009), tweets from the 2008 debate between Obama and McCain (Shamma et al., 2009), and a new dataset of tweets about health care reform that we have created. In addition to performing standard per-tweet accuracy, we also measure per-target accuracy (for health care reform) and an aggregate error metric over all users in our test set that captures how similar predicted positivity of each user is to their actual positivity. Across all datasets and measures, we find that label propagation is consistently better than the noisily supervised classifier, which in turn outperforms the lexicon-based method. Additionally, for the health care reform dataset, the label propagation approach—which uses no gold labeled tweets, just a hand-created lexicon—outperforms a maximum entropy classifier trained on gold labels. However, we do not find the follower graph to improve performance with our current implementation.

## 2 Datasets

We use several different Twitter datasets as training or evaluation resources. From the annotated datasets, only tweets with positive or negative polarity are used, so neutral tweets are ignored. While important, subjectivity detection is largely a different problem from polarity classification. For example, Pang and Lee (2004) use minimum cuts in graphs for the former and machine-learned text classification for the latter. We also do not give any special treatment to retweets, though doing so is a possible future improvement.

### 2.1 Emoticon-based training set (EMOTICON)

Emoticons are commonly exploited as noisy indicators of polarity—including by Twitter's own advanced search "with positive/negative attitude." While imperfect, there is potential for millions of tweets containing emoticons to serve as a source of noisy training material for a supervised classifier. We create such a training set from a sample of the "garden hose"[2] Twitter feed, from September to December, 2009. At the time of collection, this included up to 15% of all tweets worldwide.

From this feed, 6,265,345 tweets containing at least one of the emoticons listed in Table 1 are extracted; 5,156,277 contain a positive emoticon and

[1]Davidov et al. (2010) use 15 emoticons and 50 Twitter hashtags as proxies for sentiment in a similar manner, but their evaluation is indirect. Rather than predicting gold standard sentiment labels, they instead predict whether those same emoticons and hashtags would be appropriate for other tweets.

[2]`http://dev.twitter.com/pages/streaming_api`

| | |
|---|---|
| + | :) :D =D =) :] =] :-) :-D :-] ;) ;D ;] ;-) ;-D ;-] |
| − | :( =( :[ =[ :-( :-[ :'( :'[ D: |

Table 1: Positive and negative emoticons.

| | |
|---|---|
| + | #ff, congrats, gracias, yay, thx, smile, awesome, hello, excited, moon, loving, glad, sweet, wonderful, birthday, enjoy, goodnight, amazing, cute, bom |
| − | nickjonas, murphy, brittany, rip, triste, sad, hurts, died, snow, huhu, headache, upset, crying, throat, poor, sucks, ugh, sakit, stomach, horrible |

Table 2: Top 20 most predictive common unigram features for the positive and negative classes, in order from more predictive to less predictive.

1,109,068 contain a negative emoticon. A small number of tweets contain both negative and positive emoticons. These are permitted to appear twice, once for each label. Then, a balanced ratio of positive/negative labels is obtained by keeping only 1,109,068 of the positive tweets. Finally, a large proportion of non-English tweets are excluded by a filter that requires a tweet to have at least two words (with at least two characters) from the CMU Pronouncing Dictionary.[3] A few non-English tweets pass through this filter and some English tweets with very unusual words or incorrect spelling are dropped, but this simple strategy works well overall. The final training set contains 1,839,752 tweets, still balanced for positive and negative emoticons.

Table 2 shows the 20 most predictive unigram features of each class in the EMOMAXENT classifier (described below) that are among the 1000 most common unigrams in this dataset and are not themselves emoticons. A few non-English (but polarized) words (e.g. *gracias*, *bom*, *triste*) make it past our simple language filter and onto these lists, but the majority of the most predictive words are English. Other highly predictive words are artifacts of the particular tweet sample that comprises the EMOTICON dataset, such as 'nickjonas,' 'brittany,' and 'murphy,' the latter two explained by the abundance of negative tweets after actress Brittany Murphy's death. Most others are intuitively good markers of positive or negative polarity.

[3]The dictionary contains 133k English words, including inflected forms and proper nouns. http://www.speech.cs.cmu.edu/cgi-bin/cmudict

| Dataset | Use | Size | % Pos |
|---|---|---|---|
| STS | dev | 183 | 59.0 |
| OMD | dev | 1898 | 73.1 |
| HCR-TRAIN | train | 488 | 43.2 |
| HCR-DEV | dev | 534 | 32.2 |
| HCR-TEST | test | 396 | 38.6 |

Table 3: Basic properties of the annotated datasets used in this paper.

## 2.2 Datasets with polarity annotations

Three annotated datasets, summarized in Table 3 and described below, are used for training, development, or evaluation of polarity classifiers.

**Stanford Twitter Sentiment (STS).** Go et al. (2009) created a collection of 216 annotated tweets on various topics.[4] Of these, 108 tweets are positive and 75 are negative.

**Obama-McCain Debate (OMD).** Shamma et al. (2009) used Amazon Mechanical Turk to annotate 3,269 tweets posted during the presidential debate on September 26, 2008 between Barack Obama and John McCain. Each tweet was annotated by one or more Turkers for the categories *positive*, *negative*, *mixed*, or *other*. We filter this dataset with two constraints in order to ensure high inter-annotator agreement. First, at least three votes must have been provided for a tweet to be included. Second, more than half of the votes must have been *positive* or *negative*; the majority label is taken as the gold standard for that tweet. This results in a set of 1,898 tweets. Of these, 705 had positive gold labels and 1192 had negative gold labels, and the average inter-annotator agreement of the Turk votes for these tweets was 83.7%. To our knowledge, we are the first to perform automatic polarity classification on this dataset.

**Health Care Reform (HCR).** We create a new annotated dataset based on tweets about health care reform in the USA. This was a strongly debated

[4]http://twittersentiment.appspot.com/

topic that created a large number of polarized tweets, especially in the run up to the signing of the health care bill on March 23, 2010. We extract tweets containing the health care reform hashtag "#hcr" from early 2010; a subset of these are annotated by us and colleagues for polarity (*positive*, *negative*, *neutral*, *irrelevant*) and polarity targets (*health care reform, Obama, Democrats, Republicans, Tea Party, conservatives, liberals,* and *Stupak*). These are separated into training, dev and test sets. As with the other datasets, we restrict attention in this paper only to positive and negative tweets.[5]

### 2.3 The Twitter follower graph

One of the key ideas we test in this paper is whether social connections can be used to improve polarity classification for individual tweets and users. We construct the Twitter follower graphs for the users in the above datasets in stages using publicly available data from the Twitter API. From the full list of each user's followers, we retain only followers found within the datasets; this prunes unknown users who did not tweet about the topic and thus are unlikely to provide useful information. This method for graph construction offers nearly complete graphs, but has two main disadvantages. First, many users have raised their privacy levels over time, which hinders the ability to view their follower graph. In these cases only their tweet information is known. Secondly, due to the rapid pace of growth on Twitter, user graphs tend to grow quickly; thus our constructed graph is a representation of the user's current social graph and not the exact graph that existed at the time of the tweet.

## 3 Approach

We compare three main approaches: using lexicon-based positive/negative ratios, maximum entropy classification and label propagation.

### 3.1 Lexicon-based baseline (LEXRATIO)

A reasonable baseline to use in polarity classification is to count the number of positive and negative terms in a tweet and pick the category with more terms (O'Connor et al., 2010). This actually uses supervision at the level of word types. Like most others, we use the OpinionFinder subjectivity lexicon,[6] which contains 2,304 words annotated as positive and 4,153 words as negative. If the number of positive and negative words in a tweet is equal (including zero for both), the label is chosen at random.

### 3.2 Maximum entropy classifier (MAXENT)

The OpenNLP Maximum Entropy package[7] is used to train polarity classifiers using either EMOTICON or HCR-TRAIN, henceforth referred to as EMOMAXENT and GOLDMAXENT, respectively. After tokenizing on whitespace, unigram and bigram features are extracted. All characters are lowercased and non-alphanumeric characters are trimmed from the left and right sides of tokens. However, tokens that contain no alphanumeric characters are not trimmed. Stop words[8] are excluded as unigram features. However, bigram features are extracted before stop words are removed since many stop words are informative in the context of content words: e.g., contrast *shit* (negative) from *the shit* (very positive). The beginning and end of tweets are indicated by '$' in bigram features. Thus, the full feature set for the tweet *I love my new iPod Touch! :D* is `[love, ipod, touch, $ i, i love, love my, my ipod, ipod touch, touch :D, :D $]`. The same tokenization method is used for all datasets in this paper.

### 3.3 Label Propagation (LPROP)

Tweets are not created in isolation—each tweet is linked to other tweets by the same author, and each author is influenced by the tweets of those he or she follows. Common vocabulary and topics of discussion also connect tweets to each other. Graph-based methods such as label propagation (Zhu and Ghahramani, 2002; Baluja et al., 2008; Talukdar and Crammer, 2009) provide a natural means to represent and exploit such relationships in order to improve classification, often while requiring less supervision than with standard classification. Label propagation algorithms spread label distributions from a small set

[5] A public release of this data, along with our code, is available at https://bitbucket.org/speriosu/updown.

[6] http://www.cs.pitt.edu/mpqa/opinionfinderrelease/

[7] http://incubator.apache.org/opennlp/

[8] Taken from: http://www.ranks.nl/resources/stopwords.html

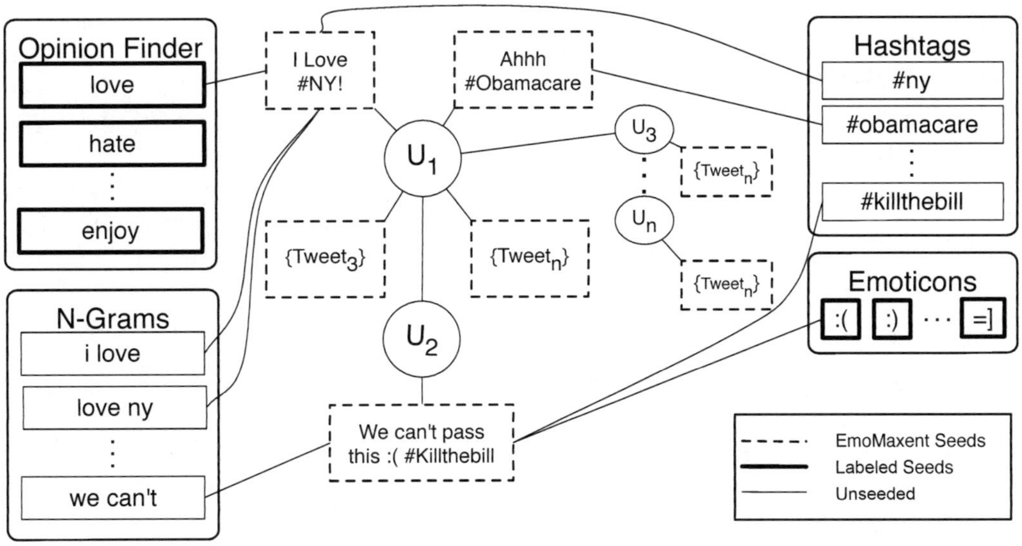


Figure 1: An illustration of our graph with All-edges and Noisy-seed (see text for description).

of nodes seeded with some initial label information (always noisy, heuristic information rather than gold instance labels in our case) throughout the graph. Label distributions are spread across a graph $G = \{V, E, W\}$ where $V$ is the set of $n$ nodes, $E$ is a set of $m$ edges and $W$ is an $n \times n$ matrix of weights, with $w_{ij}$ as the weight of edge $(i, j)$. We use Modified Adsorption (MAD) (Talukdar and Crammer, 2009) over a graph with nodes representing tweets, authors and features, while varying the seed information and the construction of the edge sets. The spreading of the label distributions can be viewed as a controlled random walk with three possible actions: (i) injecting a seeded node with its seed label, (ii) continuing the walk from the current node to a neighboring node, and (iii) abandoning the walk. MAD takes three parameters, $\mu_1$, $\mu_2$ and $\mu_3$, which control the relative importance of each of these actions, respectively. We use the Junto Label Propagation Toolkit's implementation of MAD in this paper.[9]

Modified Adsorption requires some nodes in the graph to have seed distributions, which can come for a variety of knowledge sources. We consider the following variants for seeding the graph:

- **Maxent-seed**: EMOMAXENT is trained on the EMOTICON dataset; every tweet node is seeded with its polarity predictions for the tweet.
- **Lexicon-seed**: Nodes are created for every word in the OpinionFinder lexicon. Positive words are seeded as 90% positive if they are strongly subjective and 80% positive if weakly subjective; similarly and conversely for negative words. Every tweet is connected by an edge to every word in the polarity lexicon it contains, using the weighting scheme discussed with Feature-edges below.
- **Emoticon-seed**: Nodes are created for emoticons from Table 1 and seeded as 90% positive or negative depending on their polarity.
- **Annotated-seed**: The annotations in HCR-TRAIN are used to seed the tweets from that dataset as 100% positive or negative, in accordance with the label.

We use **Noisy-seed** as a collective term for all of the above seed sets except Annotated-seed.

The other main aspect of graph construction is specifying edges and their weights. We consider the following variants:

- **Follower-edges**: When a user A follows another user B, we add an edge from A to B with a weight of 1.0, a weight that is comparable to that of a moderately frequent word in Feature-edges below.
- **Feature-edges**: Nodes are added for hashtags and the features described in §3.2 and connected to the

[9] `http://code.google.com/p/junto/`

tweets that contain them. An edge connecting a tweet $t$ to a feature $f$ has weight $w_{tf}$ using relative frequency ratios of the feature between the dataset $d$ in question and the EMOTICON dataset as a reference corpus $r$:

$$w_{tf} = \begin{cases} \log \frac{P_d(f)}{P_r(f)} & if\ P_d(f) > P_r(f) \\ 0 & o.w. \end{cases} \quad (1)$$

We use **All-edges** when combining both edge sets.

Figure 1 illustrates the connections for All-edges and Noisy-seed by example. Each user $u_n$ is attached to anyone who follows them or who they follow. Each user is also connected to the tweets they authored. Words from OpinionFinder are connected to tweets that contain those words, and similarly for hashtags, emoticons, unigrams, and bigrams. Emoticons and words from OpinionFinder are seeded according to the explanation above. All edges other than Feature-edges are given a weight of 1.0.

## 4 Results

### 4.1 Parameter tuning

We evaluated our models on the STS, OMD, and HCR-DEV datasets during development and kept HCR-TEST as a final held-out test set used once, after all relevant parameters had been set. For Modified Adsorption, 100 iterations were used, and a seed injection parameter $\mu_1$ of .005 gave the best balance of allowing seed distributions to affect other nodes without overwhelming them. The Junto default value of .01 was used for both $\mu_2$ and $\mu_3$.

### 4.2 Per-tweet accuracy

Table 4 shows the per-tweet accuracy results of the random baseline, the LEXRATIO baseline, the EMOMAXENT classifier alone, the LPROP classifier run only on Follower-edges with Maxent-seed, the LPROP classifier run on the full graph from Figure 1 only seeded with Lexicon-seed, and the LPROP classifier run on All-edges and Noisy-seed.

For all datasets, LPROP with Feature-edges and Noisy-seed outperforms or matches all other methods. For STS, our best result of 84.7% accuracy beats Go et al. (2009)'s reported best result of 82.7%. Their approach uses a Maxent classifier trained on a noisily labeled emoticon training set similar to our EMOTICON dataset. Note that they also remove neutral tweets from the test set.

| Classifier | MSE |
|---|---|
| Random | .167 |
| LEXRATIO | .170 |
| EMOMAXENT | .233 |
| LPROP (Follower-edges, Maxent-seed) | .233 |
| LPROP (All-edges, Lexicon-seed) | .187 |
| LPROP (Feature-edges, Noisy-seed) | **.148** |
| LPROP (All-edges, Noisy-seed) | **.148** |

Table 5: Mean squared error (MSE) per-user on HCR-TEST, for users with at least 3 tweets

Our semi-supervised label propagation method compares favorably to fully supervised approaches. For example, a graph with Feature-edges seeded with gold labels from HCR-TRAIN (i.e. Annotated-seed) obtains only 64.6% per-tweet accuracy on HCR-TEST. A maximent entropy classifier trained on HCR-TRAIN achieves 66.7%. Our best label propagation approach surpasses both of these at 71.2%.

We find that in general Follower-edges are not helpful as implemented here. Further work is needed to explore more nuanced ways of modeling the social graph, such as allowing leaders to influence followers more than vice versa.

### 4.3 Per-user error

In many sentiment analysis applications, it is of interest to know what the polarity of a given individual or the overall polarity toward a particular product is. Here we compare the positivity ratio predicted by our methods to that in the gold standard labels on a per-user basis, using the mean squared error between the predicted positivity ratios $ppr$ and the actual ratios $apr$ for all users:

$$MSE(ppr, apr) = \sum_i (apr_i - ppr_i)^2$$

Where $apr_i$ and $ppr_i$ are the actual and predicted positivity ratios of the $i$th user.

Table 5 gives MSE results on HCR-TEST for users with at least 3 tweets. LPROP (Feature-edges,

| Classifier | STS | OMD | HCR-DEV | HCR-TEST |
|---|---|---|---|---|
| Random | 50.0 | 50.0 | 50.0 | 50.0 |
| LEXRATIO | 72.1 | 59.1 | 54.3 | 58.1 |
| EMOMAXENT | 83.1 | 61.3 | 58.6 | 62.9 |
| LPROP (Follower-edges, Maxent-seed) | 83.1 | 61.2 | 57.9 | 62.9 |
| LPROP (All-edges, Lexicon-seed) | 70.0 | 62.6 | 64.6 | 64.6 |
| LPROP (Feature-edges, Noisy-seed) | **84.7** | **66.7** | **65.7** | **71.2** |
| LPROP (All-edges, Noisy-seed) | **84.7** | 66.5 | 65.2 | 71.0 |

Table 4: Per-tweet accuracy percentages. The models and parameters were developed while tracking performance on STS, OMD, and HCR-DEV, and HCR-TEST results were obtained from a single, blind run.

| | |
|---|---|
| + | pow pow, good debate, hack the, hack $ barackobama, barackobama, the vp, good job, to vote, john is, is to, obama did, they both, gergen, knowledge, voting for, for veterans, the veterans, america, will take |
| − | language, this was, drinking, terrorists, government, china, obama i, that we, father, obama in, mc, diplomacy, wars, afghanistan, debt, simply, financial, the spin, the bottom, bottom |

Table 7: Top 20 most positive and most negative $n$-grams in OMD after running LPROP with All-edges and Noisy-seed. Note that '$' indicates the beginning or end of a tweet.

| | |
|---|---|
| + | human, stupak, you do, sunday, fired vote for, yes on, $ we, vote yes, to vote, vote on, goal, nation, do it, up to, ago, votes, this #hcr, #hcr is, on #hcr |
| − | gop, #tlot #hcr, #tcot #tlot, 12, #topprog, medicare, #tlot, #tlot $, #ocra, cbo, tea party, tea, passes, #hhrs, $ dems, #hc, #obamacare, #sgp, dems, do not |

Table 8: Top 20 most positive and most negative $n$-grams in HCR-TEST after running LPROP with All-edges and Noisy-seed.

Noisy-seed) and LPROP (All-edges, Noisy-seed) are tied for the lowest error.

### 4.4 Per-target accuracy

Table 6 gives results on a per-target basis for the five most common targets in the HCR-TEST dataset, in order from most common to least common: *hcr*, *dems*, *obama*, *gop*, and *conservatives*. The percentages reflect the fraction of tweets correctly labeled for each target. These distributions are highly skewed: the *hcr* target covers about 69% of the tweets, while the *conservatives* target covers only about 5%. Thus performance on the *hcr* target tweets is most important for overall accuracy.

## 5 Discussion

**Polar language** An attractive property of label propagation algorithms is that label distributions can be obtained for nodes other than the tweets (and importantly, nodes that were unseeded). For example, all of the feature nodes—unigrams, bigrams, and hashtags—have a loading for the positive and negative labels. These could be used for various visualizations of the results of the polarity classification, including terms that are the most positive and negative and also highlighting or bolding such terms when showing a user individual tweets.

Table 7 shows the 20 unigrams and bigrams with the highest and lowest ratio of positive label probability to negative label probability after running LPROP with All-edges and Noisy-seed. These lists are restricted to terms that had an edge weight of at least 1.0, i.e. that were twice as frequent in OMD compared to the reference corpus, that had a raw count of at least 5 in OMD, and that didn't already appear in the OpinionFinder lexicon. Some of the terms are intuitively positive and negative, e.g. *good job* and *wars*. Others reflect more specific aspects of the OMD dataset, such as *good debate* and *afghanistan*.

Table 8 shows the top 20 for HCR-TEST. Many

| Classifier | hcr (274) | dems (27) | obama (26) | gop (22) | conservatives (20) |
|---|---|---|---|---|---|
| LEXRATIO | 58.0 | 64.8 | 69.2 | 50.0 | 52.5 |
| EMOMAXENT | 62.4 | 66.7 | 73.1 | 68.2 | 60.0 |
| LPROP (Follower-edges, Maxent-seed) | 62.4 | 66.7 | 73.1 | 68.2 | 60.0 |
| LPROP (All-edges, Lexicon-seed) | 60.6 | 85.2 | 73.1 | **86.4** | 60.0 |
| LPROP (Feature-edges, Noisy-seed) | **69.0** | **81.5** | **80.8** | **86.4** | **70.0** |
| LPROP (All-edges, Noisy-seed) | **69.0** | 77.8 | **80.8** | **86.4** | **70.0** |

Table 6: Per-target accuracy percentages for HCR-TEST. The number of tweets for each target is given in parentheses.

terms simply reflect a rallying to either pass or defeat the healthcare reform bill (*vote for, do not*). Other positive words represent more abstract concepts proponents of the bill may be expressing (*human, goal*). Conversely, opponents such as those who would attend a *tea party* are concerned about what they call *#obamacare*.

**Domain differences** There are several reasons why performance is much lower on both the OMD and HCR datasets than on STS. First, both the EMOTICON (noisy) training set and the STS dev set are general in topic. Correct estimations of the positivity and negativity of general words in the training set like *yay* and *upset* are more likely to be useful in a broad-domain evaluation set, whereas misestimations of the weights of more specific words and bigrams are likely to be washed out. In contrast, the OMD and HCR datasets contain a very different vocabulary distribution from the STS set. Words and phrases referring to specific political issues like *health care* and *iraq war* have frequencies that are orders of magnitude higher than either the EMOTICON training set or the STS dev set. Thus, misestimations of the positivity or negativity of these features will be amplified in evaluation. Lastly, expression of political opinions tends to be more nuanced than the general opinions and feelings, simply due to the complex nature of political issues. Everyone agrees that a sore throat is bad, while it is less obvious how much government involvement in health care is beneficial.

**LEXRATIO vs. EMOMAXENT** LEXRATIO has low coverage for words that tend to indicate positive and negative sentiment in particular domains. For example, STS has the tweet *In montreal for a long weekend of R&R. Much needed*, with a positive gold label. The only word in this tweet in the OpinionFinder lexicon is *long*, which is labeled as negative. Thus, LEXRATIO incorrectly classifies the tweet as negative. EMOMAXENT correctly labels this tweet positive due to features like *weekend* being strong indicators of the positive class. Similarly, the tweet *Booz Allen Hamilton has a bad ass homegrown social collaboration platform. Way cool! #ttiv* is labeled negative by LEXRATIO due to the presence of *bad*. While EMOMAXENT has a negative preference for both *bad* and *ass*, it has a strong positive preference for *bad ass*, as well as both *cool* and *way cool*.

**EMOMAXENT vs. LPROP** As seen from the per-tweet and per-user results, LPROP does consistently better than MAXENT. We now discuss one example of this improvement from the OMD set. One user authored the following four tweets:

- $t_1$: *obama +3 the conspicuousness of their presence is only matched by our absence #tweetdebate*
- $t_2$: *Fundamentally, if McCain fundamentally uses "fundamental" one more time, I'm gonna go nuts. #tweetdebate*
- $t_3$: *McCain likes the bears in Montana joke too much#tweetdebate #current*
- $t_4$: *We are less respected now... Obama #current #debate08 And I give credit to McCain... NOOO*

The gold label for $t_1$ is positive and the rest are negative. All of the LPROP classifiers correctly predicted the labels for all four tweets. EMOMAXENT missed $t_2$ and $t_3$, so this primarily negative user is incorrectly indicated as primarily positive by EMOMAXENT. LPROP gets around this by propagating sentiment polarity through unigram features in this case.

The unigram *mccain* has an edge weight to tweets that contain it of 8.6 for the OMD corpus, meaning *mccain* is much more frequent in this corpus than the reference corpus, so any sentiment associated with *mccain* is propagated strongly. In this case, the output of label propagation seeded with Noisy-seed reveals that *mccain* has negative sentiment for this dataset.

## 6 Related Work

Much work in sentiment analysis involves the use and generation of dictionaries capturing the sentiment of words. These methods range from manual approaches of developing domain-dependent lexicons (Das and Chan, 2001) to semi-automated approaches (Hu and Liu, 2004) and fully automated approaches (Turney, 2002). Melville et al. (2009) use a unified framework combining background lexical information in terms of word-class associations and refine this information for specific domains using any available training examples. They produce better results than using either a lexicon or training.

O'Connor et al. (2010) use the OpinionFinder subjectivity lexicon to label the polarity of tweets about Barack Obama and compare daily aggregate sentiment scores to the Gallup poll time series of manually gathered approval ratings of Obama. Even with this simple polarity determination, they find significant correlation between their predicted aggregate sentiment per day and the Gallup poll.

Using the OMD dataset, Shamma et al. (2009) find that amount of Twitter activity is a good predictor of topic changes during the debate, and that the content of concurrent tweets reflects a mix of the current debate topic and Twitter users' reactions to that topic. Diakopoulos and Shamma (2010) use the same dataset to develop analysis and visualization techniques to aid journalists and others in understanding the relationship between the live debate event and the timestamped tweets.

Bollen et al. (2010) perform aggregate sentiment analysis on tweets over time, comparing predicted sentiment to time series such as the stock market and crude oil prices, as well as major events such as election day and Thanksgiving. However, the authors use hand-built rules for classification based on the Profile of Mood States (POMS) and largely evaluate based on inspection.

## 7 Conclusion

We have improved upon existing tweet polarity classification methods by combining several knowledge sources with a noisily supervised label propagation algorithm. We show that a maximum entropy classifier trained with distant supervision works better than a lexicon-based ratio predictor, improving the accuracy for polarity classification on our held-out test set from 58.1% to 62.9%. By using the predictions of that classifier in combination with a graph that incorporates tweets and lexical features, we obtain even better accuracy of 71.2%.

We did not find overall gains from using the follower graph as implemented here. There is room for improvement in the way the follower graph is encoded in our graph, particularly with respect to using asymmetric relationships rather than an undirected graph, and in how follower relationships are weighted.

Another source of information that could be used to improve results is the text in pages that have been linked to from a tweet. In many cases, it is only possible to know what the polarity is by looking at the page being linked to. Our label propagation setup can incorporate this straightforwardly by adding nodes for those pages plus edges between them and all tweets that reference them.

## Acknowledgments

This research was supported by a grant from the Morris Memorial Trust Fund of the New York Community Trust. We thank Leif Johnson for providing the tweets from the Twitter firehose for the EMOTICON and HCR datasets, Partha Talukdar for the Junto label propagation toolkit, and the UT Natural Language Learning reading group for helpful feedback.

## References

Shumeet Baluja, Rohan Seth, D. Sivakumar, Yushi Jing, Jay Yagnik, Shankar Kumar, Deepak Ravichandran, and Mohamed Aly. Video suggestion and discovery for youtube: taking random walks through the view graph. In *WWW '08: Proceeding of the 17th international conference on World Wide Web*, pages 895–904, New York, NY, USA, 2008. ACM.

S. Blair-Goldensohn, K. Hannan, R. McDonald, T. Neylon, G. Reis, and J. Reynar. Building a sentiment summarizer for local service reviews. In *WWW Workshop on NLP in the Information Explosion Era (NLPIX)*, 2008. URL `http://www.ryanmcd.com/papers/local_service_summ.pdf`.

J. Bollen, A. Pepe, and H. Mao. Modeling public mood and emotion: Twitter sentiment and socio-economic phenomena. In *Proceedings of the 19th International World Wide Web Conference*, 2010.

Samuel Brody and Noemie Elhadad. An unsupervised aspect-sentiment model for online reviews. In *Human Language Technologies: The 2010 Annual Conference of the North American Chapter of the Association for Computational Linguistics*, HLT '10, pages 804–812, Stroudsburg, PA, USA, 2010. Association for Computational Linguistics. ISBN 1-932432-65-5. URL `http://portal.acm.org/citation.cfm?id=1857999.1858121`.

Yejin Choi and Claire Cardie. Adapting a polarity lexicon using integer linear programming for domain-specific sentiment classification. In *Proceedings of the 2009 Conference on Empirical Methods in Natural Language Processing*, pages 590–598. Association for Computational Linguistics, 2009. URL `http://www.aclweb.org/anthology/D/D09/D09-1062`.

S. Das and M. Chan. Extracting market sentiment from stock message boards. *Asia Pacific Finance Association, 2001*, 2001.

Dmitry Davidov, Oren Tsur, and Ari Rappoport. Enhanced sentiment learning using twitter hashtags and smileys. In *Proceedings of the 23rd International Conference on Computational Linguistics*, 2010.

Nicholas A. Diakopoulos and David A. Shamma. Characterizing debate performance via aggregated twitter sentiment. In *Proceedings of the 28th international conference on Human factors in computing systems*, pages 1195–1198, 2010.

Alec Go, Richa Bhayani, and Lei Huang. Twitter sentiment classification using distant supervision. Unpublished manuscript. Stanford University, 2009.

Minqing Hu and Bing Liu. Mining and summarizing customer reviews. In *KDD '04: Proceedings of the tenth ACM SIGKDD international conference on Knowledge discovery and data mining*, pages 168–177, New York, NY, USA, 2004. ACM. ISBN 1-58113-888-1. doi: http://doi.acm.org/10.1145/1014052.1014073.

Prem Melville, Wojciech Gryc, and Richard D. Lawrence. Sentiment analysis of blogs by combining lexical knowledge with text classification. In *KDD '09: Proceedings of the 15th ACM SIGKDD international conference on Knowledge discovery and data mining*, pages 1275–1284, New York, NY, USA, 2009. ACM. ISBN 978-1-60558-495-9. doi: http://doi.acm.org/10.1145/1557019.1557156.

Brendan O'Connor, Ramnath Balasubramanyan, Bryan R. Routledge, and Noah A. Smith. From tweets to polls: Linking text sentiment to public opinion time series. In *Proceedings of the International AAAI Conference on Weblogs and Social Media*, 2010.

B. Pang, L. Lee, and S. Vaithyanathan. Thumbs up?: sentiment classification using machine learning techniques. In *Proceedings of the ACL-02 conference on Empirical methods in natural language processing-Volume 10*, pages 79–86, 2002.

Bo Pang and Lillian Lee. A sentimental education: sentiment analysis using subjectivity summarization based on minimum cuts. In *Proceedings of the 42nd Annual Meeting on Association for Computational Linguistics*, 2004.

Bo Pang and Lillian Lee. Opinion mining and sentiment analysis. *Foundations and Trends in Information Retrieval*, 2(1-2):1–135, 2008.

Delip Rao and Deepak Ravichandran. Semi-supervised polarity lexicon induction. In *Proceedings of the 12th Conference of the European Chapter of the ACL (EACL 2009)*, pages 675–682. Association for Computational Linguistics, 2009. URL `http://www.aclweb.org/anthology/E09-1077`.

Jonathon Read. Using emoticons to reduce dependency in machine learning techniques for sentiment classification. In *Proceedings of the ACL Student Research Workshop*, ACLstudent '05, pages 43–48, Stroudsburg, PA, USA, 2005. Association for Computational Linguistics. URL `http://portal.acm.org/citation.cfm?id=1628960.1628969`.

David A. Shamma, Lyndon Kennedy, and Elizabeth F. Churchill. Tweet the debates: understanding community annotation of uncollected sources. In *Proceedings of the first SIGMM workshop on Social media*, pages 3–10, 2009.

Vikas Sindhwani and Prem Melville. Document-word co-regularization for semi-supervised sentiment analysis. In *Proceedings of IEEE International Conference on Data Mining (ICDM-08)*, 2008.

Partha Talukdar and Koby Crammer. New regularized algorithms for transductive learning. In Wray Buntine, Marko Grobelnik, Dunja Mladenic, and John Shawe-Taylor, editors, *Machine Learning and Knowledge Discovery in Databases*, volume 5782, pages 442–457. Springer Berlin / Heidelberg, 2009.

P. D. Turney. Thumbs up or thumbs down? semantic orientation applied to unsupervised classification of reviews. In *Proceedings of the 40th Annual Meeting of the Association for Computational Linguistics*, pages 417–424, 2002.

Theresa Wilson, Paul Hoffmann, Swapna Somasundaran, Jason Kessler, Janyce Wiebe, Yejin Choi, Claire Cardie, Ellen Riloff, and Siddharth Patwardhan. OpinionFinder: A system for subjectivity analysis. In *Proc. Human Language Technology Conference and Conference on Empirical Methods in Natural Language Processing (HLT/EMNLP-2005) Companion Volume (software demonstration)*, 2005.

Xiaojin Zhu and Zoubin Ghahramani. Learning from labeled and unlabeled data with label propagation. Technical Report CMU-CALD-02-107, Carnegie Mellon University, 2002.

# Unsupervised Bilingual POS Tagging with Markov Random Fields

**Desai Chen** **Chris Dyer** **Shay B. Cohen** **Noah A. Smith**
School of Computer Science
Carnegie Mellon University
Pittsburgh, PA 15213, USA
desaic@andrew.cmu.edu, {cdyer,scohen,nasmith}@cs.cmu.edu

## Abstract

In this paper, we give a treatment to the problem of bilingual part-of-speech induction with parallel data. We demonstrate that naïve optimization of log-likelihood with joint MRFs suffers from a severe problem of local maxima, and suggest an alternative – using contrastive estimation for estimation of the parameters. Our experiments show that estimating the parameters this way, using overlapping features with joint MRFs performs better than previous work on the *1984* dataset.

## 1 Introduction

This paper considers unsupervised learning of linguistic structure—specifically, parts of speech—in parallel text data. This setting, and more generally the multilingual learning scenario, has been found advantageous for a variety of unsupervised NLP tasks (Snyder et al., 2008; Cohen and Smith, 2010; Berg-Kirkpatrick et al., 2010; Das and Petrov, 2011).

We consider globally normalized Markov random fields (MRFs) as an alternative to directed models based on multinomial distributions or locally normalized log-linear distributions. This alternate parameterization allows us to introduce correlated features that, at least in principle, depend on any parts of the hidden structure. Such models, sometimes called "undirected," are widespread in *supervised* NLP; the most notable instances are conditional random fields (Lafferty et al., 2001), which have enabled rich feature engineering to incorporate knowledge and improve performance. We conjecture that the "features view" of NLP problems is also more appropriate in unsupervised settings than the contrived, acyclic causal stories required by directed models. Indeed, as we will discuss below, previous work on multilingual POS induction has had to resort to objectionable independence assumptions to avoid introducing cyclic dependencies in the causal network.

While undirected models are formally attractive, they are computationally demanding, particularly when they are used *generatively*, i.e., as joint distributions over input and output spaces. Inference and learning algorithms for these models are usually intractable on realistic datasets, so we must resort to approximations. Our emphasis here is primarily on the machinery required to support overlapping features, not on weakening independence assumptions, although we weaken them slightly. Specifically, our parameterization permits us to model the relationship between aligned words in any configuration, rather than just those that conform to an acyclic generative process, as previous work in this area has done (§2). We incorporate word prefix and suffix features (up to four characters) in an undirected version of a model designed by Snyder et al. (2008). Our experiments suggest that feature-based MRFs offer advantages over the previous approach.

## 2 Related Work

The task of unsupervised bilingual POS induction was originally suggested and explored by Snyder et al. (2008). Their work proposes a joint model over pairs of tag sequences and words that can be understood as a pair of hidden Markov models (HMMs)

*Proceedings of EMNLP 2011, Conference on Empirical Methods in Natural Language Processing*, pages 64–71,
Edinburgh, Scotland, UK, July 27–31, 2011. 

in which aligned words share states (a fixed and observable word alignment is assumed). Figure 1 gives an example for a French-English sentence pair. Following Goldwater and Griffiths (2007), the transition, emission and coupling parameters are governed by Dirichlet priors, and a token-level collapsed Gibbs sampler is used for inference. The hyperparameters of the prior distributions are inferred from data in an empirical Bayesian fashion.

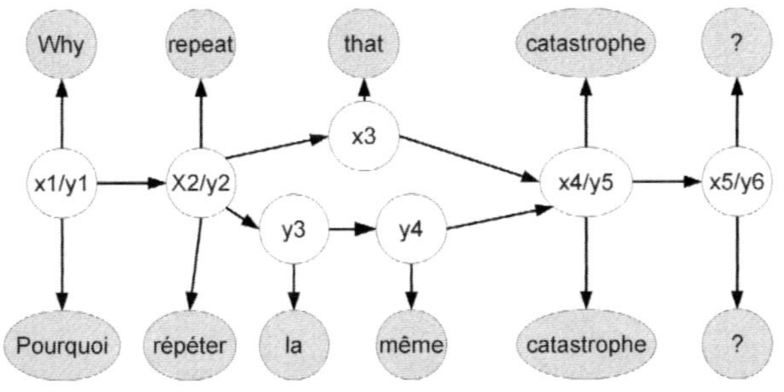


Figure 1: Bilingual Directed POS induction model

When word alignments are monotonic (i.e., there are no crossing links in the alignment graph), the model of Snyder et al. is straightforward to construct. However, crossing alignment links pose a problem: they induce cycles in the tag sequence graph, which corresponds to an ill-defined probability model. Their solution is to eliminate such alignment pairs (their algorithm for doing so is discussed below). Unfortunately, this is a potentially a serious loss of information. Crossing alignments often correspond to systematic word order differences between languages (e.g., SVO vs. SOV languages). As such, leaving them out prevents useful information about entire subsets of POS types from exploiting of bilingual context.

In the monolingual setting, Smith and Eisner (2005) showed similarly that a POS induction model can be improved with spelling features (prefixes and suffixes of words), and Haghighi and Klein (2006) describe an MRF-based monolingual POS induction model that uses features. An example of such a monolingual model is shown in Figure 2. Both papers developed different approximations of the computationally expensive partition function. Haghighi and Klein (2006) approximated by ignoring all sentences of length greater than some maximum, and the "contrastive estimation" of Smith and Eisner (2005) approximates the partition function with a set

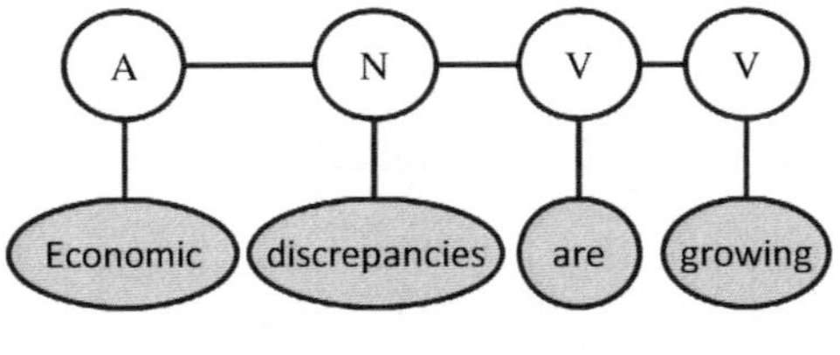


Figure 2: Monolingual MRF tag model (Haghighi and Klein, 2006)

of automatically distorted training examples which are compactly represented in WFSTs.

Das and Petrov (2011) also consider the problem of unsupervised bilingual POS induction. They make use of independent conventional HMM monolingual tagging models that are parameterized with feature-rich log-linear models (Berg-Kirkpatrick et al., 2010). However, training is constrained with tag dictionaries inferred using bilingual contexts derived from aligned parallel data. In this way, the complex inference and modeling challenges associated with a bilingual tagging model are avoided.

Finally, multilingual POS induction has also been considered without using parallel data. Cohen et al. (2011) present a multilingual estimation technique for part-of-speech tagging (and grammar induction), where the lack of parallel data is compensated by the use of labeled data for some languages and unlabeled data for other languages.

## 3 Model

Our model is a Markov random field whose random variables correspond to words in two parallel sentences and POS tags for those words. Let $\mathbf{s} = \langle s_1, \ldots, s_{N_s} \rangle$ and $\mathbf{t} = \langle t_1, \ldots, t_{N_t} \rangle$ denote the two word sequences; these correspond to $N_s + N_t$ observed random variables.[1] Let $\mathbf{x}$ and $\mathbf{y}$ denote the sequences of POS tags for $\mathbf{s}$ and $\mathbf{t}$, respectively. These are the hidden variables whose values we seek to infer. We assume that a word alignment is provided for the sentences. Let $A \subseteq \{1, \ldots, N_s\} \times \{1, \ldots N_t\}$ denote the word correspondences specified by the alignment. The MRF's unnormalized probability $S$

[1]We use "source" and "target" but the two are completely symmetric in our undirected framework.

assigns:

$$S(\mathbf{s},\mathbf{t},\mathbf{x},\mathbf{y} \mid A,\mathbf{w}) = \exp \mathbf{w}^\top \Bigg( \sum_{i=1}^{N_s} \mathbf{f}_{\text{s-emit}}(s_i, x_i) + \sum_{i=2}^{N_s} \mathbf{f}_{\text{s-tran}}(x_{i-1}, x_i) + \sum_{i=1}^{N_t} \mathbf{f}_{\text{t-emit}}(t_i, y_i) + \sum_{i=2}^{N_t} \mathbf{f}_{\text{t-tran}}(y_{i-1}, y_i) + \sum_{(i,j)\in A} \mathbf{f}_{\text{align-POS}}(x_i, y_j) \Bigg)$$

where $\mathbf{w}$ is a numerical vector of feature weights that parameterizes the model. Each $\mathbf{f}_\bullet$ corresponds to features on pairs of random variables; a source POS tag and word, two adjacent source POS tags, similarly for the target side, and aligned source/target POS pairs. For simplicity, we let $\mathbf{f}$ denote the sum of these five feature vectors. (In most settings, each feature/coordinate will be specific to one of the five addends.) In this paper, the features are indicators for each possible value of the pair of random variables, plus prefix and suffix features for words (up to four characters). These features encode information similar to the Bayesian bilingual HMM discussed in §2. Future work might explore extensions to this basic feature set.

The marginal probability of the words is given by:

$$p(\mathbf{s},\mathbf{t} \mid A,\mathbf{w}) = \frac{\sum_{\mathbf{x},\mathbf{y}} S(\mathbf{x},\mathbf{y},\mathbf{s},\mathbf{t} \mid A,\mathbf{w})}{\sum_{\mathbf{s}',\mathbf{t}'} \sum_{\mathbf{x},\mathbf{y}} S(\mathbf{s}',\mathbf{t}',\mathbf{x},\mathbf{y} \mid A,\mathbf{w})}.$$

Maximum likelihood estimation would choose weights $\mathbf{w}$ to optimize a product of quantities like the above, across the training data.

A key advantage of this representation is that any alignments may be present. In directed models, crossing links create forbidden cycles in the graphical model. For example, Figure 3 shows a crossing link between "Economic discrepancies" and "divergences economiques." Snyder et al. (2008) dealt with this problem by deleting word correspondences that created cycles. The authors deleted crossing links by considering each alignment link in the order of the source sentence, deleting it if it crossed previous links. Deleting crossing links removes some information about word correspondence.

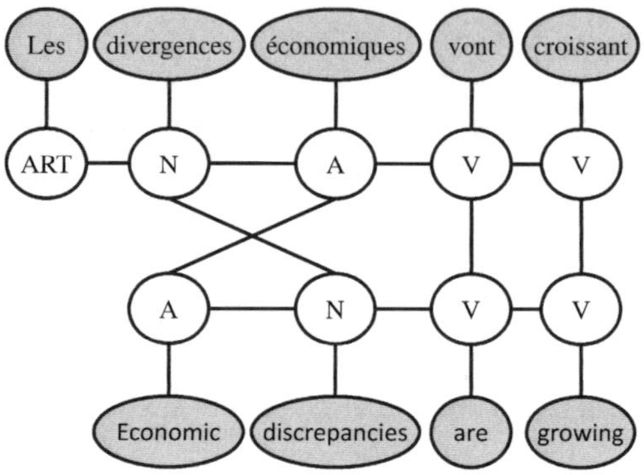


Figure 3: Bilingual tag model.

## 4 Inference and Parameter Learning

When using traditional generative models, such as hidden Markov models, the unsupervised setting lends itself well to maximizing joint log-likelihood, leading to a model that performs well (Snyder et al., 2008). However, as we show in the following analysis, maximizing joint log-likelihood for a joint Markov random field with arbitrary features suffers from serious issues which are related to the complexity of the optimized objective surface.

### 4.1 MLE with Gradient Descent

For notational simplicity, we assume a single pair of sentences $\mathbf{s}$ and $\mathbf{t}$; generalizing to multiple training instances is straightforward. The marginalized log-likelihood of the data given $\mathbf{w}$ is

$$\mathcal{L}(\mathbf{w}) = \log p(\mathbf{s},\mathbf{t} \mid \mathbf{w}) = \log \frac{\sum_{\mathbf{x},\mathbf{y}} S(\mathbf{x},\mathbf{y},\mathbf{s},\mathbf{t} \mid \mathbf{w})}{\sum_{\mathbf{s}',\mathbf{t}'} \sum_{\mathbf{x},\mathbf{y}} S(\mathbf{x},\mathbf{y},\mathbf{s}',\mathbf{t}' \mid \mathbf{w})}.$$

In general, maximizing marginalized log-likelihood is a non-concave optimization problem. Iterative hill-climbing methods (e.g., expectation-maximization and gradient-based optimization) will lead only to local maxima, and these may be quite shallow. Our analysis suggests that the problem is exacerbated when we move from directed to undirected models. We next describe a simple experiment that gives insight into the problem.

We created a small synthetic monolingual data set for sequence labeling. Our synthetic data consists of the following five sequences of observations: $\{(0\ 1\ 2\ 3), (1\ 2\ 3\ 0), (2\ 3\ 0\ 1), (3\ 0\ 1\ 2), (0\ 1\ 2\ 3)\}$. We then maximized the marginalized log-likelihood for two models: a hidden Markov model and an MRF. Both use the same set features, only the MRF is globally normalized. The number of hidden states in both models is 4.

The global maximium in both cases would be achieved when the emission probabilities (or feature weights, in the case of MRF) map each observation symbol to a single state. When we tested whether this happens in practice, we noticed that it indeed happens for hidden Markov models. The MRF, however, tended to use fewer than four tags in the emission feature weights, i.e., for half of the tags, all emission feature weights were close to 0. This effect also appeared in our real data experiments.

The reason for this problem with the MRF, we believe, is that the parameter space of the MRF is underconstrained. HMMs locally normalize the emission probabilities, which implies that a tag cannot "disappear"—a total probability mass of 1 must always be allocated to the observation symbols. With MRFs, however, there is no such constraint. Further, effective deletion of a state $y$ requires zeroing out transition probabilities from all other states to $y$, a large number of parameters that are completely decoupled within the model.

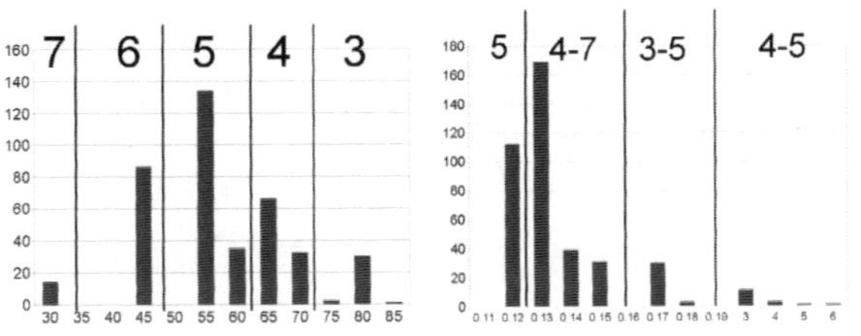


(a) likelihood (b) contrastive objective

Figure 4: Histograms of local optima found by optimizing the length neighborhood objective (a) and the contrastive objective (b) on a synthetic dataset with 8 sentences of length 7. The weights are initialized uniformly at random in the interval $[-1, 1]$. We plot frequency versus negated log-likelihood (lower horizontal values are better). An HMM always finds a solution that uses all available tags. The numbers at the top are numbers of tags used by each local optimum.

Our bilingual model is more complex than the above example, and we found in preliminary experiments that the effect persists there, as well. In the following section, we propose a remedy to this problem based on contrastive estimation (Smith and Eisner, 2005).

### 4.2 Contrastive Estimation

Contrastive estimation maximizes a modified version of the log-likelihood. In the modified version, it is the normalization constant of the log-likelihood that changes: it is limited to a sum over possible elements in a *neighborhood* of the observed instances. More specifically, in our bilingual tagging model, we would define a neighborhood function for sentences, $N(\mathbf{s}, \mathbf{t})$ which maps a pair of sentences to a set of pairs of sentences. Using this neighborhood function, we maximize the following objective function:

$$\begin{aligned}
&\mathcal{L}_{\text{ce}}(\mathbf{w}) \\
&= \log p(\mathbf{S} = \mathbf{s}, \mathbf{T} = \mathbf{t} \mid \mathbf{S} \in N_1(\mathbf{s}), \mathbf{T} \in N_2(\mathbf{t}), \mathbf{w}) \\
&= \log \frac{\sum_{\mathbf{x},\mathbf{y}} S(\mathbf{s}, \mathbf{t}, \mathbf{x}, \mathbf{y} \mid \mathbf{w})}{\sum_{\mathbf{s}',\mathbf{t}' \in N(\mathbf{s},\mathbf{t})} \sum_{\mathbf{x},\mathbf{y}} S(\mathbf{s}', \mathbf{t}', \mathbf{x}, \mathbf{y} \mid \mathbf{w})}.
\end{aligned} \tag{1}$$

We define the neighborhood function using a cross-product of monolingual neighborhoods: $N(\mathbf{s}, \mathbf{t}) = N_1(\mathbf{s}) \times N_1(\mathbf{t})$. $N_1$ is the "dynasearch" neighborhood function (Potts and van de Velde, 1995; Congram et al., 2002), used for contrastive estimation previously by Smith (2006). This neighborhood defines a subset of permutations of a sequence $\mathbf{s}$, based on local transpositions. Specifically, a permutation of $\mathbf{s}$ is in $N_1(\mathbf{s})$ if it can be derived from $\mathbf{s}$ through swaps of any adjacent pairs of words, with the constraint that each word only be moved once. This neighborhood can be compactly represented with a finite-state machine of size $O(N_s)$ but encodes a number of sequences equal to the $N_s$th Fibonacci number.

**Monolingual Analysis** To show that contrastive estimation indeed gives a remedy to the local maximum problem, we return to the monolingual synthetic data example from §4.1 and apply contrastive estimation on this problem. The neighborhood we use is the dynasearch neighborhood. In Figure 4b we compare the maxima identified using MLE with the monolingual MRF model to the maxima identified by contrastive estimation. The results are conclusive: MLE tends to get stuck much more often in local maxima than contrastive estimation.

Following an analysis of the feature weights found by contrastive estimation, we found that contrastive estimation puts more weight on the transition features than emission features, i.e., the transition features weights have larger absolute values than emission feature weights. We believe that this could explain why contrastive estimation finds better local maximum that plain MLE, but we leave exploration of this effect for future work.

It is interesting to note that even though the contrastive objective tends to use more tags available in the dictionary than the likelihood objective does, the maximum objective that we were able to find does not correspond to the tagging that uses all available tags, unlike with HMM, where the maximum that achieved highest likelihood also uses all available tags.

### 4.3 Optimizing the Contrastive Objective

To optimize the objective in Eq. 1 we use a generic optimization technique based on the gradient. Using the chain rule for derivatives, we can derive the partial derivative of the log-likelihood with respect to a weight $w_i$:

$$\frac{\partial \mathcal{L}_{\text{ce}}(\mathbf{w})}{\partial w_i} = \mathbb{E}_{p(\mathbf{X},\mathbf{Y}|\mathbf{s},\mathbf{t},\mathbf{w})}[f_i] - \mathbb{E}_{p(\mathbf{S},\mathbf{T},\mathbf{X},\mathbf{Y}|\mathbf{S}\in N_1(\mathbf{s}),\mathbf{T}\in N_1(\mathbf{t}),\mathbf{w})}[f_i]$$

The second term corresponds to a computationally expensive inference problem, because of the loops in the graphical model. This situation is different from previous work on linear chain-structured MRFs (Smith and Eisner, 2005; Haghighi and Klein, 2006), where exact inference is possible. To overcome this problem, we use Gibbs sampling to obtain the two expectations needed by the gradient. This technique is closely related to methods like stochastic expectation-maximization (Andrieu et al., 2003) and to contrastive divergence (Hinton, 2000).

The training algorithm iterates between sampling part-of-speech tags and sampling permutations of words to compute the expected value of features. To sample permutations, the sampler iterates through the sentences and decides, for each sentence, whether to swap a pair of adjacent tags and words or not. The Markov blanket for computing the probability of swapping a pair of tags and words is shown in Figure 5. We run the algorithm for a fixed number (50) of iterations. By testing on a development set, we observed that the accuracy may increase after 50 iterations, but we chose this small number of iterations for speed.

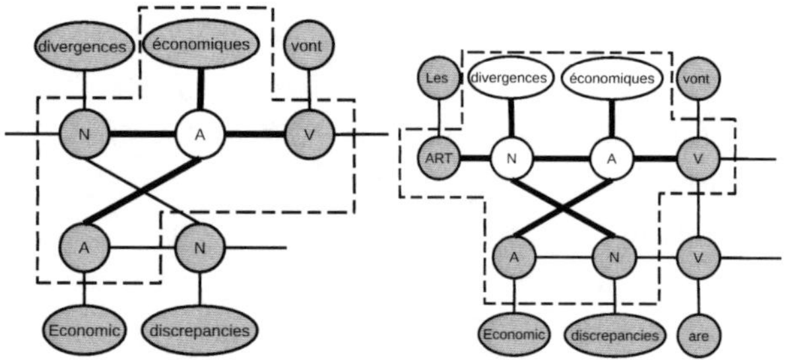


Figure 5: Markov blanket of a tag (left) and of a pair of adjacent tags and words (right).

In preliminary experiments we considered stochastic gradient descent, with online updating. We found this led to low-accuracy local optima, and opted for gradient descent with batch updates in our implementation. The step size was chosen to limit the maximum absolute value of the update in any weight to 0.1. Preliminary experiments showed only harmful effects from regularization, so we did not use it. These issues deserve further analysis and experimentation in future research.

## 5 Experiments

We next describe experiments using our undirected model to unsupervisedly learn POS tags.

With unsupervised part-of-speech tagging, it is common practice to use a full or partial dictionary that maps words to possible part-of-speech tags. The goal of the learner is then to discern which tag a word should take among the tags available for that word. Indeed, in all of our experiments we make use of a tag dictionary. We consider both a *complete* tag dictionary, where all of the POS tags for all words in the data are known,[2] and a smaller tag dictionary that only provides possible tags for the 100

[2]Of course, additional POS tags may be possible for a given word that were not in evidence in our finite dataset.

most frequent words in each language, leaving the other words completely ambiguous. The former dictionary makes the problem easier by reducing ambiguity; it also speeds up inference.

Our experiments focus on the Orwell novel *1984* dataset for our experiments, the same data used by Snyder et al. (2008). It consists of parallel text of the *1984* novel in English, Bulgarian, Slovene and Serbian (Erjavec, 2004), totalling 5,969 sentences in each language. The *1984* datset uses fourteen part-of-speech tags, two of which denote punctuation. The tag sets for English and other languages have minor differences in determiners and particles.

We use the last 25% of sentences in the dataset as a test set, following previous work. The dataset is manually annotated with part-of-speech tags. We use automatically induced word alignments using Giza++ (Och and Ney, 2003). The data show very regular patterns of tags that are aligned together: words with the same tag in two languages tend to be aligned with each other.

When a complete tag dictionary derived from the Slavic language data is available, the level of ambiguity is very low. The baseline of choosing random tags for each word gives an accuracy in the low 80s. For English, we use an extended tag dictionary built from the Wall Street Journal and the *1984* data. The English tag dictionary is much more ambiguous because it is obtained from a much larger dataset. The random baseline gives an accuracy of around 56%. (See Table 1.)

In our first set of experiments (§5.1), we perform a "sanity check" with a monolingual version of the MRF that we described in earlier sections. We compare it against plain HMM to assure that the MRFs behave well in the unsupervised setting.

In our second set of experiments (§5.2), we compare the bilingual HMM model from Snyder et al. (2008) to the joint MRF model. We show that using an MRF has an advantage over an HMM model in the partial tag dictionary setting.

### 5.1 Monolingual Experiments

We turn now to two monolingual experiments that verify our model's suitability for the tagging problem.

| Language | Random | HMM | MRF |
|---|---|---|---|
| Bulgarian | 82.7 | 88.9 | 93.5 |
| English | 56.2 | 90.7 | 87.0 |
| Serbian | 83.4 | 85.1 | 89.3 |
| Slovene | 84.7 | 87.4 | 94.5 |

Table 1: Unsupervised monolingual tagging accuracies with complete tag dictionary on *1984* data.

**Supervised Learning** As a very primitive comparison, we trained a monolingual supervised MRF model to compare to the results of supervised HMMs. The training procedure is based on sampling, just like the unsupervised estimation method described in §4.3. The only difference is that there is no need to sample the words because the tags are the only random variables to be marginalized over. Our model and HMM give very close performance with difference in accuracy less than 0.1%. This shows that the MRF is capable of representing an equivalent model represented by the HMM. It also shows that gradient descent with MCMC approximate inference is capable of finding a good model with the weights initialized to all 0s.

**Unsupervised Learning** We trained our model under the monolingual setting as a sanity check for our approximate training algorithm. Our model under monolingual mode is exactly the same as the models introduced in §2. We ran our model on the *1984* data with the complete tag dictionary. A comparison between our result and monolingual directed model is shown in Table 1. "Random" is obtained by choosing a random tag for each word according to the tag dictionary. "HMM" is a Bayesian HMM implemented by (Snyder et al., 2008). We also implemented a basic (non-Bayesian) HMM. We trained the HMM with EM and obtained rsults similar to the Bayesian HMM (not shown).

### 5.2 Billingual Results

Table 2 gives the full results in the bilingual setting for the *1984* dataset with a partial tag dictionary. In general, MRFs do better than their directed counterparts, the HMMs. Interestingly enough, removing crossing links from the data has only a slight adverse effect. It appears like the prefix and suffix features are more important than having crossing links. Re-

| Language pair | HMM | MRF | MRF w/o cross. | MRF w/o spell. |
|---|---|---|---|---|
| English | 71.3 | 73.3± 0.6 | 73.4± 0.6 | 67.4± 0.9 |
| Bulgarian | 62.6 | 62.3± 0.3 | 63.8± 0.4 | 55.2± 0.5 |
| Serbian | 54.1 | 55.7± 0.2 | 54.6± 0.3 | 47.7± 0.5 |
| Slovene | 59.7 | 61.4± 0.3 | 60.4± 0.3 | 56.7± 0.4 |
| English | 66.5 | 73.3± 0.3 | 73.4± 0.2 | 62.3± 0.5 |
| Slovene | 53.8 | 59.7± 2.5 | 57.6± 2.0 | 52.1± 1.3 |
| Bulgarian | 54.2 | 58.1± 0.1 | 56.3± 1.3 | 58.0± 0.2 |
| Serbian | 56.9 | 58.6± 0.3 | 59.0± 1.2 | 55.1± 0.3 |
| English | 68.2 | 72.8± 0.6 | 72.7± 0.6 | 65.7± 0.4 |
| Serbian | 54.7 | 58.5± 0.6 | 57.7± 0.3 | 54.2± 0.3 |
| Bulgarian | 55.9 | 59.8± 0.1 | 60.3± 0.5 | 55.0± 0.4 |
| Slovene | 58.5 | 61.4± 0.3 | 61.6± 0.4 | 58.1± 0.6 |
| Average | 59.7 | 62.9 | 62.5 | 56.5 |

Table 2: Unsupervised bilingual tagging accuracies with tag dictionary only for the top 100 frequent words. "HMM" is the result reported by (Snyder et al., 2008). "MRF" is our contrastive model averaged over ten runs. "MRF w/o cross." is our model trained without crossing links, like Snyder et al.'s HMM. "MRF w/o spell." is our model without prefix and suffix features. Numbers appearing next to results are standard deviations over the ten runs.

| Language | w/ cross. | w/o cross. |
|---|---|---|
| French | 73.8 | 70.3 |
| English | 56.0 | 59.2 |

Table 3: Effect of removing crossing links when learning French and English in a bilingual setting.

moving the prefix and suffix features gives substantially lower results on average, results even below plain HMMs.

The reason that crossing links do not change the results much could be related to fact that most of the sentence pairs in the *1984* dataset do not contain many crossing links (only 5% of links cross another link). To see whether crossing links do have an effect when they come in larger number, we tested our model on French-English data. We aligned 10,000 sentences from the Europarl corpus (Koehn, 2005), resulting in 87K crossing links out of a total of 673K links. Using the Penn treebank (Marcus et al., 1993) and the French treebank (Abeillé et al., 2003) to evaluate the model, results are given in Table 3. It is evident that crossing links have a larger effect here, but it is mixed: crossing links improve performance for French while harming it for English.

## 6 Conclusion

In this paper, we explored the capabilities of joint MRFs for modeling bilingual part-of-speech models. Exact inference with dynamic programming is not applicable, forcing us to experiment with approximate inference techniques. We demonstrated that using contrastive estimation together with Gibbs sampling for the calculation of the gradient of the objective function leads to better results in unsupervised bilingual POS induction.

Our experiments also show that the advantage of using MRFs does not necessarily come from the fact that we can use non-monotonic alignments in our model, but instead from the ability to use overlapping features such as prefix and suffix features for the vocabulary in the data.

## Acknowledgments

We thank the reviewers and members of the ARK group for helpful comments on this work. This research was supported in part by the NSF through grant IIS-0915187 and the U. S. Army Research Laboratory and the U. S. Army Research Office under contract/grant number W911NF-10-1-0533.

## References


A. Abeillé, L. Clément, and F. Toussenel. 2003. Building a treebank for French. In A. Abeillé, editor, *Treebanks*. Kluwer, Dordrecht.

C. Andrieu, N. de Freitas, A. Doucet, and M. I. Jordan. 2003. An introduction to MCMC for machine learning. *Machine Learning*, 50:5–43.

T. Berg-Kirkpatrick, A. Bouchard-Cote, J. DeNero, and D. Klein. 2010. Unsupervised learning with features. In *Proceedings of NAACL*.

S. B. Cohen and N. A. Smith. 2010. Covariance in unsupervised learning of probabilistic grammars. *Journal of Machine Learning Research*, 11:3017–3051.

S. B. Cohen, D. Das, and N. A. Smith. 2011. Unsupervised structure prediction with non-parallel multilingual guidance. In *Proceedings of EMNLP*.

R. K. Congram, C. N. Potts, and S. L. van de Velde. 2002. An iterated Dynasearch algorithm for the single-machine total weighted tardiness scheduling problem. *Informs Journal On Computing*, 14(1):52–67.

D. Das and S. Petrov. 2011. Unsupervised part-of-speech tagging with bilingual graph-based projections. In *Procedings of ACL*.

T. Erjavec. 2004. MULTEXT-East version 3: Multilingual morphosyntactic specifications, lexicons and corpora. In *Proceedings of LREC*.

S. Goldwater and T. Griffiths. 2007. A fully Bayesian approach to unsupervised part-of-speech tagging. In *Proc. of ACL*.

A. Haghighi and D. Klein. 2006. Prototype-driven learning for sequence models. In *Proceedings of HLT-NAACL*.

G. E. Hinton. 2000. Training products of experts by minimizing contrastive divergence. Technical Report GCNU TR 2000-004, University College London.

P. Koehn. 2005. Europarl: A parallel corpus for statistical machine translation. In *MT Summit 2005*.

J. D. Lafferty, A. McCallum, and F. C. N. Pereira. 2001. Conditional random fields: Probabilistic models for segmenting and labeling sequence data. In *Proceedings of ICML*.

M. P. Marcus, B. Santorini, and M. A. Marcinkiewicz. 1993. Building a large annotated corpus of English: The Penn treebank. *Computational Linguistics*, 19:313–330.

F. Och and H. Ney. 2003. A systematic comparison of various statistical alignment models. *Computational Linguistics*, 29(1):19–51.

C. N. Potts and S. L. van de Velde. 1995. Dynasearch–iterative local improvement by dynamic programming. Part I: The traveling salesman problem. *Technical report*.

N. A. Smith and J. Eisner. 2005. Contrastive estimation: training log-linear models on unlabeled data. In *Proc. of ACL*.

N. A. Smith. 2006. *Novel Estimation Methods for Unsupervised Discovery of Latent Structure in Natural Language Text*. Ph.D. thesis, Johns Hopkins University.

B. Snyder, T. Naseem, J. Eisenstein, and R. Barzilay. 2008. Unsupervised multilingual learning for POS tagging. In *Proceedings of EMNLP*.

# Unsupervised Concept Annotation using Latent Dirichlet Allocation and Segmental Methods

**Nathalie Camelin, Boris Detienne, Stéphane Huet, Dominique Quadri and Fabrice Lefèvre**
LIA - University of Avignon, BP 91228
84911 Avignon Cedex 09, France
{nathalie.camelin,boris.detienne,stephane.huet,dominique.quadri,fabrice.lefevre}@univ-avignon.fr

## Abstract

Training efficient statistical approaches for natural language understanding generally requires data with segmental semantic annotations. Unfortunately, building such resources is costly. In this paper, we propose an approach that produces annotations in an unsupervised way. The first step is an implementation of latent Dirichlet allocation that produces a set of topics with probabilities for each topic to be associated with a word in a sentence. This knowledge is then used as a bootstrap to infer a segmentation of a word sentence into topics using either integer linear optimisation or stochastic word alignment models (IBM models) to produce the final semantic annotation. The relation between automatically-derived topics and task-dependent concepts is evaluated on a spoken dialogue task with an available reference annotation.

## 1 Introduction

Spoken dialogue systems in the field of information query are basically used to interface a database with users using speech. When probabilistic models are used in such systems, good performance can only be reached at the price of collecting a lot of field data, which must be transcribed and annotated at the semantic level. It becomes then possible to train efficient models in a supervised manner. However, the annotation process is costly and as a consequence represents a real difficulty hindering the widespread development of these systems. Therefore any means to avoid it would be profitable as portability to new tasks, domains or languages would be greatly facilitated.

To give a full description of the architecture of a dialogue system is out of the scope of this paper. Instead we limit ourselves to briefly recall that once a speech recognizer has transcribed the signal it is common (though avoidable for very simple tasks) to use a module dedicated to extract the meaning of the user's queries. This meaning representation is then conveyed to an interaction manager that decides upon the next best action to perform considering the current user's input and the dialogue history. One of the very first steps to build the spoken language understanding (SLU) module is the identification of literal concepts in the word sequence hypothesised by the speech recogniser. An example of a semantic representation in terms of literal concept is given in Figure 1. Once the concepts are identified they can be further composed to form the overall meaning of the sentence, for instance by means of a tree representation based on hierarchical semantic frames.

To address the issue of concept tagging several techniques are available. Some of these techniques now classical rely on probabilistic models, that can be either discriminative or generative. Among these, the most efficiently studied this last decade are: hidden Markov models, finite state transducers, maximum entropy Markov models, support vector machines, dynamic fields (CRF). In (Hahn et al., 2010) it is shown that CRFs obtain the best performance on a tourist information retrieval task in French (MEDIA (Bonneau-Maynard et al., 2005)), but also in two other comparable corpora in Italian and Polish.

To be able to apply any such technique, basic con-

*Proceedings of EMNLP 2011, Conference on Empirical Methods in Natural Language Processing*, pages 72–81,
Edinburgh, Scotland, UK, July 27–31, 2011. 

| words | concept | normalized value |
| --- | --- | --- |
| donnez-moi | null | |
| le | refLink-coRef | singular |
| tarif | object | payment-amount-room |
| puisque | connectProp | imply |
| je voudrais | null | |
| une chambre | number-room | 1 |
| qui coûte | object | payment-amount-room |
| pas plus de | comparative-payment | less than |
| cinquante | payment-amount-integer-room | 50 |
| euros | payment-unit | euro |

Figure 1: Semantic concept representation for the query *"give me the rate since I'd like a room charged not more than fifty euros"*.

cept units have to be defined by an expert. In the best case, most of these concepts can be derived straightforwardly from the pieces of information lurking in the database tables (mainly table fields but not exclusively). Some others are general (dialogic units but also generic entities such as number, dates, etc). However, to provide an efficient and usable information to the reasoning modules (the dialogue manager in our case) concepts have to be fine-grained enough and application-dependent (even general concepts might have to be tailored to peculiar uses). To that extent it seems out of reach to derive the concept definitions using a fully automatic procedure. Anyhow the process can be bootstrapped, for instance by induction of semantic classes such as in (Siu and Meng, 1999) or (Iosif et al., 2006). Our assumption here is that the most time-consuming parts of concept inventory and data tagging could be obtained in an unsupervised way even though a final (but hopefully minimal) manual procedure is still required to tag the classes so as to manually correct automatic annotation.

Unlike the previous attempts cited above which developed *ad hoc* approaches, we investigate here the use of broad-spectrum knowledge extraction methods. The notion most related to that of concept in SLU is the topic, as used in information retrieval systems. Anyhow for a long time, the topic detection task was limited to associate a single topic to a document and thus was not fitted to our requirements. The recently proposed LDA technique allows to have a probabilistic representation of a document as a mixture of topics. Then multiple topics can co-occur inside a document and the same topic can be repeated. From these characteristics it is possible to consider the application of LDA to unsupervised concept inventory and concept tagging for SLU. A shortcoming is that LDA does not modelize at all the sequentiality of the data. To address this issue we propose to conclude the procedure with a final step to introduce specific constraints for a correct segmentation of the data: the assignments of topics proposed by LDA are modified to be more segmentally coherent.

The paper is organised as follows. Principles of automatic induction of semantic classes are presented in Section 2, followed by the presentation of an induction system based on LDA. The additional step of segmentation is presented in Section 3 with two variants: stochastic word alignment (GIZA) and integer linear programming (ILP). Then evaluations and results are reported in Section 4 on the French MEDIA dialogue task.

## 2 Automatic induction of semantic classes

### 2.1 Context modeling

The idea of automatic induction of semantic classes is based on the assumption that concepts often share the same context (syntactic or lexical). Implemented systems are based on the observation of co-occurring words according to two different ways. The observation of consecutive words (bigrams or trigrams) enables the generation of lexical compounds supposed to follow syntactic rules. The comparison of right and left contexts considering pairs of words enables to cluster words (and word compounds) into semantic classes.

In (Siu and Meng, 1999) and (Pargellis et al., 2001), iterative systems are presented. Their implementations differ in the metrics chosen to evaluate the similarity during the generation of syntactic rules and semantic classes, but also in the number of words taken into account in a word context and the order of successive steps (which ones to generate first: syntactic rules or semantic classes?). An iterative procedure is executed to obtain a sufficient set of rules in order to automatically extract knowledge from the data.

While there may be still room for improvement in these techniques we decided instead to investigate general knowledge extraction approaches in order to evaluate their potential. For that purpose a global strategy based on an unsupervised machine learning technique is adopted in our work to produce semantic classes.

## 2.2 Implementation of an automatic induction system based on LDA

Several approaches are available for topic detection in the context of knowledge extraction and information retrieval. They all more or less rely on the projection of the documents of interest in a semantic space to extract meaningful information. However, as the considered spaces (initial document words and latent semantics) are discrete the performance of the proposed approaches for the topic extraction tasks are pretty unstable, and also greatly depend on the quantity of data available. In this work we were motivated by the recent development of a very attractive technique with major distinct features such as the detection of multiple topics in a single document. LDA (Blei et al., 2003) is the first principled description of a Dirichlet-based model of mixtures of latent variables. LDA will be used in our work to annotate the dialogue data in terms of topics in an unsupervised manner. Then the relation between automatic topics and expected concepts will be addressed manually.

Basically LDA is a generative probabilistic model for text documents. LDA follows the assumption that a set of observations can be explained by latent variables. More specifically documents are represented by a mixture of topics (latent variables) and topics are characterized by distributions over words. The LDA parameters are $\{\alpha, \beta\}$. $\alpha$ represents the Dirichlet parameters of $K$ latent topic mixtures as $\alpha = [\alpha_1, \alpha_2, \dots, \alpha_K]$. $\beta$ is a matrix representing a multinomial distribution in the form of a conditional probability table $\beta_{k,w} = P(w|k)$. Based on this representation, LDA can estimate the probability of a new document $d$ of $N$ words $d = [w_1, w_2, \dots, w_N]$ using the following procedure.

A topic mixture vector $\theta$ is drawn from the Dirichlet distribution (with parameter $\alpha$). The corresponding topic sequence $\kappa = [k_1, k_2, \dots, k_N]$ is generated for the whole document accordingly to a multinomial distribution (with parameter $\theta$). Finally each word is generated by the word-topic multinomial distribution (with parameter $\beta$, that is $p(w_i|k_i, \beta)$). After this procedure, the joint probability of $\theta$, $\kappa$ and $d$ is then:

$$p(\theta, \kappa, d|\alpha, \beta) = p(\theta|\alpha) \prod_{i=1}^{N} p(k_i|\theta) p(w_i|k_i, \beta) \quad (1)$$

To obtain the marginal probability of $d$, a final integration over $\theta$ and a summation over all possible topics considering a word is necessary:

$$p(d|\alpha, \beta) = \int p(\theta|\alpha) \left( \prod_{i=1}^{N} \sum_{k_i} p(k_i|\theta) p(w_i|k_i, \beta) \right) \quad (2)$$

The framework is comparable to that of probabilistic latent semantic analysis, but the topic multinomial distribution in LDA is assumed to be sampled from a Dirichlet prior and is not linked to training documents. This approach is illustrated in Figure 2.

Training of the $\alpha$ and $\beta$ parameters is possible using a corpus of documents, with a fixed number of topics to predict. A variational inference procedure is described in (Blei et al., 2003) which alleviates the intractability due to the coupling between $\theta$ and $\beta$ in the summation over the latent topics. Once the parameters for the Dirichlet and multinomial distributions are available, topic scores can be derived for any given document or word sequence.

In recent years, several studies have been carried out in language processing based on LDA. For instance, (Tam and Schultz, 2006) worked on unsupervised language model adaptation; (Celikyilmaz et al., 2010) ranked candidate passages in a question-answering system; (Phan et al., 2008) implemented LDA to classify short and sparse web texts.

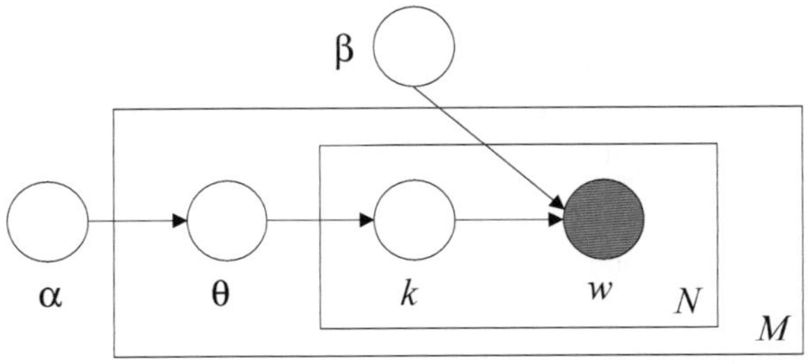


Figure 2: Graphical representation for LDA variables (from (Blei et al., 2003)). The grey circle is the only observable variable.

In our work LDA is employed to annotate each user's utterance of a dialogue corpus with topic. Utterances longer than one word are included in the training set as its sequence of *words*. Once the model has been trained, inference on data corpus assigns the topic with the highest probability to each word in a document. This probability is computed from the probability of the topic to appear in the document and the probability of the word to be generated by the topic. As a consequence we obtain a full topic annotation of the utterance.

Notice that LDA considers a user utterance as a bag of words. This implies that each topic is assigned to a word without any consideration for its immediate context. An additional segmental process is required if we want to introduce some context information in the topic assignment.

## 3 Segmental annotation

### 3.1 Benefits of a segmental annotation

The segmental annotation of the data is not a strict requirement for language understanding. Up to quite recently, most approaches for literal interpretation were limited to lexical-concept relations; for instance this is the case of the Phoenix system (Ward, 1991) based on the detection of keywords. However in an NLP perspective, the segmental approach allows to connect the various levels of sentence analysis (lexical, syntactic and semantic). Even though, in order to simplify its application, segments are generally designed specifically for the semantic annotation and do not have any constraint on their relation with the actual syntactic units (chunks, phrasal groups, etc). To get relieved of such constraints not only simplifies the annotation process itself but as ultimately the interpretation module is to be used inside a spoken dialogue system, data will be noisy and generally bound the performance of the syntactic analysers (due to highly spontaneous and ungrammatical utterances from the users, combined with errors from the speech recognizer).

Another interesting property of segmental approach is to offer a convenient way to dissociate the detection of a conceptual unit from the extraction of its associated value. The value corresponds to the normalisation of the surface form (see last column in 1); for instance if the segment "not more than" is associated to the concept *comparative-payment*, its value is "less than". The same value would be associated to "not exceeding" or "inferior to". Value extraction requires a link between concepts and words based on which the normalisation problem can be addressed by means of regular expressions or concept-dependent language models (even allowing integrated approaches such as described in (Lefèvre, 2007)). In the case of global approaches (not segmental), value extraction must be dealt with directly at the level of the conceptual unit tagging, as in (Mairesse et al., 2009). This additional level is very complex (as some values may not be enumerable, such as numbers and dates) and is only affordable when the number of authorised values (for the enumerable cases) is low.

To refine the LDA output, the topic-to-word alignment is discarded and an automatic procedure is used to derive the best alignment between topics and words. While the underlying probabilistic models are pretty comparable, the major interest of this approach is to separate the tasks of detecting topics and aligning topics with words. It is then possible to introduce additional constraints (such as locality, number of segments, limits on repetitions etc) in the latter task which would otherwise hinder topic detection. Conversely the alignment is self-coherent and able to question the associations proposed during topic detection with respect to its own constraints only. Two approaches were designed to this purpose: one based on IBM alignment models and another one based on integer linear optimisation.

### 3.2 Alignment with IBM models (GIZA)

Once topic assignments for the documents in the corpus have been proposed by LDA, a filtering process is done to keep only the most relevant topics of each document. The $\chi_{max}$ most probable topics are kept according to the probability $p(k|w_i, d)$ that topic $k$ generated the word $w_i$ of the document $d$. $\chi_{max}$ is a value fixed empirically according to the expected set of topics in a sentence. Then, the obtained topic sequences are disconnected from the words. At this point, the topic and word sequences can be considered as a translation pair to produce a word-topic parallel corpus. These data can be used with classical approaches in machine translation to align source and target sentences at the word level. Since these alignment models can align several words with a single topic, only the first occurrence is kept for consecutive repetitions of the same topic. These models are expected to correct some errors made by LDA, and to assign in particular words previously associated with discarded topics to more likely ones.

In our experiments the statistical word alignment toolkit GIZA++ (Och and Ney, 2003) is used to train the so-called IBM models 1-4 as well as the HMM model. To be able to train the most informative IBM model 4, the following training pipeline was considered: 5 iterations of IBM1, 5 iterations of HMM, 3 iterations of IBM3 and 3 iterations of IBM4. The IBM4 model obtained at the last iteration is finally used to align words and topics. In order to improve alignment, IBM models are usually trained in both directions (words towards concepts and *vice versa*) and symmetrised by combining them. For this purpose, we resorted to the default symmetrization heuristics used by MOSES, a widely used machine translation system toolkit (Koehn et al., 2007).

### 3.3 Alignment with Integer Linear Programming (ILP)

Another approach to the re-alignment of LDA outputs is based on a general optimisation technique. ILP is a widely used tool for modelling and solving combinatorial optimisation problems. It broadly aims at modelling a decision process as a set of equations or inequations (called *constraints*) which are linear with regards to so-called *decision variables*. An ILP is also composed of a linear *objective function*. Solving an ILP consists in assigning values to decision variables, such that all constraints are satisfied and the objective function is optimised. We refer to (Chen et al., 2010) for an overview of applications and methods of ILP.

We provide two ILP formulations for solving the topic assignment problem related to a given document. They both take as input data an ordered set $d$ of words $w_i$, $i = 1...N$, a set of $K$ available topics and, for each word $w_i \in d$ and topic $k = 1...K$, the natural logarithm of the probability $p(k|w_i, d)$ that $k$ is assigned to $w_i$ in the considered document $d$. Model $[ILP]$ simply finds the highest-probability assignment of one topic to each word in the document, such that at most $\chi_{max}$ different topics are assigned.

$$[ILP] : \max \sum_{i=1}^{N} \sum_{k=1}^{K} log(p(k|w_i, d)) \; x_{ik} \quad (3)$$

$$\sum_{k=1}^{K} x_{ik} = 1 \qquad i \quad (4)$$

$$y_k - x_{ik} \geq 0 \qquad i, k \quad (5)$$

$$\sum_{k=1}^{K} y_k \leq \chi_{max} \quad (6)$$

$$x_{ik} \in \{0, 1\} \qquad i, k$$

$$y_k \in \{0, 1\} \qquad k$$

In this model, decision variable $x_{ik}$ is equal to 1 if topic $k$ is assigned to word $w_i$, and equal to 0 otherwise. Constraints (4) ensure that exactly one topic is assigned to each word. Decision variable $y_k$ is equal to 1 if topic $k$ is used. Constraints (5) force variable $y_k$ to take a value of 1 if at least one variable $x_{ik}$ is not null. Moreover, Constraints (6) limit the total number of topics used. The objective function (3) merely states that we want to maximize the total probability of the assignment. Through this model, our assignment problem is identified as a *p-centre* problem (see (ReVelle and Eiselt, 2005) for a survey on such location problems).

Numerical experiments show that $[ILP]$ tends to give sparse assignments: most of the time, adjacent words are assigned to different topics even if the total number of topics is correct. To prevent this unnatural behaviour, we modified $[ILP]$ to consider groups of consecutive words instead of isolated words. Model $[ILP\_seg]$ partitions the document into segments of consecutive words, and assigns one topic to each segment, such that at most $\chi_{max}$ segments are created. For the sake of convenience, we denote by $\bar{p}(k|w_{ij},d) = \sum_{l=i}^{j} log(p(k|w_l,d))$ the logarithm of the probability that topic $k$ is assigned to all words from $i$ to $j$ in the current document.

$$[ILP\_seg] : \max \sum_{i=1}^{N} \sum_{j=i}^{N} \sum_{k=1}^{K} \bar{p}(k|w_{ij},d)\, x_{ijk} \quad (7)$$

$$\sum_{j=1}^{i} \sum_{l=i}^{N} \sum_{k=1}^{K} x_{jlk} = 1 \qquad i \quad (8)$$

$$\sum_{i=1}^{N} \sum_{j=i}^{N} \sum_{k=1}^{K} x_{ijk} \leq \chi_{max} \quad (9)$$

$$x_{ijk} \in \{0,1\} \qquad i,j,k$$

In this model, decision variable $x_{ijk}$ is equal to 1 if topic $k$ is assigned to all words from $i$ to $j$, and 0 otherwise. Constraints (8) ensure that each word belongs to a segment that is assigned a topic. Constraints (9) limit the number of segments. Due to the small size of the instances considered in this paper, both $[ILP]$ and $[ILP\_seg]$ are well solved by a direct application of an ILP solver.

## 4 Evaluation and results

### 4.1 MEDIA corpus

The MEDIA corpus is used to evaluate the proposed approach and to compare the various configurations. MEDIA is a French corpus related to the domain of tourism information and hotel booking (Bonneau-Maynard et al., 2005). 1,257 dialogues were recorded from 250 speakers with a wizard of Oz technique (a human agent mimics an automatic system). This dataset contains 17k user utterances and 123,538 words, for a total of 2,470 distinct words.

The MEDIA data have been manually transcribed and semantically annotated. The semantic annotation uses 75 concepts (*e.g. location, hotel-state, time-month...*). Each concept is supported by a sequence of words, the *concept support*. The *null* concept is used to annotate every words segment that does not support any of the 74 other concepts (and does not bear any information wrt the task). On average, a concept support contains 2.1 words, 3.4 concepts are included in a utterance and 32% of the utterances are restrained to a single word (generally "yes" or "no"). Table 1 gives the proportions of utterances according to the number of concepts in the utterance.

| # concepts | 1 | 2 | 3 | [4,72] |
|---|---|---|---|---|
| % utterances | 49.4 | 14.1 | 7.9 | 28.6 |

Table 1: Proportion of user utterances as a function of the number of concepts in the utterance.

Notice that each utterance contains at least one concept (the *null* label being considered as a concept). As shown in Table 2, some concepts are supported by few segments. For example, 33 concepts are represented by less than 100 concept supports. Considering that, we can foresee that finding these poorly represented concepts will be hard for LDA.

| [1,100[ | [100,500[ | [500,1k[ | [1k,9k[ | [9k,15k] |
|---|---|---|---|---|
| 33 | 21 | 6 | 14 | 1 (*null*) |

Table 2: Number of concepts according to their occurrence range.

### 4.2 Evaluation protocol

Unlike previous studies, we chose a fully automatic way to evaluate the systems. In (Siu and Meng, 1999), a manual process is introduced to reject induced classes or rules that are not relevant to the task and also to name the semantic classes with the appropriate label. Thus, they were able to evaluate their semi-supervised annotation on the ATIS corpus. In (Pargellis et al., 2001), the relevance of the generated semantic classes was manually evaluated giving a mark to each induced semantic rule.

To evaluate the unsupervised procedure it is necessary to associate each induced topic with a MEDIA concept. To that purpose, the reference annotation is used to align topics with MEDIA concepts at the word level. A co-occurrence matrix is computed and each topic is associated with its most co-occurring concept.

As MEDIA reference concepts are very fine-grained, we also define a *high-level* concept hierarchy containing 18 clusters of concepts. For example, a high-level concept *payment* is created from the 4 concepts *payment-meansOfPayment, payment-currency, payment-total-amount, payment-approx-amount*; a high-level concept *location* corresponds to 12 concepts (*location-country, location-district, location-street, ...*). Thus, two levels of concepts are considered for the evaluation: *high-level* and *fine-level*.

The evaluation is presented in terms of the classical F-measure, defined as a combination of precision and recall measures. Two levels are also considered to measure topic assignment quality:

- *alignment* corresponds to a full evaluation where each word is considered and associated with one topic;
- *generation* corresponds to the set of topics generated for a turn (no order, no word-alignment).

### 4.3 System descriptions

Four systems are evaluated in our experiments.

$[LDA]$ is the result of the unsupervised learning of LDA models using GIBBSLDA++ tool[1]. It assigns the most probable topic to each word occurrence in a document as described in Section 2.2. This approach requires prior estimation of the number of clusters that are expected to be found in the data. To find an optimal number of clusters, we adjusted the number $K$ of topics around the 75 reference concepts. 2k training iterations were made using default values for $\alpha$ and $\beta$.

$[GIZA]$ is the system based on the GIZA++ toolkit[2] which re-aligns for each sentence the topic sequence assigned by $[LDA]$ to word sequence as described in Section 3.2.

$[ILP]$ and $[ILP\_seg]$ systems are the results of the ILP solver IBM ILOG CPLEX[3] applied to the models described in Section 3.3.

For the three last systems, the value $\chi_{max}$ has to be fixed according to the desired concept annotation. As on average a concept support contains 2.1 words, $\chi_{max}$ is defined empirically according to the number of words: with $i = [\![2,4]\!]$: $\chi_{max} = i$ with $i = [\![5,10]\!]$ words: $\chi_{max} = i - 2$ and for utterances containing more than 10 words: $\chi_{max} = i/2$.

For the sake of simplicity, single-word utterances are processed separately with prior knowledge. City names, months, days or answers (*e.g.* "yes", "no", "yeah") and numbers are identified in these one-word utterances.

### 4.4 Results

Examples of topics generated by $[LDA]$, with $K = 100$ topics, are shown in Table 3.

Plots comparing the different systems implemented w.r.t. the different evaluation levels in terms of F-measure are reported in Figures 3, 4, 5 and 6 (*high-level* vs *fine-level*, *alignment* vs *generation*).

The $[LDA]$ system generates topics which are

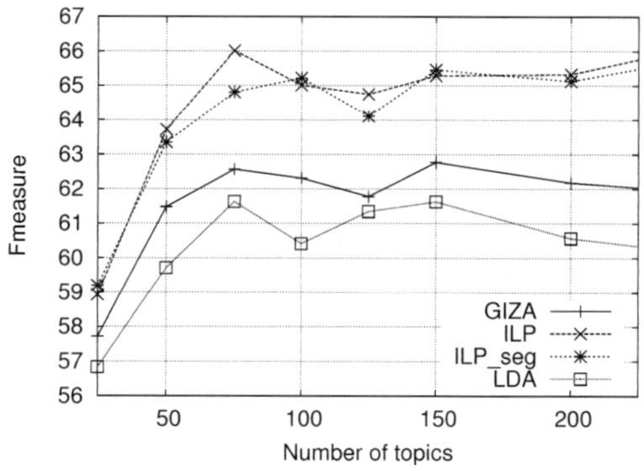


Figure 3: F-measure of the high-level concept generation as a function of the number of topics.

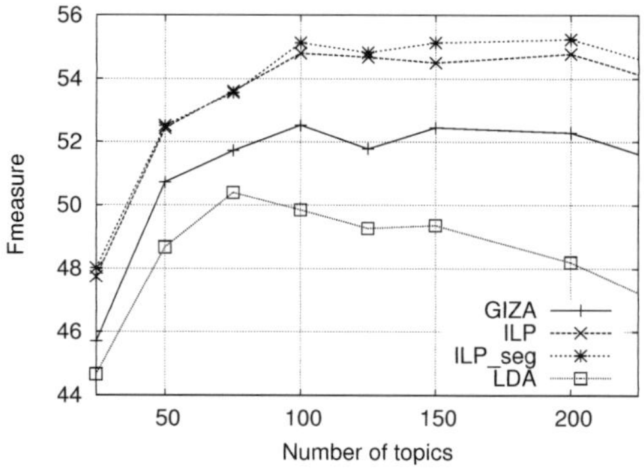


Figure 4: F-measure of the high-level concept alignment as a function of the number of topics.

[1] http://gibbslda.sourceforge.net/

[2] http://code.google.com/p/giza-pp/

[3] http://www-01.ibm.com/software/integration/optimization/cplex-optimizer/

| Topic 0 *information* | | Topic 13 *time-date* | | Topic 18 *sightseeing* | | Topic 35 *politeness* | | Topic 33 *location* | | Topic 43 *answer-yes* | |
|---|---|---|---|---|---|---|---|---|---|---|---|
| words | prob. | words | prob. | words | prob. | words | prob. | words | prob. | words | prob. |
| d' | 0.28 | du | 0.16 | de | 0.30 | au | 0.31 | de | 0.30 | oui | 0.62 |
| plus | 0.17 | au | 0.11 | la | 0.24 | revoir | 0.27 | Paris | 0.12 | et | 0.02 |
| informations | 0.16 | quinze | 0.08 | tour | 0.02 | madame | 0.09 | la | 0.06 | absolument | 0.008 |
| autres | 0.10 | dix-huit | 0.07 | vue | 0.02 | merci | 0.08 | près | 0.06 | autre | 0.008 |
| détails | 0.03 | décembre | 0.06 | Eiffel | 0.02 | bonne | 0.01 | proche | 0.05 | donc | 0.007 |
| obtenir | 0.03 | mars | 0.06 | sur | 0.02 | journée | 0.01 | Lyon | 0.03 | jour | 0.005 |
| alors | 0.01 | dix-sept | 0.04 | mer | 0.01 | villes | 0.004 | aux | 0.02 | Notre-Dame | 0.004 |
| souhaite | 0.003 | nuits | 0.04 | sauna | 0.01 | bientôt | 0.003 | gare | 0.02 | d'accord | 0.004 |

Table 3: Examples of topics discovered by LDA ($K = 100$).

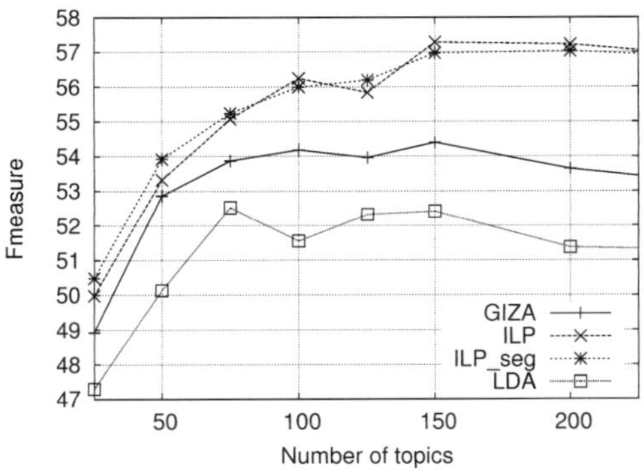


Figure 5: F-measure of the fine-level concept generation as a function of the number of topics.

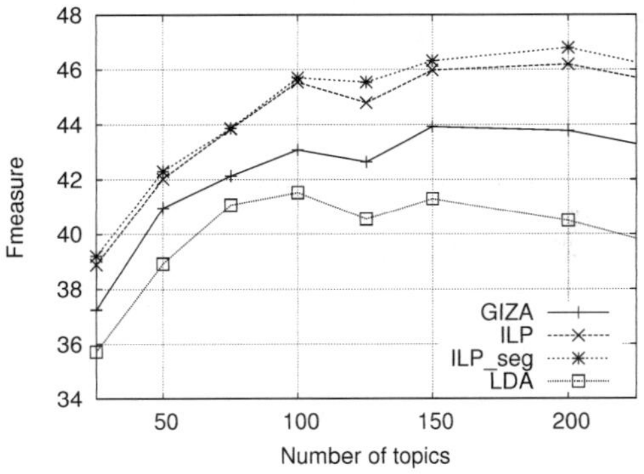


Figure 6: F-measure of the fine-level concept alignment as a function of the number of topics.

correctly correlated with the *high-level* concepts. It can be observed that the bag of 75 topics reaches an F-measure of 61.5% (Fig. 3). When not enough topics are required from $[LDA]$, induced topics are too wide to fit the fine-grained concept annotation of MEDIA. On the other hand if too many topics are required, the performance of bag of high-level topics stays the same while a substantial decrease of the F-measure is observed in the *alignment* evaluation (Fig. 4). This effect can be explained by the automatic alignment method chosen to transpose topics into reference concepts. Indeed, the increase of the number of topics makes them co-occur with many concepts, which often leads to assign them to the most frequent concept *null* in the studied corpus.

From the *high-level* to *fine-level* concept evaluations, results globally decrease by 10%. An additional global loss of 10% is also observed for both the *generation* and *alignment* scorings. In the *fine-level* evaluation, a maximum F-measure of 52.2% is observed for the *generation* of 75 topics (Fig. 5) whereas the F-measure decreases to 41.5% in the *alignment* evaluation (Fig. 6).

To conclude on the $[LDA]$ system, we can see that it generates topics having a good correlation with the *high-level* concepts, seemingly the best representation level between topics and concepts. From these results it seems obvious that an additional step is needed to obtain a more accurate segmental annotation, which is expected with the following systems.

The $[GIZA]$ system improves the results. It is very likely that the filtering process helps to discard the irrelevant topics. Therefore, the automatic alignment between words and the filtered topics induced by $[LDA]$ with IBM models seems more robust when more topics (a higher value for $K$) is required from $[LDA]$, specifically in *high-level* concept *alignment* (Fig. 4).

Systems based on the ILP technique perform better than other systems whatever the evaluation. Considering $[LDA]$ as the baseline, we can expect significant gains of performance. For example, an F-measure of 66% is observed for the ILP systems considering the *high-level* concept *generation* for 75 topics (Figure 4), where the maximum for $[LDA]$ was 61.5%, and an F-measure of 55% is observed (instead of 50.5% for $[LDA]$) considering the *high-level* concept *alignment*.

No significant difference was finally measured between both ILP models for the concept generation evaluations. Even though $[ILP\_seg]$ seems to obtain slightly better results in the *alignment* evaluation. This could be expected since $[ILP\_seg]$ intrinsically yields alignments with grouped topics, closer to the reference alignment used for the evaluation.

It is worth noticing that unlike $[LDA]$ system behaviour, the results of $[ILP]$ are not affected when more topics are generated by $[LDA]$. A large number of topics enables $[ILP]$ to pick up the best topic for a given segment among in a longer selection list. As for $[LDA]$, the same losses are observed between *high-level* and *fine-level* concepts and *generation* and *alignment* paradigms. Nevertheless, an F-measure of 54.8% is observed at the *high-level* concept in *alignement* evaluation (Figure 4) that corresponds to a precision of 56.2% and a recall of 53.5%, which is not so low considering a fully-automatic high-level annotation system.

## 5 Conclusions and perspectives

In this paper an unsupervised approach for concept extraction and segmental annotation has been proposed and evaluated. Based on two steps (topic inventory and assignment with LDA, then re-segmentation with either IBM alignment models or ILP) the technique has been shown to offer performance above 50% for the retrieval of reference concepts. It confirms the applicability of the technique to practical tasks with an expected gain in data production.

Future work will investigate the use of $n$-grams to increase LDA accuracy to provide better hypotheses for the following segmentation method. Besides, other levels of data representation will be examined (use of lemmas, *a priori* semantic classes like city names...) in order to better generalise on the data.


## ACKNOWLEDGEMENTS

This work is supported by the ANR funded project PORT-MEDIA (www.port-media.org) and the LIA OptimNLP project (www.lia.univ-avignon.fr).


## References


D.M. Blei, A.Y. Ng, and M.I. Jordan. 2003. Latent dirichlet allocation. *The Journal of Machine Learning Research*, 3:993–1022.

H. Bonneau-Maynard, S. Rosset, C. Ayache, A. Kuhn, and D. Mostefa. 2005. Semantic annotation of the french media dialog corpus. In *Proceedings of the 9th European Conference on Speech Communication and Technology*.

A. Celikyilmaz, D. Hakkani-Tur, and G. Tur. 2010. Lda based similarity modeling for question answering. In *Proceedings of the NAACL HLT 2010 Workshop on Semantic Search*, pages 1–9. Association for Computational Linguistics.

Der-San Chen, Robert G. Batson, and Yu Dang. 2010. *Applied Integer Programming: Modeling and Solution*. Wiley, January.

Stefan Hahn, Marco Dinarelli, Christian Raymond, Fabrice Lefvre, Patrick Lehnen, Renato De Mori, Alessandro Moschitti, Hermann Ney, and Giuseppe Riccardi. 2010. Comparing stochastic approaches to spoken language understanding in multiple languages. *IEEE Transactions on Audio, Speech and Language Processing*, PP(99):1.

E. Iosif, A. Tegos, A. Pangos, E. Fosler-Lussier, and A. Potamianos. 2006. Unsupervised combination of metrics for semantic class induction. In *Proceedings of the IEEE Spoken Language Technology Workshop*, pages 86–89.

Philipp Koehn, Hieu Hoang, Alexandra Birch, Chris Callison-Burch, Marcello Federico, Nicola Bertoldi, Brooke Cowan, Wade Shen, Christine Moran, Richard Zens, Chris Dyer, Ondrej Bojar, Alexandra Constantin, and Evan Herbst. 2007. Moses: Open source toolkit for statistical machine translation. In *Proceedings of ACL, Companion Volume*, pages 177–180, Prague, Czech Republic.

F. Lefèvre. 2007. Dynamic bayesian networks and discriminative classifiers for multi-stage semantic interpretation. In *Proceedings of ICASSP*, Honolulu, Hawai.

F. Mairesse, M. Gašić, F. Jurčíček, S. Keizer, B. Thomson, K. Yu, and S. Young. 2009. Spoken language understanding from unaligned data using discriminative classification models. In *Proceedings of ICASSP*, Taipei, Taiwan.

Franz Josef Och and Hermann Ney. 2003. A systematic comparison of various statistical alignment models. *Computational Linguistics*, 29(1):19–51.

A. Pargellis, E. Fosler-Lussier, A. Potamianos, and C.H. Lee. 2001. Metrics for measuring domain independence of semantic classes. In *Proceedings of the 7th European Conference on Speech Communication and Technology*.

X.H. Phan, L.M. Nguyen, and S. Horiguchi. 2008. Learning to classify short and sparse text & web with hidden topics from large-scale data collections. In *Proceeding of the 17th international conference on World Wide Web*, pages 91–100. ACM.

C. S. ReVelle and H. A. Eiselt. 2005. Location analysis: A synthesis and survey. *European Journal of Operational Research*, 165(1):1–19, August.

K.C. Siu and H.M. Meng. 1999. Semi-automatic acquisition of domain-specific semantic structures. In *Proceedings of the 6th European Conference on Speech Communication and Technology*.

Y.C. Tam and T. Schultz. 2006. Unsupervised language model adaptation using latent semantic marginals. In *Proceedings of INTERSPEECH*, pages 2206–2209.

W Ward. 1991. Understanding Spontaneous Speech. In *Proceedings of ICASSP*, pages 365–368, Toronto, Canada.

# Unsupervised Mining of Lexical Variants from Noisy Text

**Stephan Gouws***, **Dirk Hovy** and **Donald Metzler**
stephan@ml.sun.ac.za, {dirkh, metzler}@isi.edu
USC Information Sciences Institute
Marina del Rey, CA
90292, USA

## Abstract

The amount of data produced in user-generated content continues to grow at a staggering rate. However, the text found in these media can deviate wildly from the standard rules of orthography, syntax and even semantics and present significant problems to downstream applications which make use of this noisy data. In this paper we present a novel unsupervised method for extracting domain-specific lexical variants given a large volume of text. We demonstrate the utility of this method by applying it to normalize text messages found in the online social media service, Twitter, into their most likely standard English versions. Our method yields a 20% reduction in word error rate over an existing state-of-the-art approach.

## 1 Introduction

The amount of data produced in user-generated content, e.g. in online social media, and from machine-generated sources such as optical character recognition (OCR) and automatic speech recognition (ASR), surpasses that found in more traditional media by orders of magnitude and continues to grow at a staggering rate. However, the text found in these media can deviate wildly from the standard rules of orthography, syntax and even semantics and present significant problems to downstream applications which make use of this 'noisy' data. In social media this noise might result from the need for social identity, simple spelling errors due to high input cost associated with the device (e.g. typing on a mobile phone), space constraints imposed by the specific medium or even a user's location (Gouws et al., 2011). In machine-generated texts, noise might result from imperfect inputs, imperfect conversion algorithms, or various degrees of each.

Recently, several works have looked at the process of *normalizing* these 'noisy' types of text into more standard English, or in other words, to convert the various forms of idiosyncratic spelling and writing errors found in these media into what would normally be considered standard English orthography. Many of these works rely on supervised methods which share the common burden of requiring training data in the form of noisy input and clean output pairs. The problem with developing large amounts of annotated training data is that it is costly and requires annotators with sufficient expertise. However, the volume of data that is available in these media makes this a suitable domain for applying semi- and even fully unsupervised methods.

One interesting observation is that these noisy out-of-vocabulary (OOV) words are typically formed through some semi-deterministic process which doesn't render them *completely* indiscernible at a lexical level from the original words they are meant to represent. We therefore refer to these OOV tokens as *lexical variants* of the clean in-vocabulary (IV) tokens they are derived from. For instance, in social media '2morrow' '2morow' and '2mrw' still share at least *some* lexical resemblance with 'tomorrow', due to the fact that it is mainly the

*This work was done while the first author was a visiting student at ISI from the MIH Media Lab at Stellenbosch University, South Africa.

*Proceedings of EMNLP 2011, Conference on Empirical Methods in Natural Language Processing*, pages 82–90,
Edinburgh, Scotland, UK, July 27–31, 2011. 

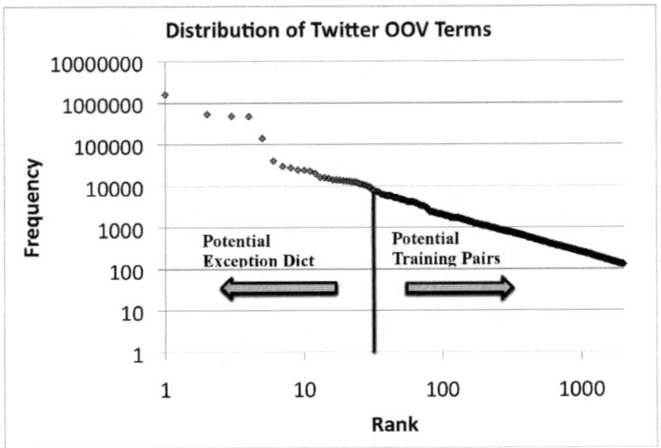


Figure 1: A plot of the OOV distribution found in Twitter. Also indicated is the potential for using (OOV,most-likely-IV) training pairs found on this curve for either exception dictionary entries (the most frequent pairs), or for learning lexical transformations (the long tail). The threshold between the two (vertical bar) is domain-specific.

result of a phonetic transliteration procedure. Also, 'computer' and 'conpu7er' share strong lexical overlap, and might be the result of noise in the OCR process.

As with many aspects of NLP, the distribution of these OOV tokens resemble a power law distribution (see Figure 1 for the OOV distribution in Twitter). Thus, some words are commonly converted to some OOV representation (e.g. domain-specific abbreviations in social media, or words which are commonly incorrectly detected in OCR) and these account for most of the errors, with the rest making up the long tail. If one could somehow automatically extract a list of all the domain-specific OOV tokens found in a collection of texts, along with the most likely clean word (or words) each represents, then this could play a key role in for instance normalizing individual messages. Very frequent (noisy, clean) pairs at the head of the distribution could be used for extracting common domain-specific abbreviations, and word-pairs in the long tail may be used as input to learning algorithms for automatically learning the types of transformations found in these media, as shown in Figure 1.

For example, taking Twitter as our target domain, examples for learning common exception pairs may include '*gf*'→'*girlfriend*'. For learning types of lexical transformations, one might learn from '*thinking*'→'*thinkin*' and '*walking*'→'*walkin*' that '*ng*' could go to '*n*' (known as 'g-clipping').

In this paper we present a novel unsupervised method for extracting an approximation to such a domain-specific list of (noisy, clean) pairs, given only a large volume of representative text. We furthermore demonstrate the utility of this method by applying it to normalize text messages found in the online social media service, Twitter, into their most likely standard English versions.

The primary contributions of this paper are:

- We present an unsupervised method that mines (noisy, clean) pairs and requires only large amounts of domain-specific noisy data
- We demonstrate the utility of this method by incorporating it into a standard method for noisy text normalization, which results in a significant reduction in the word error rate compared to the original method.

## 2 Training Pair Mining

Given a large corpus of noisy text, our challenge is to automatically mine pairs of domain-specific lexical variants that can be used as training data for a variety of natural language processing tasks. The key challenge is how to develop an effective approach that is both domain-specific and robust to noisy corpora. Our proposed approach requires nothing more than a large "common English" corpus (e.g., a large newswire corpus) and a large corpus of domain text (e.g., a large corpus of Twitter data, a query log, OCR output, etc.). Using these two sources of evidence, the approach mines domain-specific lexical variants in a fully unsupervised manner.

Before describing the details of our approach, we first describe the characteristics that we would like the mined lexical variants to have. First, the variants should be *semantically related* to each other. Pairs of words that are lexically similar, but semantically unrelated are not of particular interest since such pairs can be found using basic edit distance-based approaches. Second, the variants should be *domain-specific*. Variants that capture common English lexical variations (e.g., "running" and "run") can be captured using standard normalization procedures, such

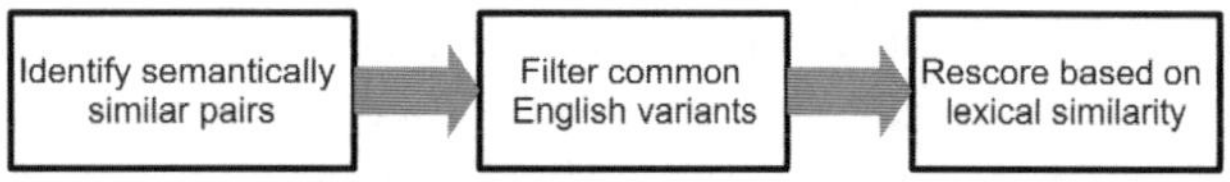


Figure 2: Flow chart illustrating our procedure for mining pairs of lexical variants.

as stemming. Instead, we are interested in identifying domain-specific variations (e.g., "u" and "you" in the SMS and Twitter domains) that cannot easily be handled by existing approaches. Finally, the variants should be *lexically similar*, by definition. Hence, ideal variants will be domain-specific, lexically similar, and semantically related.

To mine such variants we synthesize ideas from natural language processing and large-scale text mining to derive a novel mining procedure. Our procedure can be divided into three atomic steps. First we identify semantically similar pairs, then we filter out common English variants, and finally we rescore the resulting list based on lexical similarity (see Figure 2). The remainder of this section describes the complete details of each of these steps.

### 2.1 Identifying Semantically Similar Pairs

The first step of our mining procedure harvests semantically similar pairs of terms from both the common English corpus and the domain corpus. There are many different ways to measure semantic relatedness. In this work, we use distributional similarity as our measure of semantic similarity. However, since we are taking a fully unsupervised approach, we do not know *a priori* which pairs of terms may be related to each other. Hence, we must compute the semantic similarity between all possible pairs of terms within the lexicon. To solve this computationally challenging task, we use a large-scale all-pairs distributional similarity approach similar to the one originally proposed by Pasca and Dienes (Pasca and Dienes, 2005). Our implementation, which makes use of Hadoop's MapReduce distributed programming paradigm, can efficiently compute all-pairs distributional similarity over very large corpora (e.g., the Twitter pairs we use later were mined from a corpus of half a billion Twitter messages).

Using a similar strategy as Pasca and Dienes, we define term contexts as the bigrams that appear to the left and to the right of a given word (Pasca and Dienes, 2005). Following standard practice, the contextual vectors are weighted according to pointwise mutual information and the similarity between the vectors is computed using the cosine similarity metric (Lin and Pantel, 2001; Bhagat and Ravichandran, 2008). It is important to note that there are many other possible ways to compute distributional and semantic similarity, and that just about any approach can be used within our framework. The approach used here was chosen because we had an existing implementation. Indeed, other approaches may be more apt for other data sets and tasks.

This approach is applied to both the common English corpus and the domain corpus. This yields two sets of semantically (distributionally) similar word pairs that will ultimately be used to distill unsupervised lexical variants.

### 2.2 Filtering Common English Variants

Given these two sets of semantically similar word pairs, the next step in our procedure is designed to identify the domain-specific pairs by filtering out the common English variants. The procedure that we follow is very simple, yet highly effective. Given the semantically similar word pairs harvested from the domain corpus, we eliminate all of the pairs that are also found in the semantically similar common English pairs.

Any type of "common English" corpus can be used for this purpose, depending on the task. However, we found that a large corpus of newswire articles tends to work well. Most of the semantically similar word pairs harvested from such a corpus are common lexical variants and synonyms. By eliminating these common variants from the harvested domain corpus pairs, we are left with only the domain-specific semantically similar word pairs.

### 2.3 Lexical Similarity-Based Re-ordering

The first step of our mining procedure identified semantically similar term pairs using distributional similarity, while the second identified those that were domain-specific by filtering out common English variants. The third, and final, step of our procedure re-orders the output of the second step to account for lexical similarity.

For each word pair (from the second step of our procedure), we compute two scores: 1) a semantic similarity score, and 2) a lexical similarity score. The final score of the pair is then simply the product of the two scores. In this work, we use the cosine similarity score as our semantic similarity score, since it is already computed during the first step of our procedure.

In the social media domain, as in the mobile texting domain, compressed writing schemes typically involve deleting characters or replacing one or more characters with some other characters. For example, users might delete vowels (*'tomorrow'*→*'tmrrw'*), or replace *'ph'* with its phonetic equivalent *'f'*, as in *'phone'*→*'fone'*. We make use of a subsequence similarity function (Lodhi et al., 2002) which can still capture the structural overlap (in the form of string subsequences) between the remaining unchanged letters in the noisy word and the original clean word from which it was derived. In this work we use a subsequence length of 2, but as with the other steps in our procedure, this one is purposefully defined in a general way. Any semantic similarity score, lexical similarity score, and combination function can be used in practice.

The output of the entire procedure is a scored list of word pairs that are semantically related, domain-specific, and lexically similar, thereby exhibiting the characteristics that we initially defined as important. We treat these (scored) pairs as *pseudo training data* that has been derived in a fully unsupervised manner. We anticipate that these pairs will serve as powerful training data for a variety of tasks, such as noisy text normalization, which we will return to in Section 3.

### 2.4 Example and Error Analysis

As an illustrative example of this procedure in practice, Table 1 shows the actual output of our system for each step of the mining procedure. To generate this example, we used a corpus of 2GB of English news articles as our "common English" corpus and a corpus of approximately 500 million Twitter messages as our domain corpus. In this way, our goal is to identify Twitter-specific lexical variants, which we will use in the next section to normalize noisy Twitter messages.

Column (A) of the table shows that our distributional similarity approach is capable of identifying a variety of semantically similar terms in the Twitter corpus. However, the list contains a large number of common English variants that are not specific to Twitter. Column (B) shows the outcome of eliminating all of the pairs that were found in the newswire corpus. Many of the common pairs have been eliminated and the list now contains mostly Twitter-specific variants. Finally, Column (C) shows the result of re-ordering the domain-specific pairs to account for lexical similarity.

| Rank | Precision |
|---|---|
| P@50 | 0.90 |
| P@100 | 0.88 |

Table 2: Precision at 50 and 100 of the induced exception dictionary.

In our specific case, the output of step 1 yielded a list of roughly 3.3M potential word variants. Filtering out common English variants reduced this to about 314K pairs. In order to estimate the quality of the list we computed the precision at 50 and at 100 for which the results are shown in Table 2. Furthermore, we find that up to position 500 the pairs are still of reasonable quality. Thereafter, the number of errors start to increase noticeably. In particular, we find that the most common types of errors are

1. Number-related: e.g. '30' and '30pm' (due to incorrect tokenization), or '5800' and '5530';
2. Lemma-related: e.g. 'incorrect' and 'incorrectly'; and
3. Negations: e.g. 'could' and 'couldnt'.

Performance can thus be improved by making use of better tokenization, lemmatizing words, filtering out common negations and filtering out pairs of numbers.

Still, the resulting pairs satisfy all of our desired qualities rather well, and hence we hypothesize would serve as useful training data for a number of different Twitter-related natural language processing tasks. Indeed, we will now describe one such possible application and empirically validate the utility of the automatically mined pairs.

| (A) | (B) | (C) |
|---|---|---|
| i ↔ you | u ↔ you | ur ↔ your |
| my ↔ the | seeking ↔ seeks | wit ↔ with |
| u ↔ you | 2 ↔ to | to ↔ too |
| is ↔ was | lost ↔ won | goin ↔ going |
| a ↔ the | q ↔ que | kno ↔ know |
| i ↔ we | f*ck ↔ hell | about ↔ bout |
| my ↔ your | feat ↔ ft | wat ↔ what |
| and ↔ but | bday ↔ birthday | jus ↔ just |
| seeking ↔ seeks | ff ↔ followfriday | talkin ↔ talking |
| me ↔ you | yang ↔ yg | gettin ↔ getting |
| 2 ↔ to | wit ↔ with | doin ↔ doing |
| am ↔ was | a ↔ my | so ↔ soo |
| are ↔ were | are ↔ r | you ↔ your |
| lost ↔ won | amazing ↔ awesome | dnt ↔ dont |
| he ↔ she | til ↔ till | bday ↔ birthday |
| q ↔ que | fav ↔ favorite | nothin ↔ nothing |
| it ↔ that | mostly ↔ partly | people ↔ ppl |
| f*ck ↔ hell | northbound ↔ southbound | lil ↔ little |
| can ↔ could | hung ↔ toned | sayin ↔ saying |
| im ↔ its | love ↔ miss | so ↔ sooo |

Table 1: Column (A) shows the highest weighted distributionally similar terms harvested from a large Twitter corpus. Column (B) shows which pairs from (A) remain after filtering out distributionally similar word pairs mined from a large news corpus. Column (C) shows the effect of reordering the pairs from (B) using a string similarity kernel.

## 3 Deriving A Common Exception Dictionary for Text Normalization as a Use Case for Mining Lexical Variants

As discussed in Section 1, these training pairs may aid methods which attempt to normalize noisy text by translating from the ill-formed text into standard English. Since the OOV distribution in noisy text mostly resemble a power law distribution (see Figure 1), one may use the highest scoring training pairs to induce 'exception dictionaries' (lists of *(noisy word)→(most likely clean word)*) of the most common domain-specific abbreviations found in the text.

We will demonstrate the utility of our derived pairs in one specific use case, namely inducing a domain-specific exception dictionary to augment a vanilla normalization method. We leave the second proposed use-case, namely using pairs in the long tail for learning transformation rules, for future work.

We evaluate the first use case in Section 4.

### 3.1 Baseline Normalization Method

We make use of a competitive heuristic text normalization method over Twitter data as a baseline, and compare its accuracy to an augmented method which makes use of an automatically induced exception dictionary (using the method described in Section 2) as a first step, before resorting to the same baseline method as a 'back-off' for words not found in the dictionary.

As we point out in Section 5, there are various metaphors within which the noisy text normalization problem has been approached. In general, however, the problem of noisy text normalization may be approached by using a three step process (Gouws et al., 2011):

1. In the **out-of-vocabulary (OOV) detection** step, we detect unknown words which are candidates for normalization

2. In the **candidate selection** step, we find the weighted lists of most likely candidates (from a list of in-vocabulary (IV) words) for the OOV words and group them into a confusion set. The

confusion sets are then appended to one another to create a confusion- network or lattice

3. Finally, in the **decoding** step, we use a language model to rescore the confusion network, and then find the most likely posterior path (Viterbi path) through this network.

The words at each node in the resulting posterior Viterbi path represents the words of the hypothesized original clean sentence.

In this work, we reimplement the method described in Contractor (2010) as our baseline method. We next describe the details of this method in the context of the framework presented above. See (Gouws et al., 2011) for more details.

**OOV DETECTION** is a crucial part of the normalizaton process, since false-positives will result in undesirable attempts to 'correct' IV words, hence bringing down the method's accuracy. We implement OOV detection as a simple lexicon-lookup procedure, with heuristics for handling specific out-of-vocabulary-but-valid tokens such as hash tags and @usernames.

**CANDIDATE SELECTION** involves comparing an unknown OOV word to a list of words which are deemed in-vocabulary, and producing a top-K ranked list with candidate words and their estimated probabilities of relevance as output. This process requires a function with which to compute the similarity or alternatively, distance, between two words. More traditional string-similarity functions like the simple Lehvenshtein string edit distance do not fare too well in this domain.

We implement the IBM-similarity (Contractor et al., 2010) which employs a slightly more advanced similarity function. It finds the length of the longest common subsequence (LCS) between two strings $s_1$ and $s_2$, normalized by the edit distance (ED) between the consonants in each string (referred to as the 'consonant skeleton' (CS)), thus

$$\text{sim}(s_1, s_2) = \frac{\text{LCS}(s_1, s_2)}{\text{ED}(\text{CS}(s_1), \text{CS}(s_2))}$$

Finally, the **DECODING** step takes an input word lattice (lattice of concatenated, weighted confusion sets), and produces a new lattice by incorporating the probabilities from an $n$-gram language model with the prior probabilities in the lattice to produce a reranked posterior lattice. The most likely (Viterbi) path through this lattice represents the decoded clean output. We use SRI-LM (Stolcke, 2002) for this.

### 3.2 Augmenting the Baseline: Our Method

In order to demonstrate the utility of the mined lexical variant pairs, we first construct a (noisy, clean) lookup table from the mined pairs. We (arbitrarily) use the 50 mined pairs with the highest overall combined score (see Section 2.3) for the exception dictionary. For each pair, we map the OOV term (noisy and typically shorter) to the IV term (clean and usually longer). The exception lookup list is then used to augment the baseline method (see Section 3.1) in the following way: When the method encounters a new word, it first checks to see if the word is in the exception dictionary. If it is, we normalize to the value in the dictionary. If it is not, we pass the ill-formed word to the baseline method to proceed as normal.

## 4 Evaluation

### 4.1 Dataset

We make use of the Twitter dataset discussed in Han (2011). It consists of a random sampling of 549 English tweets, annotated by three independent annotators. All OOV words were pre-identified and the annotators were requested to determine the standard form (gold standard) for each ill-formed word.

### 4.2 Evaluation Metrics

In this study, we are interested in measuring the quality of our mined training pairs by evaluating its utility on an external task: Using the training pairs to induce a (noisy→clean) exception dictionary to augment the working of a standard noisy text normalization system. Hence, our focus is entirely on the accuracy of the candidate selection procedure as defined in Section 3.1. We compute this accuracy in terms of the word error rate (WER), defined as the number of token substitutions, insertions or deletions one has to make to turn the system output into the gold standard, normalized by the total number of tokens in the output. In order to remove the possible bias introduced by our very basic OOV-detection

| Method | WER | % Change |
|---|---|---|
| Naive baseline | 10.7% | – |
| IBM-baseline | 7.8% | −27.1% |
| Our method | **5.6%** | **−47.7%** |

Table 3: Word error rate (WER, lower is better) results of our method against a naive baseline and the much stronger IBM-baseline (Contractor et al., 2010). We also show the relative change in WER for our method and the IBM-baseline compared to the naive baseline.

mechanism, we evaluate the output of all systems only on the *oracle pairs*. Oracle pairs are defined as the (input,system-output,gold) pairs where input and gold do not match. In other words, we remove the possible confounding impact of imperfect OOV detection on the accuracy of the normalization process by assuming a perfect OOV-detection step.

### 4.3 Discussion of Results

The results of our experiments are displayed in Table 3. It is important to note that the focus is not on achieving the best WER compared to other systems (although we achieve very competitive scores), but to evaluate the *added utility* of integrating an exception dictionary which is based purely on the mined (noisy, clean) pairs with an already competitive baseline method.

The 'naive baseline' shows the results if we make no changes to the input tokens for all oracle pairs. Therefore it reflects the total level of errors that are present in the corpus.

The IBM-method is seen to reduce the amount of errors by a substantial 27.1%. However, the augmented method results in a further 20.6% reduction in errors, for a total reduction of 47.7% of all errors in the dataset, compared to the IBM-baseline's 27.1%.

Since we replace matches in the dictionary indiscriminately, and since the dictionary comprise those pairs that typically occur most frequently in the corpus from which they were mined, it is important to note that if these pairs are of poor quality, then their sheer frequency will drive the overall system accuracy down. Therefore, the accuracy of these pairs are strongly reflected in the WER performance of the augmented method.

| Noisy | Clean | % Oracle Pairs |
|---|---|---|
| u | you | 8.7 |
| n | and | 1.4 |
| ppl | people | 1 |
| da | the | 1 |
| w | with | 0.7 |
| cuz | because | 0.5 |
| y | why | 0.5 |
| yu | you | 0.5 |
| lil | little | 0.5 |
| dat | that | 0.5 |
| wat | what | 0.4 |
| tha | the | 0.4 |
| kno | know | 0.4 |
| r | are | 0.4 |

Table 4: Error analysis for all (noisy, clean) normalizations missed by the vanilla IBM-baseline method, but included in the top-50 pairs used for constructing the exception dictionary. We also show the percentage of all oracle pairs that are corrected by including each pair in an exception dictionary.

Table 4 shows the errors missed by the IBM-baseline, but contained in the mined exception dictionary. We also show each pair's frequency of occurrence in the oracle pairs (hence its contribution towards lowering WER).

## 5 Related work

To the best of our knowledge, we are the first to address the problem of mining pairs of lexical variants from noisy text in an unsupervised and purely statistical manner that does not require aligned noisy and clean messages. To obtain aligned clean and noisy text without annotated data implies the use of some normalizing method first. Yvon (2010) presents one such approach, where they generate exception dictionaries from their finite-state system's normalized output. However, their method is still trained on annotated training pairs, and hence supervised. A related direction is 'transliteration mining' (Jiampojamarn et al., 2010) which aims to automatically obtain bilingual lists of names written in different scripts. They also employ string-similarity measures to find similar string pairs written in different scripts. However, their input data is constrained to Wikipedia articles written in different languages, whereas we impose no constrains on our input data, and merely require a large collection thereof.

Noisy text normalization, on the other hand, has recently received a lot of focus. Most works construe the problem in the metaphors of either machine translation (MT) (Bangalore et al., 2002; Aw et al., 2006; Kaufmann and Kalita, 2010), spelling correction (Choudhury et al., 2007; Cook and Stevenson, 2009), or automated speech recognition (ASR) (Kobus et al., 2008). For our evaluation, we developed an implementation of Contractor (2010) which works on the same general approach as Han (2011).

## 6 Conclusions and Future Work

The ability to automatically extract lexical variants from large noisy corpora has many practical applications, including noisy text normalization, query spelling suggestion, fixing OCR errors, and so on. This paper developed a novel methodology for automatically mining such pairs from a large domain-specific corpus. The approach makes use of distributional similarity for measuring semantic similarity, a novel approach for filtering common English pairs by comparing against pairs mined from a large news corpus, and a substring similarity measure for re-ordering the pairs according to their lexical similarity.

To demonstrate the utility of the method, we used automatically mined pairs to construct an unsupervised exception dictionary, that was used in conjunction with a string similarity measure, to form a highly effective hybrid noisy text normalization technique. By exploiting the properties of the power law distribution, the exception dictionary can successfully correct a large number of cases, while the heuristic string similarity-based approach handled many of the less common test cases from the tail of the distribution. The hybrid approach showed substantial reductions in WER (around 20%) versus the string similarity approach, hence validating our proposed approach.

For future work we are interested in exploiting the (noisy, clean) pairs contained in the long tail as input to learning algorithms for acquiring domain-specific lexical transformations.

## Acknowledgments

Stephan Gouws would like to thank MIH Holdings Ltd. for financial support during the course of this work.

## References

A.T. Aw, M. Zhang, J. Xiao, and J. Su. 2006. A phrase-based statistical model for SMS text normalization. In *Proceedings of the COLING/ACL on Main conference poster sessions*, pages 33–40. Association for Computational Linguistics.

S. Bangalore, V. Murdock, and G. Riccardi. 2002. Bootstrapping bilingual data using consensus translation for a multilingual instant messaging system. In *Proceedings of the 19th International Conference on Computational Linguistics Volume 1*, pages 1–7. Association for Computational Linguistics.

Rahul Bhagat and Deepak Ravichandran. 2008. Large scale acquisition of paraphrases for learning surface patterns. In *Proceedings of ACL-08: HLT*, pages 674–682, Columbus, Ohio, June. Association for Computational Linguistics.

M. Choudhury, R. Saraf, V. Jain, A. Mukherjee, S. Sarkar, and A. Basu. 2007. Investigation and modeling of the structure of texting language. *International Journal on Document Analysis and Recognition*, 10(3):157–174.

D. Contractor, T.A. Faruquie, and L.V. Subramaniam. 2010. Unsupervised cleansing of noisy text. In *Proceedings of the 23rd International Conference on Computational Linguistics: Posters*, pages 189–196. Association for Computational Linguistics.

P. Cook and S. Stevenson. 2009. An unsupervised model for text message normalization. In *Proceedings of the Workshop on Computational Approaches to Linguistic Creativity*, pages 71–78. Association for Computational Linguistics.

S. Gouws, D. Metzler, C. Cai, and E. Hovy. 2011. Contextual Bearing on Linguistic Variation in Social Media. In *Proceedings of the ACL-11 Workshop on Language in Social Media*. Association for Computational Linguistics.

Bo Han and Timothy Baldwin. 2011. Lexical Normalisation of Short Text Messages: Makn Sens a #twitter. In *Proceedings of the 49th Annual Meeting of the Association for Computational Linguistics: Human Language Technologies*. Association for Computational Linguistics.

S. Jiampojamarn, K. Dwyer, S. Bergsma, A. Bhargava, Q. Dou, M.Y. Kim, and G. Kondrak. 2010. Transliteration generation and mining with limited training resources. In *Proceedings of the 2010 Named Entities Workshop*, pages 39–47. Association for Computational Linguistics.

M. Kaufmann and J. Kalita. 2010. Syntactic Normalization of Twitter Messages. In *International Conference on Natural Language Processing, Kharagpur, India.*

C. Kobus, F. Yvon, and G. Damnati. 2008. Normalizing SMS: are two metaphors better than one? In *Proceedings of the 22nd International Conference on Computational Linguistics-Volume 1*, pages 441–448. Association for Computational Linguistics.

Dekang Lin and Patrick Pantel. 2001. Discovery of inference rules for question-answering. *Nat. Lang. Eng.*, 7:343–360, December.

H. Lodhi, C. Saunders, J. Shawe-Taylor, N. Cristianini, and C. Watkins. 2002. Text classification using string kernels. *The Journal of Machine Learning Research*, 2:419–444.

Marius Pasca and Pter Dienes. 2005. Aligning needles in a haystack: Paraphrase acquisition across the web. In Robert Dale, Kam-Fai Wong, Jian Su, and Oi Yee Kwong, editors, *Natural Language Processing IJCNLP 2005*, volume 3651 of *Lecture Notes in Computer Science*, pages 119–130. Springer Berlin / Heidelberg.

A. Stolcke. 2002. SRILM-an extensible language modeling toolkit. In *Proceedings of the International Conference on Spoken Language Processing*, volume 2, pages 901–904. Citeseer.

F. Yvon. 2010. Rewriting the orthography of sms messages. *Journal of Natural Language Engineering*, 16(02):133–159.

# Lightly-Supervised Training for Hierarchical Phrase-Based Machine Translation

**Matthias Huck**[1] and **David Vilar**[1,2] and **Daniel Stein**[1] and **Hermann Ney**[1]

[1] Human Language Technology and Pattern Recognition Group, RWTH Aachen University
<surname>@cs.rwth-aachen.de

[2] DFKI GmbH
Berlin, Germany
david.vilar@dfki.de

## Abstract

In this paper we apply lightly-supervised training to a hierarchical phrase-based statistical machine translation system. We employ bitexts that have been built by automatically translating large amounts of monolingual data as additional parallel training corpora. We explore different ways of using this additional data to improve our system.

Our results show that integrating a second translation model with only non-hierarchical phrases extracted from the automatically generated bitexts is a reasonable approach. The translation performance matches the result we achieve with a joint extraction on all training bitexts while the system is kept smaller due to a considerably lower overall number of phrases.

## 1 Introduction

We investigate the impact of an employment of large amounts of unsupervised parallel data as training data for a statistical machine translation (SMT) system. The unsupervised parallel data is created by automatically translating monolingual source language corpora. This approach is called *lightly-supervised training* in the literature and has been introduced by Schwenk (2008). In contrast to Schwenk, we do not apply lightly-supervised training to a conventional phrase-based system (Och et al., 1999; Koehn et al., 2003) but to a hierarchical phrase-based translation (HPBT) system.

In hierarchical phrase-based translation (Chiang, 2005) a weighted synchronous context-free grammar is induced from parallel text, the search is based on CYK+ parsing (Chappelier and Rajman, 1998) and typically carried out using the cube pruning algorithm (Huang and Chiang, 2007). In addition to the contiguous *lexical phrases* as in standard phrase-based translation, the hierarchical phrase-based paradigm also allows for phrases with gaps which are called *hierarchical phrases*. A generic non-terminal symbol serves as a placeholder that marks the gaps.

In this paper we study several different ways of incorporating unsupervised training data into a hierarchical system. The basic techniques we employ are the use of multiple translation models and a distinction of the hierarchical and the non-hierarchical (i.e. lexical) part of the translation model. We report experimental results on the large-scale NIST Arabic-English translation task and show that lightly-supervised training yields significant gains over the baseline.

## 2 Related Work

Large-scale lightly-supervised training for SMT as we define it in this paper has been first carried out by Schwenk (2008). Schwenk translates a large amount of monolingual French data with an initial Moses (Koehn et al., 2007) baseline system into English. In Schwenk's original work, an additional bilingual dictionary is added to the baseline. With lightly-supervised training, Schwenk achieves improvements of around one BLEU point over the baseline. In a later work (Schwenk and Senellart, 2009) he applies the same method for translation model adaptation on an Arabic-French task with

*Proceedings of EMNLP 2011, Conference on Empirical Methods in Natural Language Processing*, pages 91–96, Edinburgh, Scotland, UK, July 27–31, 2011. 

gains of up to 3.5 points BLEU. [1]

Hierarchical phrase-based translation has been pioneered by David Chiang (Chiang, 2005; Chiang, 2007) with his Hiero system. The hierarchical paradigm has been implemented and extended by several groups since, some have published their software as open source (Li et al., 2009; Hoang et al., 2009; Vilar et al., 2010).

Combining multiple translation models has been investigated for domain adaptation by Foster and Kuhn (2007) and Koehn and Schroeder (2007) before. Heger et al. (2010) exploit the distinction between hierarchical and lexical phrases in a similar way as we do. They train phrase translation probabilities with forced alignment using a conventional phrase-based system (Wuebker et al., 2010) and employ them for the lexical phrases while the hierarchical phrases stay untouched.

## 3 Using the Unsupervised Data

The most straightforward way of trying to improve the baseline with lightly-supervised training would be to concatenate the human-generated parallel data and the unsupervised data and to jointly extract phrases from the unified parallel data (after having trained word alignments for the unsupervised bitexts as well). This method is simple and expected to be effective usually. There may however be two drawbacks: First, the reliability and the amount of parallel sentences may differ between the human-generated and the unsupervised part of the training data. It might be desirable to run separate extractions on the two corpora in order to be able to distinguish and weight phrases (or rather their scores) according to their origin during decoding. Second, if we incorporate large amounts of additional unsupervised data, the amount of phrases that are extracted may become much larger. We would want to avoid blowing up our phrase table sizes without an appropriate effect on translation quality. This holds in particular in the case of hierarchical phrases. Phrase-based machine translation systems are usually able to correctly handle local context dependencies, but often have problems in producing a fluent sentence structure across long distances. It is thus an intuitive supposition that using hierarchical phrases extracted from unsupervised data in addition to the hierarchical phrases extracted from the presumably more reliable human-generated bitexts does not increase translation quality. We will compare a joint extraction to the usage of two separate translation models (either without separate weighting, with a binary feature, or as a log-linear mixture). We will further check if including hierarchical phrases from the unsupervised data is beneficial or not.

[1] Schwenk names the method *lightly-supervised training* because the topics that are covered in the monolingual source language data that is being translated may potentially also be covered by parts of the language model training data of the system which is used to translate them. This can be considered as a form of light supervision. We loosely apply the term *lightly-supervised training* if we mean the process of utilizing a machine translation system to produce additional bitexts that are used as training data, but still refer to the automatically produced bilingual corpora as *unsupervised data*.

| | Arabic | English |
|---|---|---|
| Sentences | 2 514 413 | |
| Running words | 54 324 372 | 55 348 390 |
| Vocabulary | 264 528 | 207 780 |
| Singletons | 115 171 | 91 390 |

Table 1: Data statistics for the preprocessed Arabic-English parallel training corpus. In the corpus, numerical quantities have been replaced by a special category symbol.

| | dev (MT06) | test (MT08) |
|---|---|---|
| Sentences | 1 797 | 1 360 |
| Running words | 49 677 | 45 095 |
| Vocabulary | 9 274 | 9 387 |
| OOV [%] | 0.5 | 0.4 |

Table 2: Data statistics for the preprocessed Arabic part of the dev and test corpora. In the corpus, numerical quantities have been replaced by a special category symbol.

## 4 Experiments

We use the open source Jane toolkit (Vilar et al., 2010) for our experiments, a hierarchical phrase-based translation software written in C++.

### 4.1 Baseline System

The baseline system has been trained using a human-generated parallel corpus of 2.5M Arabic-English sentence pairs. Word alignments in both directions were produced with GIZA++ and symmetrized according to the refined method that was suggested by Och and Ney (2003).

The models integrated into our baseline system are: phrase translation probabilities and lexical translation probabilities for both translation directions, length penalties on word and phrase level, three binary features marking hierarchical phrases, glue rule, and rules with non-terminals at the boundaries, four simple additional count- and length-based binary features, and a large 4-gram language model with modified Kneser-Ney smoothing that was trained with the SRILM toolkit (Stolcke, 2002).

We ran the cube pruning algorithm, the depth of the hierarchical recursion was restricted to one by using shallow rules as proposed by Iglesias et al. (2009).

The scaling factors of the log-linear model combination have been optimized towards BLEU with MERT (Och, 2003) on the MT06 NIST test corpus. MT08 was employed as held-out test data. Detailed statistics for the parallel training data are given in Table 1, for the development and the test corpus in Table 2.

### 4.2 Unsupervised Data

The unsupervised data that we integrate has been created by automatic translations of parts of the Arabic LDC Gigaword corpus (mostly from the HYT collection) with a standard phrase-based system (Koehn et al., 2003). We thus in fact conduct a cross-system and cross-paradigm variant of lightly-supervised training. Translating the monolingual Arabic data has been performed by LIUM, Le Mans, France. We thank Holger Schwenk for kindly providing the translations.

The score computed by the decoder for each translation has been normalized with respect to the sentence length and used to select the most reliable sentence pairs. Word alignments for the unsupervised data have been produced in the same way as for the baseline bilingual training data. We report the statistics of the unsupervised data in Table 3.

### 4.3 Translation Models

We extracted three different phrase tables, one from the baseline human-generated parallel data only, one from the unsupervised data only, and one joint phrase table from the concatenation of the baseline data and the unsupervised data. We will denote the different extractions as *baseline*, *unsupervised*, and *joint*, respectively.

| | Arabic | English |
|---|---|---|
| Sentences | 4 743 763 | |
| Running words | 121 478 207 | 134 227 697 |
| Vocabulary | 306 152 | 237 645 |
| Singletons | 130 981 | 102 251 |

Table 3: Data statistics for the Arabic-English unsupervised training corpus after selection of the most reliable sentence pairs. In the corpus, numerical quantities have been replaced by a special category symbol.

The conventional restrictions have been applied for phrase extraction in all conditions, i.e. a maximum length of ten words on source and target side for lexical phrases, a length limit of five (including non-terminal symbols) on source side and ten on target side for hierarchical phrases, and at most two non-terminals per rule which are not allowed to be adjacent on the source side. To limit the number of hierarchical phrases, a minimum count cutoff of one and an extraction pruning threshold of 0.1 have been applied to them. Note that we did not prune lexical phrases.

Statistics on the phrase table sizes are presented in Table 4.[2] In total the joint extraction results in almost three times as many phrases as the baseline extraction. The extraction from the unsupervised data exclusively results in more than two times as many hierarchical phrases as from the baseline data. The sum of the number of hierarchical phrases from baseline and unsupervised extraction is very close to the number of hierarchical phrases from the joint extraction. If we discard the hierarchical phrases extracted from the unsupervised data and use the lexical part of the unsupervised phrase table (27.3M phrases) as a second translation model in addition to the baseline phrase table (67.0M phrases), the overall number of phrases is increased by only 41% compared to the baseline system.

[2]The phrase tables have been filtered towards the phrases needed for the translation of a given collection of test corpora.

| | number of phrases | | |
|---|---|---|---|
| | lexical | hierarchical | total |
| extraction from baseline data | 19.8M | 47.2M | 67.0M |
| extraction from unsupervised data | 27.3M | 115.6M | 142.9M |
| phrases present in both tables | 15.0M | 40.1M | 55.1M |
| joint extraction baseline + unsupervised | 32.1M | 166.5M | 198.6M |

Table 4: Phrase table sizes. The phrase tables have been filtered towards a larger set of test corpora containing a total of 2.3 million running words.

| | dev (MT06) | | test (MT08) | |
|---|---|---|---|---|
| | BLEU [%] | TER [%] | BLEU [%] | TER [%] |
| HPBT baseline | 44.1 | 49.9 | $44.4_{\pm 0.9}$ | $49.4_{\pm 0.8}$ |
| HPBT unsupervised only | 45.3 | 48.8 | 45.2 | 49.1 |
| joint extraction baseline + unsupervised | 45.6 | 48.7 | **45.4**$_{\pm 0.9}$ | $49.1_{\pm 0.8}$ |
| baseline hierarchical phrases + unsupervised lexical phrases | 45.1 | 49.1 | 45.2 | 49.2 |
| baseline hierarchical phrases + joint extraction lexical phrases | 45.3 | 48.7 | 45.3 | 49.1 |
| baseline + unsupervised lexical phrases | 45.3 | 48.9 | 45.3 | 49.0 |
| baseline + unsupervised lexical phrases (with binary feature) | 45.3 | 48.8 | **45.4** | 49.0 |
| baseline + unsupervised lexical phrases (separate scaling factors) | 45.3 | 48.9 | 45.0 | 49.3 |
| baseline + unsupervised full table | 45.6 | 48.6 | 45.1 | 48.9 |
| baseline + unsupervised full table (with binary feature) | 45.5 | 48.6 | 45.2 | 48.8 |
| baseline + unsupervised full table (separate scaling factors) | 45.5 | 48.7 | 45.3 | 49.0 |

Table 5: Results for the NIST Arabic-English translation task (truecase). The 90% confidence interval is given for the baseline system as well as for the system with joint phrase extraction. Results in bold are significantly better than the baseline.

### 4.4 Experimental Results

The empirical evaluation of all our systems on the two standard metrics BLEU (Papineni et al., 2002) and TER (Snover et al., 2006) is presented in Table 5. We have also checked the results for statistical significance over the baseline. The confidence intervals have been computed using bootstrapping for BLEU and Cochran's approximate ratio variance for TER (Leusch and Ney, 2009).

When we combine the full baseline phrase table with the unsupervised phrase table or the lexical part of it, we either use common scaling factors for their source-to-target and target-to-source translation costs, or we use common scaling factors but mark entries from the unsupervised table with a binary feature, or we optimize the four translation features separately for each of the two tables as part of the log-linear model combination.

Including the unsupervised data leads to a substantial gain on the unseen test set of up to +1.0% BLEU absolute. The different ways of combining the manually produced data with the unsupervised have little impact on translation quality. This holds specifically for the combination with only the lexical phrases, which, when marked with a binary feature, is able to obtain the same results as the full (joint extraction) system but with much less phrases. We compared the decoding speed of these two setups and observed that the system with less phrases is clearly faster (5.5 vs. 2.6 words per second, measured on MT08). The memory requirements of the systems do not differ greatly as we are using a binarized representation of the phrase table with on-demand loading. All setups consume slightly less than 16 gigabytes of RAM.

## 5 Conclusion

We presented several approaches of applying lightly-supervised training to hierarchical phrase-based machine translation. Using the additional automatically produced bitexts we have been able to obtain considerable gains compared to the baseline on the large-scale NIST Arabic-to-English translation task. We showed that a joint phrase extraction from human-generated and automatically generated parallel training data is not required to achieve significant improvements. The same translation quality can be achieved by adding a second translation model with only lexical phrases extracted from the automatically created bitexts. The overall amount of phrases can thus be kept much smaller.

## Acknowledgments

The authors would like to thank Holger Schwenk from LIUM, Le Mans, France, for making the automatic translations of the Arabic LDC Gigaword corpus available. This work was partly supported by the Defense Advanced Research Projects Agency (DARPA) under Contract No. HR0011-08-C-0110. Any opinions, findings and conclusions or recommendations expressed in this material are those of the authors and do not necessarily reflect the views of the DARPA.

## References

Jean-Cédric Chappelier and Martin Rajman. 1998. A Generalized CYK Algorithm for Parsing Stochastic CFG. In *Proc. of the First Workshop on Tabulation in Parsing and Deduction*, pages 133–137, April.

David Chiang. 2005. A Hierarchical Phrase-Based Model for Statistical Machine Translation. In *Proc. of the 43rd Annual Meeting of the Assoc. for Computational Linguistics (ACL)*, pages 263–270, Ann Arbor, MI, June.

David Chiang. 2007. Hierarchical Phrase-Based Translation. *Computational Linguistics*, 33(2):201–228, June.

George Foster and Roland Kuhn. 2007. Mixture-model adaptation for SMT. In *Proc. of the Second Workshop on Statistical Machine Translation*, pages 128–135, Prague, Czech Republic, June.

Carmen Heger, Joern Wuebker, David Vilar, and Hermann Ney. 2010. A Combination of Hierarchical Systems with Forced Alignments from Phrase-Based Systems. In *Proc. of the Int. Workshop on Spoken Language Translation (IWSLT)*, Paris, France, December.

Hieu Hoang, Philipp Koehn, and Adam Lopez. 2009. A Unified Framework for Phrase-Based, Hierarchical, and Syntax-Based Statistical Machine Translation. In *Proc. of the Int. Workshop on Spoken Language Translation (IWSLT)*, pages 152–159, Tokyo, Japan.

Liang Huang and David Chiang. 2007. Forest Rescoring: Faster Decoding with Integrated Language Models. In *Proc. of the Annual Meeting of the Assoc. for Computational Linguistics (ACL)*, pages 144–151, Prague, Czech Republic, June.

Gonzalo Iglesias, Adrià de Gispert, Eduardo R. Banga, and William Byrne. 2009. Rule Filtering by Pattern for Efficient Hierarchical Translation. In *Proc. of the 12th Conf. of the Europ. Chapter of the Assoc. for Computational Linguistics (EACL)*, pages 380–388, Athens, Greece, March.

Philipp Koehn and Josh Schroeder. 2007. Experiments in domain adaptation for statistical machine translation. In *Proc. of the Second Workshop on Statistical Machine Translation*, pages 224–227, Prague, Czech Republic, June.

Philipp Koehn, Franz Joseph Och, and Daniel Marcu. 2003. Statistical Phrase-Based Translation. In *Proc. of the Human Language Technology Conf. / North American Chapter of the Assoc. for Computational Linguistics (HLT-NAACL)*, pages 127–133, Edmonton, Canada, May/June.

P. Koehn, H. Hoang, A. Birch, C. Callison-Burch, M. Federico, N. Bertoldi, B. Cowan, W. Shen, C. Moran, R. Zens, et al. 2007. Moses: Open Source Toolkit for Statistical Machine Translation. In *Proc. of the Annual Meeting of the Assoc. for Computational Linguistics (ACL)*, pages 177–180, Prague, Czech Republic, June.

Gregor Leusch and Hermann Ney. 2009. Edit distances with block movements and error rate confidence estimates. *Machine Translation*, December.

Zhifei Li, Chris Callison-Burch, Chris Dyer, Sanjeev Khudanpur, Lane Schwartz, Wren Thornton, Jonathan Weese, and Omar Zaidan. 2009. Joshua: An Open Source Toolkit for Parsing-Based Machine Translation. In *Proc. of the Workshop on Statistical Machine Translation*, pages 135–139, Athens, Greece, March.

Franz Josef Och and Hermann Ney. 2003. A Systematic Comparison of Various Statistical Alignment Models. *Computational Linguistics*, 29(1):19–51, March.

Franz Josef Och, Christoph Tillmann, and Hermann Ney. 1999. Improved Alignment Models for Statistical Machine Translation. In *Proc. of the Joint SIGDAT Conf. on Empirical Methods in Natural Language Processing and Very Large Corpora (EMNLP99)*, pages 20–28, University of Maryland, College Park, MD, June.

Franz Josef Och. 2003. Minimum Error Rate Training for Statistical Machine Translation. In *Proc. of the Annual Meeting of the Assoc. for Computational Linguistics (ACL)*, pages 160–167, Sapporo, Japan, July.

Kishore Papineni, Salim Roukos, Todd Ward, and Wei-Jing Zhu. 2002. Bleu: a Method for Automatic Evaluation of Machine Translation. In *Proc. of the 40th Annual Meeting of the Assoc. for Computational Linguistics (ACL)*, pages 311–318, Philadelphia, PA, July.

Holger Schwenk and Jean Senellart. 2009. Translation Model Adaptation for an Arabic/French News Translation System by Lightly-Supervised Training. In *MT Summit XII*, Ottawa, Ontario, Canada, August.

Holger Schwenk. 2008. Investigations on Large-Scale Lightly-Supervised Training for Statistical Machine Translation. In *Proc. of the Int. Workshop on Spoken Language Translation (IWSLT)*, pages 182–189, Waikiki, Hawaii, October.

Matthew Snover, Bonnie Dorr, Richard Schwartz, Linnea Micciulla, and John Makhoul. 2006. A Study of Translation Edit Rate with Targeted Human Annotation. In *Conf. of the Assoc. for Machine Translation in the Americas (AMTA)*, pages 223–231, Cambridge, MA, August.

Andreas Stolcke. 2002. SRILM – an Extensible Language Modeling Toolkit. In *Proc. of the Int. Conf. on Spoken Language Processing (ICSLP)*, volume 3, Denver, CO, September.

David Vilar, Daniel Stein, Matthias Huck, and Hermann Ney. 2010. Jane: Open Source Hierarchical Translation, Extended with Reordering and Lexicon Models. In *ACL 2010 Joint Fifth Workshop on Statistical Machine Translation and Metrics MATR*, pages 262–270, Uppsala, Sweden, July.

Joern Wuebker, Arne Mauser, and Hermann Ney. 2010. Training Phrase Translation Models with Leaving-One-Out. In *Proc. of the Annual Meeting of the Assoc. for Computational Linguistics (ACL)*, pages 475–484, Uppsala, Sweden, July.

# Unsupervised Alignment for Segmental-based Language Understanding

**Stéphane Huet** and **Fabrice Lefèvre**
Université d'Avignon, LIA-CERI, France
{stephane.huet,fabrice.lefevre}@univ-avignon.fr

## Abstract

Recent years' most efficient approaches for language understanding are statistical. These approaches benefit from a segmental semantic annotation of corpora. To reduce the production cost of such corpora, this paper proposes a method that is able to match first identified concepts with word sequences in an unsupervised way. This method based on automatic alignment is used by an understanding system based on conditional random fields and is evaluated on a spoken dialogue task using either manual or automatic transcripts.

## 1 Introduction

One of the very first step to build a spoken language understanding (SLU) module for dialogue systems is the extraction of literal concepts from word sequences hypothesised by a speech recogniser. To address this issue of concept tagging, several techniques are available. These techniques rely on models, now classic, that can be either discriminant or generative. Among these, we can cite: hidden Markov models, finite state transducers, maximal entropy Markov models, support vector machines, dynamic Bayesian networks (DBNs) or conditional Markov random fields (CRFs) (Lafferty et al., 2001). In (Hahn et al., 2011), it is shown that CRFs obtain the best performance on a reference task (MEDIA) in French (Bonneau-Maynard et al., 2005), but also on two other comparable corpora in Italian and Polish. Besides, the comparison of the understanding results of manually vs automatically transcribed utterances has shown the robustness of CRFs.

Among the approaches evaluated in (Hahn et al., 2011) was a method using log-linear models comparable to those used in stochastic machine translation, which turned out to have lower performance than CRF. In this paper, we further exploit the idea of applying automatic translation techniques to language understanding but limiting ourselves to the objective of obtaining a segmental annotation of training data.

In many former approaches literal interpretation was limited to list lexical-concept relations; for instance this is the case of the PHOENIX system (Ward, 1991) based on the detection of keywords. The segmental approach allows a finer-grained analysis considering sentences as segment sequences during interpretation. This characteristic enables the approach to correctly connect the various levels of sentence analysis (lexical, syntactic and semantic). However, in order to simplify its practical application, segments have been designed specifically for semantic annotation and do not integrate any constraint in their relation with the syntactic units (chunks, phrasal groups, etc.). Not only it simplifies the annotation process itself but as the overall objective is to use the interpretation module inside a spoken dialogue system, transcribed speech data are noisy and generally bound the performance of syntactic analysers (due to highly spontaneous and ungrammatical utterances from the users, combined with errors from the speech recognizer).

Among other interesting proprieties, segmental approaches offer a convenient way to dissociate the detection of a conceptual unit from the estimation of its associated value. The value corresponds to the normalisation of the surface form. For instance, if

*Proceedings of EMNLP 2011, Conference on Empirical Methods in Natural Language Processing*, pages 97–104,
Edinburgh, Scotland, UK, July 27–31, 2011. 

the segment "no later than eleven" is associated with the concept `departure-time`, its value is "morning"; the same value is associated with the segments "between 8 and noon" or "in the morning". The value estimation requires a link between concepts and sentence words. Then it becomes possible to treat the normalisation problem by means of regular expressions or concept-dependent language models (allowing an integrated approach such as described in (Lefèvre, 2007)). In the case of global approaches (not segmental), value detection must be directly incorporated in the conceptual units to identify, as in (Mairesse et al., 2009). The additional level is a real burden and is only affordable when the number of authorised values is low.

Obviously a major drawback of the approach is its cost: associating concept tags with a dialogue transcription is already a tedious task and its complexity is largely increased by the requirement for a precise delimitation of the support (lexical segment) corresponding to each tag. The SLU evaluation campaign MEDIA has been the first opportunity to collect and distribute a reasonably-sized corpus endowed with segmental annotations.

Anyhow the difficulty remains unchanged each time a corpus has to be collected for a new task. We propose in this study a new method that reduces the effort required to build training data for segmental annotation models. Making the assumption that the concepts evoked in a sentence are automatically detected beforehand or provided by an expert, we study how to associate them with their lexical supports without *prior* knowledge. A conceptual segmental annotation is obtained using alignment techniques designed to align multilingual parallel corpora in the machine translation domain. This annotation can be considered as unsupervised since it is done without a training corpus with links between word sequences and concepts.

We present in the paper the necessary adaptations for the application of the alignment techniques in this new context. They have been kept to their minimal so as to maintain the highest level of generality, which in return benefits from the availability of existing software tools. Using a reference annotation, we evaluate the alignment quality from the unsupervised approach in two interesting situations depending on whether the correct order of the concepts is known or not. Finally, the end-to-end evaluation of the approach is made by measuring the impact of the alignments on the CRF-based understanding system.

After a brief recall of the conceptual decoding principles in Section 2, the principles of automatic alignment of parallel corpora are described in Section 3 along with the specificities due to the alignment of semantic concepts. Section 4 presents the experiments and comments on the results, while Section 5 concludes the paper.

## 2 Segmental conceptual decoding

If literal interpretation can be seen as the translation of natural language to the set of semantic tag sequences, then the methods and models of machine translation can be used. Since the number of concepts is generally much lower than the vocabulary size, this particular type of translation can also be considered as a mere classification problem in which the conceptual constituents represent the class to identify. Interpretation can thus be performed by methods and models of classification.

Discriminant approaches model the conditional probability distribution of the semantic constituent sequence (or concepts) $c_1 \dots c_n$ considering a word sequence $w_1 \dots w_T$: $P(c_1^n|w_1^T)$. In generative approaches, the joint probability $P(c_1^n, w_1^T)$ is modelized instead and can be used to compute inferences either for prediction/decoding or parameter training.

Generative models (such as hidden Markov models) have been first introduced to address the understanding problem with stochastic approaches (Levin and Pieraccini, 1995). Recent variants offer more degrees of freedom in modeling (see for instance (He and Young, 2005) or (Lefèvre, 2007)). Since then log-linear models have clearly shown their superiority for tasks of sequence tagging (Hahn et al., 2011).

Several variants of log-linear models differ in their conditional variable independence assumptions and use different normalisation steps. CRFs (Lafferty et al., 2001) represent linear chains of random independent variables, all conditioned over the entire sequence and the normalisation is global over the sequence.

Some generative approaches such as DBNs make inferences in multi-level models (Lefèvre, 2007)

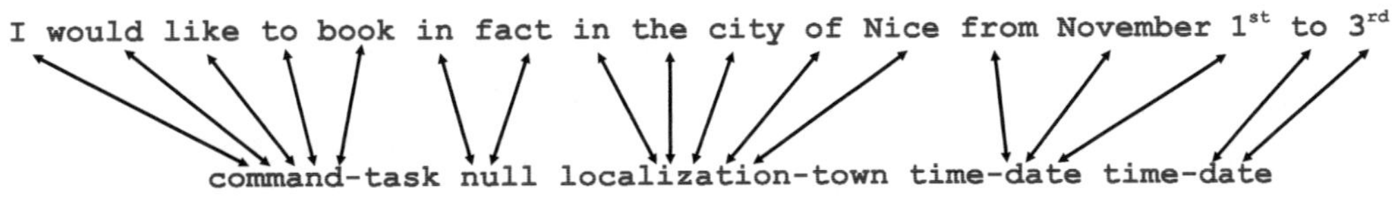


Figure 1: Example of an alignment of words with their conceptual units.

and intrinsically take into account segmentation. For models unable to handle multi-level representations (as CRF), it is convenient to represent segments directly at the tag level. For this purpose the BIO formalism can be used: B is added to tags starting a segment, I to tags inside a segment and O to out-of-domain tags (if these are not already handled through a specific NULL tag). In the case displayed in Figure 1, the concept sequence becomes: `B-cmd-task I-cmd-task I-cmd-task B-null I-null B-loc-town I-loc-town I-loc-town I-loc-town I-loc-town B-time-date I-time-date B-time-date I-time-date I-time-date`.

## 3 Semantic concept alignment

Automatic alignment is a major issue in machine translation. For example, word-based alignments are used to generate phrase tables that are core components for many current statistical machine translation systems (Koehn et al., 2007). The alignment task aims at finding the mapping between words of two sentences in relation of translation. It faces several difficulties:

- some source words are not associated with a translated word;
- others are translated by several words;
- matched words may occur at different positions in both sentences according to the syntactic rules of the considered languages.

Several statistical models have been proposed to align two sentences (Brown et al., 1993). One of their main interests is their ability to be built in an unsupervised way from a parallel corpus aligned at the sentence level, but not at the word level. Formally, from a sentence $S = s_1 \dots s_m$ expressed in a source language and its translation $T = t_1 \dots t_n$ expressed in a target language, an IBM-style alignment $A = a_1 \dots a_m$ connects each source word to a target word ($a_j \in \{1, ..., n\}$) or to the so-called NULL token which accounts for untranslated target words. IBM statistical models evaluate the translation of $S$ into $T$ from the computation of $P(S, A|T)$; the best alignment $\hat{A}$ can be deduced from this criterion using the Viterbi algorithm:

$$\hat{A} = \text{argmax}_A P(S, A|T) \ . \quad (1)$$

IBM models differ according to their complexity level. IBM1 model makes the strong assumption that alignments are independent and can be evaluated only through the transfer probabilities $P(s_i|t_j)$. The HMM model, which is an improvement over IBM2, adds a new parameter $P(a_j|a_{j-1}, n)$ that assumes a first-order dependency between alignment variables. The next models (IBM3 to IBM5) are mainly based on two types of parameters:

- distortion, which measures how words of $T$ are reordered with respect to the index of the words from $S$ they are aligned with,
- fertility, which measures the usual number of words that are aligned with a target word $t_j$.

In order to improve alignments, IBM models are usually applied in both translation directions. These two alignments are then symmetrized by combining them. This last step is done via heuristic methods; a common approach is to start with the intersection and then iteratively add links from the union (Och et al., 1999).

If we have at our disposal a method that can find concepts contained in an utterance, segmental annotation can be obtained by aligning words $S = w_1^T$ with the found concepts $T = c_1^n$ (Fig. 1). Concepts are ideally generated in the correct order with respect to the word segments of the analysed utterance. In a more pragmatic way, concepts are likely to be produced as bag-of-concepts rather than ordered sequences.

Statistical alignment methods used in machine translation are relevant in our context if we consider that the target language is the concept language. There are nevertheless differences with genuine language translation. First, each word is aligned to at most one concept, while a concept is aligned with one word or more. Consequently, it is expected that word fertilities are one for the alignment of words toward concepts and concept fertilities are one or more in the reverse direction. Another consequence is that NULL words are useless in our context. These specificities of the alignment process raise some difficulties with regard to IBM models. Indeed, according to the way probabilities are computed, the alignment of concepts toward words only allows one word to be chosen per concept, which prevents this direction from having a sufficient number of links between words and concepts.

Another significant difference with translation is related to the translated token order. While word order is not random in a natural language and follows syntactic rules, it is not the case anymore when a word sequence have to be aligned with a bag-of-concepts. HMM and IBM2 to IBM5 models have parameters that assume that the index of a matched source word or the indices of the translations of the adjacent target words bear on the index of target words. Therefore, the randomness of the concept indices can disrupt performance obtained with these models, contrary to IBM1. As shown in the next section, it is appropriate to find ways to explicitly re-order concept sequences than to let the distortion parameters handle the problem alone.

## 4 Experiments and results

### 4.1 Experimental setup

The evaluation of the introduced methods was carried out on the MEDIA corpus (Bonneau Maynard et al., 2008). This corpus consists of human-machine dialogues collected with a wizard of Oz procedure in the domain of negotiation of tourist services. Produced for a realistic task, it is annotated with 145 semantic concepts and their values (more than 2k in total for the enumerable cases). The audio data are distributed with their manual transcripts and automatic speech recognition (ASR) hypotheses. The corpus is divided into three parts: a training set (approximatively 12k utterances), a development set (1.2k) and a test set (3k).

The experiments led on the alignment methods were evaluated on the development corpus using MGIZA++ (Gao and Vogel, 2008), a multi-thread version of GIZA++ (Och and Ney, 2003) which also allows previously trained IBM alignments models to be applied on the development and test corpora.[1] The conceptual tagging process was evaluated on the test corpus, using WAPITI (Lavergne et al., 2010) to train the CRF models. Several setups have been tested:

- manual vs ASR transcriptions,
- inclusion (or not) of values during the error computation.

Several concept orderings (before automatic alignment) have also been considered:

- a first ideal one, which takes reference concept sequences as they are, aka **sequential order**;
- two more realistic variants that sort concepts either **alphabetically** or **randomly**, in order to simulate bag-of-concepts. Alphabetical order is introduced solely to show that a particular order (which is not related to the natural order) might misled the alignment process by introducing undue regularities.

To give a rough idea, these experiments required a few minutes of computing time to train alignment models of 12k utterances, a few hours to train CRF models (using 8 CPUs on our cluster of Xeon CPUs) and a few seconds to apply alignment and CRF models in order to decode the test corpus.

### 4.2 Experimental results for alignment

Alignment quality is estimated using the *alignment error rate* (AER), a metric often employed in machine translation (Och and Ney, 2000). If $H$ stands for hypothesis alignments and $R$ for reference alignments, AER is computed by the following relation:[2]

$$AER = 1 - \frac{2 \times |H \cap R|}{|H| + |R|} \quad . \tag{2}$$

[1] With `previousa`, `previoust`, `previousn`, etc parameters.

[2] This equation is a simplification of the usually provided one because all alignments are considered as sure in our case.

In our context, this metrics is evaluated by representing a link between source and target identities by $(w_i, c_j)$, instead of the usual indices $(i, j)$. Indeed, alignments are then used to tag words. Besides, concepts to align have positions that differ from the ones in the reference when they are reordered to simulate bags-of-concepts.

As mentioned in the introduction, we resort to widely used tools for alignment in order to be as general as possible in our approach. We do not modify the algorithms and rely on their generality to deal with specificities of the studied domain. To train iteratively the alignment models, we use the same pipeline as in MOSES, a widely used machine translation system (Koehn et al., 2007):

1. 5 iterations of IBM1,
2. 5 iterations of HMM,
3. 3 iterations of IBM3 then
4. 3 iterations of IBM4.

To measure the quality of the built models, the model obtained at the last iteration of this chain is applied on the development corpus.

All the words of an utterance should normally be associated with one concept, which makes the IBM models' NULL word useless. However, in the MEDIA corpus, a `null` semantic concept is associated with words that do not correspond to a concept relevant for the tourist domain and may be omitted by counting on the probability with the NULL word included in the IBM models. Two versions were specifically created to test this hypothesis: one with all the reference concept sequences and another without the `null` tags. The results measured when taking into account these tags (AER of 14.2 %) are far better than the ones obtained when they are discarded (AER of 27.4 %), in the word → concept alignment direction.[3] We decided therefore to keep the `null` in all the experiments.

Table 1 presents the alignment results measured on the development corpus according to the way concepts are reordered with respect to the reference and according to the considered alignment direction. The three first lines exhibit the results obtained with the last IBM4 iteration. As expected, the AER measured with this model in the concept → word direction (second line), which can only associate at most one word per concept, is clearly higher than the one obtained in the opposite direction (first line). Quite surprisingly, an improvement in terms of AER (third line) over the best direction (first line) is observed using the default MOSES heuristics (called *grow-diag-final*) that symmetrizes alignments obtained in both directions.

IBM1 models, contrary to other models, do not take into account word index inside source and target sentences, which makes them relevant to deal with bag-of-concepts. Therefore, we measured how AER varies when using models previously built in the training chain. The results obtained by applying IBM1 and by symmetrizing alignments (last line), show finally that these simple models lead to lower performance than the one measured with IBM4 or even HMM (last line), the concepts being ordered alphabetically or randomly (two last columns).

The previous experiments have shown that alignment is clearly of lower quality when algorithms are faced with bags-of-concepts instead of well-ordered sequences. In order to reduce this phenomenon, sequences are reordered after a first alignment $\mathcal{A}_1$ generated by the symmetrized IBM4 model. Two strategies have been considered to fix the new position of each concept $c_i$. The first one averages the indices of the words $w_i$ that are aligned with $c_i$ according to $\mathcal{A}_1$:

$$\text{pos}_1(c_j) = \frac{\sum_{is.t.(i,j)\in\mathcal{A}_1} i}{\text{Card}(\{(i,j) \in \mathcal{A}_1\})} \quad . \tag{3}$$

The second one weights each word index with their transfer probabilities determined by IBM4:

$$\text{pos}_2(c_j) = \frac{\sum_{is.t.(i,j)\in\mathcal{A}_1} i \times f(w_i, c_j)}{\sum_{is.t.(i,j)\in\mathcal{A}_1} f(w_i, c_j)} \tag{4}$$

where

$$f(w_i, c_j) = \lambda P(c_j|w_i) + (1 - \lambda) P(w_i|c_j) \tag{5}$$

and $\lambda$ is a coefficient fixed on the development corpus.

Training alignment models on the corpus reordered according to $\text{pos}_1$ (Tab. 2, second column)

[3] For a fair comparison between both setups, the `null` concept was ignored in $H$ and $R$ for this series of experiments.

| | Sequential order | Alphabetic order | Random order |
|---|---|---|---|
| word → concept IBM4 | 14.4 | 29.2 | 28.6 |
| concept → word IBM4 | 40.9 | 51.6 | 49.0 |
| symmetrized IBM4 | **12.8** | **27.3** | **25.7** |
| symmetrized IBM1 | 33.2 | 33.2 | 33.1 |
| symmetrized HMM | 14.8 | 29.9 | 28.7 |

Table 1: AER (%) measured on the MEDIA development corpus with respect to the alignment model used and its direction.

| | Initial | 1st reordering iteration | | Last reordering iteration |
|---|---|---|---|---|
| | | $pos_1$ | $pos_2$ | $pos_2$ |
| Alphabetic order | 27.3 | 22.2 | 21.0 | **19.4** |
| Random order | 25.7 | 21.9 | 20.2 | **18.5** |

Table 2: AER (%) measured on the MEDIA development corpus according to the strategy used to reorder concepts.

or $pos_2$ (third column) leads to a significant improvement of the AER. This reordering step can be repeated as long as performance goes on improving. By proceeding like this until step 3 for the alphabetic order and until step 7 for the random order, values of AER below 20 % (last column) are finally obtained. It is noteworthy that random reordering has better results than alphabetic reordering. Indeed, HMM, IBM3 and IBM4 models have probabilities that are more biased in this latter case, where the same sequences occur more often although many are not in the reference.

### 4.3 Experimental results for spoken language understanding

In order to measure how spoken language understanding is disturbed by erroneous alignments, CRFs parameters are trained under two conditions: one where concept tagging is performed by an expert and one where corpora are obtained using automatic alignment. The performance criterion used to evaluate the understanding task is the *concept error rate* (CER). CER is computed in a similar way as word error rate (WER) used in speech recognition; it is obtained from the Levenshtein alignment between both hypothesized and reference sequences as the ratio of the sum of the concepts in the hypothesis substituted, inserted or omitted on the total number of concepts in the manual reference annotation. The `null` concept is not considered during the score computation. The CER can also take into account the normalized values in addition to the concept tags.

Starting from a state-of-the-art system (Manual column), degradations due to various alignment conditions are reported in Table 3. It can be noted that the absolute increase in CER is at most 8.0 % (from 17.6 to 25.6 with values) when models are trained on the corpus aligned with IBM models; the ordering information brings it back to 3.7 % (17.6 to 21.3), and finally with automatic transcription the impact of the automatic alignments is smaller (resp. 5.8 % and 2.0 %). As expected random order is preferable to alphabetic order (slight gain of 1 %).

In Table 4, the random order alignments are used but this time the $n$-best lists of alignments are considered and not only the 1-best hypotheses. Instead of training CRFs with only one version of the alignment for a concept-word sequence pair, we filter out from the $n$-best lists the alignments having a probability above a given threshold. It can be observed that varying this confidence threshold allows an improvement of the SLU performance (CER can be reduced by 0.8 % for manual transcription and 0.4 % for automatic transcription). However, this improvement is not propagated to scores with values (CER was reduced at best by 0.1 for manual transcription and was increased for automatic tran-

| | Manual | Automatic alignments: Sequential | Alphabetic order | Random order |
|---|---|---|---|---|
| Manual transcription | 13.9 (17.6) | 17.7 (21.3) | 22.6 (26.4) | 22.0 (25.6) |
| ASR transcription (wer 31 %) | 24.7 (29.8) | 27.1 (31.8) | 31.5 (36.4) | 30.6 (35.6) |

Table 3: CER (%) measured for concept decoding on the MEDIA test corpus with several alignment methods of the training data. Inside parenthesis, CER for concepts and values.

scription). After closer inspection of the scoring alignments, an explanation for this setback is that the manually-designed rules used for value extraction are perturbed by loose segmentation. This is particularly the case for the concept used to annotate co-references, which has confusions between the values `singular` and `plural` (e.g. "this" is singular and "those" plural). This issue can be solved by an *ad hoc* adaptation of the rules. However, it would infringe our objective of relying upon unsupervised approaches and minimizing human expertise. Therefore, a better answer would be to resort to a probabilistic scheme also for value extraction (as proposed in (Lefèvre, 2007)).

The optimal configuration (confidence threshold of 0.3, 4th row of Table 4) is close to the baseline 1-best system in terms of the number of training utterances. We also tried a slightly different setup which adds the filtered alignments to the former corpus before CRF parameter training (i.e. the 1-best is not filtered in the $n$-best list). In that case performance remains pretty stable with respect to the filtering process (CER is around 21.4 % for concepts and 25.2 % for concept+value for thresholds between 0.1 and 0.7).

## 5 Conclusion

In this study an unsupervised approach is proposed to the problem of conceptual unit alignment for spoken language understanding. We show that unsupervised statistical word alignment from the machine translation domain can be used in this context to associate semantic concepts with word sequences. The quality of the derived alignment, already good in the general case (< 20 % of errors on the word-concept associations), is improved by knowledge of the correct unit order (< 15 %). The impact of automatic alignments on the understanding performance is an absolute increase of +8 % in terms of CER, but is reduced to less than +4 % in the ordered case. When automatic transcripts are used, these gaps decrease to +6 % and below +3 % respectively. From these results we do believe that the cost vs performance ratio is in favour of the proposed method.

## Acknowledgements

This work is partially supported by the ANR funded project PORT-MEDIA.[4]

## References

Hélène Bonneau-Maynard, Sophie Rosset, Christelle Ayache, Anne Kuhn, and Djamel Mostefa. 2005. Semantic annotation of the MEDIA corpus for spoken dialog. In *Proceedings of Eurospeech*, pages 3457–3460, Lisboa, Portugal.

Hélène Bonneau Maynard, Alexandre Denis, Frédéric Béchet, Laurence Devillers, F. Lefèvre, Matthieu Quignard, Sophie Rosset, and Jeanne Villaneau. 2008. MEDIA : évaluation de la compréhension dans les systèmes de dialogue. In *L'évaluation des technologies de traitement de la langue, les campagnes Technolangue*, pages 209–232. Hermès, Lavoisier.

Peter F. Brown, Stephen A. Della Pietra, Vincent J. Della Pietra, and Robert L. Mercer. 1993. The mathematics of statistical machine translation: Parameter estimation. *Computational Linguistics*, 19(2):263–311.

Qin Gao and Stephan Vogel. 2008. Parallel implementations of word alignment tool. In *Software Engineering, Testing, and Quality Assurance for Natural Language Processing*, pages 49–57, Columbus, OH, USA.

Stefan Hahn, Marco Dinarelli, Christian Raymond, Fabrice Lefèvre, Patrick Lehen, Renato De Mori, Alessandro Moschitti, Hermann Ney, and Giuseppe Riccardi. 2011. Comparing stochastic approaches to spoken language understanding in multiple languages. *IEEE Transactions on Audio, Speech and Language Processing (TASLP)*, 19(6):1569–1583.

[4] `www.port-media.org`

| | # train utterances | Manual transcription | ASR transcription (WER = 31 %) |
|---|---|---|---|
| 1-best | 12795 | 22.0 (25.6) | 30.6 (**35.6**) |
| filtered 10-best (conf thres = 0.1) | 18955 | 21.7 (25.8) | 31.2 (36.9) |
| filtered 10-best (conf thres = 0.2) | 15322 | 21.3 (**25.5**) | 30.7 (36.3) |
| filtered 10-best (conf thres = 0.3) | 13374 | **21.2** (25.7) | **30.2** (36.0) |
| filtered 10-best (conf thres = 0.5) | 10963 | 21.4 (25.7) | 30.6 (36.2) |
| filtered 10-best (conf thres = 0.7) | 9647 | 25.4 (29.1) | 32.9 (38.2) |

Table 4: CER (%) measured for concept decoding on the MEDIA test corpus with filtered $n$-best lists of random order alignments of the training data. Inside parenthesis, CER for concepts and values.


Yulan He and Steve Young. 2005. Spoken language understanding using the hidden vector state model. *Speech Communication*, 48(3–4):262–275.

Philipp Koehn, Hieu Hoang, Alexandra Birch, Chris Callison-Burch, Marcello Federico, Nicola Bertoldi, Brooke Cowan, Wade Shen, Christine Moran, Richard Zens, Chris Dyer, Ondrej Bojar, Alexandra Constantin, and Evan Herbst. 2007. Moses: Open source toolkit for statistical machine translation. In *Proceedings of ACL, Companion Volume*, pages 177–180, Prague, Czech Republic.

John Lafferty, Andrew McCallum, and Fernando Pereira. 2001. Conditional random fields: Probabilistic models for segmenting and labeling sequence data. In *Proceedings of ICML*, pages 282–289, Williamstown, MA, USA.

Thomas Lavergne, Olivier Cappé, and François Yvon. 2010. Practical very large scale CRFs. In *Proceedings of ACL*, pages 504–513, Uppsala, Sweden.

Fabrice Lefèvre. 2007. Dynamic bayesian networks and discriminative classifiers for multi-stage semantic interpretation. In *Proceedings of ICASSP*, Honolulu, Hawai.

Esther Levin and Roberto Pieraccini. 1995. Concept-based spontaneous speech understanding system. In *Proceedings of Eurospeech*, pages 555–558, Madrid, Spain.

François Mairesse, Milica Gašić, Filip Jurčíček, Simon Keizer, Blaise Thomson, Kai Yu, and Steve Young. 2009. Spoken language understanding from unaligned data using discriminative classification models. In *Proceedings of ICASSP*, Taipei, Taiwan.

Franz Joseph Och and Hermann Ney. 2000. A comparison of alignment models for statistical machine translation. In *Proceedings of Coling*, volume 2, pages 1086–1090, Saarbrücken, Germany.

Franz Josef Och and Hermann Ney. 2003. A systematic comparison of various statistical alignment models. *Computational Linguistics*, 29(1):19–51.

Franz Josef Och, Christoph Tillmann, and Hermann Ney. 1999. Improved alignment models for statistical machine translation. In *Proceedings of the Joint SIGDAT Conference on Empirical Methods in Natural Language Processing and Very Large Corpora*, pages 20–28, College Park, MD, USA.

Wayne Ward. 1991. Understanding spontaneous speech: the Phoenix system. In *Proceedings of ICASSP*, pages 365–368, Toronto, Canada.

# Unsupervised Name Ambiguity Resolution Using A Generative Model

**Zornitsa Kozareva and Sujith Ravi**
USC Information Sciences Institute
4676 Admiralty Way
Marina del Rey, CA 90292-6695
{kozareva, sravi}@isi.edu

## Abstract

Resolving ambiguity associated with names found on the Web, Wikipedia or medical texts is a very challenging task, which has been of great interest to the research community. We propose a novel approach to disambiguating names using Latent Dirichlet Allocation, where the learned topics represent the underlying senses of the ambiguous name. We conduct a detailed evaluation on multiple data sets containing ambiguous person, location and organization names and for multiple languages such as English, Spanish, Romanian and Bulgarian. We conduct comparative studies with existing approaches and show a substantial improvement of 15 to 35% in task accuracy.

## 1 Introduction

Recently, ambiguity resolution for names found on the Web (Artiles et al., 2007), Wikipedia articles (Bunescu and Pasca, 2006), news texts (Pedersen et al., 2005) and medical literature (Ginter et al., 2004) has become an active area of research. Like words, names are ambiguous and can refer to multiple entities. For example, a Web search for *Jerry Hobbs* on Google returns a mixture of documents associated with two different entities in the top 10 search results. One refers to a computational linguist at University of Southern California and the other refers to a fugitive and murderer. Disambiguating the names and identifying the correct entity is very important especially for Web search applications since 11-17% of the Web search queries are composed of person name and a term (Artiles et al., 2009a).

In the past, there has been a substantial body of work in the area of name disambiguation under a variety of different names and using diverse set of approaches. Some refer to the task as *cross-document coreference resolution* (Bagga and Baldwin, 1998), *name discrimination* (Pedersen et al., 2005) or *Web People Search* (WebPS) (Artiles et al., 2007). The majority of the approaches focus on person name ambiguity (Chen and Martin, 2007; Artiles et al., 2010), some have also explored organization and location name disambiguation (Pedersen et al., 2006).

The intuition behind most approaches follows the distributional hypothesis (Harris, 1954) according to which ambiguous names sharing the same contexts tend to refer to the same individual. To model these characteristics, Bunescu and Pasca (2006) and Cucerzan (2007) incorporate information from Wikipedia articles, Artiles et al. (2007) use Web page content, Mann and Yarowsky (2003) extract biographic facts. The approaches used in the WebPS tasks mainly rely on bag-of-words representations (Artiles et al., 2007; Chen and Martin, 2007; Artiles et al., 2009b). Most methods suffer from a common drawback—they rely on surface features such as word co-occurrences, which are insufficient to capture hidden information pertaining to the entities (senses) associated with the documents.

We take a novel approach for tackling the problem of name ambiguity using an unsupervised topic modeling framework. To our knowledge, no one has yet explored the disambiguation of names using Latent Dirichlet Allocation (LDA) nor has shown LDA's behavior on multiple data sources and settings. Our motivation for using an unsupervised

*Proceedings of EMNLP 2011, Conference on Empirical Methods in Natural Language Processing*, pages 105–112,
Edinburgh, Scotland, UK, July 27–31, 2011. 

topic modeling framework for name disambiguation is based on the advantages generative models offer in contrast to the existing ones. For instance, topic models such as Latent Dirichlet allocation (LDA) method (Blei et al., 2003) have been widely used in the literature for other applications to uncover hidden (or latent) groupings underlying a set of observations. Topic models are capable of handling ambiguity and distinguishing between uses of words with multiple meanings depending on context. Thereby, they provide a natural fit for our name disambiguation task, where latent topics correspond to the entities (name senses) representing the documents for an ambiguous name. Identifying these latent topics helps us identify the particular sense of a given ambiguous name that is used in the context of a particular document and hence resolve name ambiguity. In addition, this approach offers several advantages—(1) entities (senses) can be learnt automatically from a collection of documents in an unsupervised manner, (2) efficient methods already exist for performing inference in this model so we can easily scale to Web data, and (3) unlike typical approaches, we can easily apply our learnt model to resolve name ambiguity for unseen documents.
The main contributions of this paper are:

- We propose a novel model for name disambiguation using Latent Dirichlet Allocation.
- Unlike previous approaches, which are designed for specific tasks, corpora and languages, we conduct a detailed evaluation taking into consideration the multiple properties of the data and names.
- Our experimental study shows that LDA can be used as a general name disambiguation framework, which can be successfully applied on any *corpora* (i.e. Web, news, Wikipedia), *languages* (i.e. English, Spanish, Romanian and Bulgarian) and *types of ambiguous names* (i.e. people, organizations, locations).
- We conduct a comparative study with existing state-of-the-art clustering approaches and show substantial improvements of 15 to 35% in task accuracy.

The rest of the paper is organized as follows. In Section 2 we describe related work. Section 3 describes the Latent Dirichlet Allocation model used to disambiguate the names. Section 4 describes the experiments we have conducted on multiple data sets and languages. Finally, we conclude in Section 5.

## 2 Related Work

Ambiguous names have been disambiguated with varying success from structured texts (Pedersen et al., 2006), semi-structured texts such as Wikipedia articles (Bunescu and Pasca, 2006; Cucerzan, 2007) or unstructured texts such as those found on the Web (Pedersen and Kulkarni, 2007; Artiles et al., 2009b). Most approaches (Artiles et al., 2009b; Chen et al., 2009; Lan et al., 2009) focus on person name disambiguation, while others (Pedersen et al., 2006) also explore ambiguity in organization and location names. In the medical domain, Hatzivassiloglou et al. (2001) and Ginter et al. (2004) tackle the problem of gene and protein name disambiguation.

Due to the high interest in this task, researchers have explored a wide range of approaches and features. Among the most common and efficient ones are those based on clustering and bag-of-words representation (Pedersen et al., 2005; Artiles et al., 2009b). Mann and Yarowsky (2003) extract biographic facts such as date or place of birth, occupation, relatives among others to help resolve ambiguous names of people. Others (Bunescu and Pasca, 2006; Cucerzan, 2007; Nguyen and Cao, 2008) work on Wikipedia articles, using infobox and link information. Pedersen et al. (2006) rely on second order co-occurrence vectors. A few others (Matthias, 2005; Wan et al., 2005; Popescu and Magnini, 2007) identify names of people, locations and organizations and use them as a source of evidence to measure the similarity between documents containing the ambiguous names. The most similar work to ours is that of Song et al. (2007) who use a topic-based modeling approach for name disambiguation. However, their method explicitly tries to model the distribution of latent topics with regard to person names and words appearing within documents whereas in our method, the latent topics represent the underlying entities (name senses) for an ambiguous name.

Unlike the previous approaches which were specifically designed and evaluated on the WebPS task or a corpus such as Wikipedia or the Web, in this paper we show a novel unsupervised topic modeling approach for name disambiguation for any corpora (i.e. Web, news, Wikipedia), languages (i.e. English, Spanish, Romanian and Bulgarian) and semantic categories (i.e. people, location and organization). The obtained results show substantial improvements over the existing approaches.

## 3 Name Disambiguation with LDA

Recently, topic modeling methods have found widespread applications in NLP for various tasks such as summarization (Daumé III and Marcu, 2006), inferring concept-attribute attachments (Reisinger and Pasca, 2009), selectional preferences (Ritter et al., 2010) and cross-document co-reference resolution (Haghighi and Klein, 2010).

Topic models such as LDA are generative models for documents and represent hidden or latent topics (where a topic is a probability distribution over words) underlying the semantic structure of documents. An important use for methods such as LDA is to infer the set of topics associated with a given document (or a collection of documents). Next, we present a novel approach for the task of name disambiguation using unsupervised topic models.

### 3.1 Method Description

Given a document corpus $D$ associated with a certain ambiguous name, our task is to group the documents into $K$ sets such that each document set corresponds to one particular entity (sense) for the ambiguous name. We first formulate the name disambiguation problem as a topic modeling task and then apply the standard LDA method to infer hidden topics (senses). Our generative story is as follows:

**for** each name sense $s_k$ where $k \in \{1, ..., K\}$ **do**
  Generate $\beta_{s_k}$ according to $Dir(\eta)$
**end for**
**for** each document $i$ in the corpus $D$ **do**
  Choose $\theta_i \sim Dir(\alpha)$
  **for** each word $w_{i,j}$ where $j \in \{1, ..., N_i\}$ **do**
    Choose a sense $z_{i,j} \sim Multinomial(\theta_i)$
    Choose a word $w_{i,j} \sim Multinomial(\beta_{z_{i,j}})$
  **end for**
**end for**

### 3.2 Inference

We perform inference on this model using collapsed Gibbs sampling, where each of the hidden sense variables $z_{i,j}$ are sampled conditioned on an assignment for all other variables, while integrating over all possible parameter settings (Griffiths and Steyvers, 2002). We use the MALLET (McCallum, 2002) implementation of LDA for our experiments. We ran LDA with different parameter settings on a held out data set and found that the following configuration resulted in the best performance. We set the hyperparameter $\eta$ to the default value of 0.01. For the name discrimination task, we have to choose from a smaller set of name senses and each document is representative of a single sense, so we use a sparse prior ($\alpha$=0.1). On the other hand, the Web People Search data is more noisy and also involves a large number of senses, so we use a higher prior ($\alpha$=50).

For the name discrimination task (Section 4.1), we are given a set of senses to choose from and hence we can use this value to fix the number of topics (senses) $K$ in LDA. However, it is possible that the number of senses may be unknown to us apriori. For example, it is difficult to identify all the senses associated with names of people on the Web. In such scenarios, we set the value of $K$ to a fixed value. For experiments on Web People Search, we set $K = 40$, which is roughly the average number of senses associated with people names on the Web. An alternative strategy is to automatically choose the number of senses based on the model that leads to the highest posterior probability (Griffiths and Steyvers, 2004). It is easy to incorporate this technique into our model, but we leave this for future work.

### 3.3 Interpreting Name Senses From Topics

As a result of training, our model outputs the topic (sense) distributions for each document in the corpus. Although the LDA model can assign multiple senses to a document, the name disambiguation task specifies that each document should be assigned only to a single name sense. Hence, for each document $i$ we assign it the most probable sense from its sense distribution. This allows us to cluster all the documents in $D$ into $K$ sets.

To evaluate our results against the gold standard

data, we further need to find a mapping between our document clusters and the true name sense labels. For each cluster $k$, we identify the true sense labels (using the gold data) for every document which was assigned to sense $k$ in our output, and pick the majority sense label $label_{k_{maj.}}$ as being representative of the entire cluster (i.e., all documents in cluster $k$ will be labeled as belonging to sense $label_{k_{maj.}}$). Finally, we evaluate our labeling against the gold data.

## 4 Experimental Evaluation

Our objective is to study LDA's performance on multiple datasets, name categories and languages. For this purpose, we evaluate our approach on two tasks: *name discrimination* and *Web People Search*, which are described in the next subsections. We use freely available data from (Pedersen et al., 2006) and (Artiles et al., 2009b), which enable us to compare performance against existing methods.

### 4.1 Name Discrimination

Pedersen et al. (2006) create ambiguous data by conflating together tuples of non-ambiguous well known names. The goal is to cluster the contexts containing the conflated names such that the original and correct names are re-discovered. This task is known as *name discrimination*.

An advantage of the name conflation process is that data can be easily created for any type of names and languages. In our study, we use the whole data set developed by Pedersen et al. (2006) for the English, Spanish, Romanian and Bulgarian languages.

Table 1 shows the conflated names and the semantic category they belong to (i.e. person, organization or location) together with the distribution of the instances for each underlying entity in the name. In total there are eight person, eight location and three organization conflated name pairs which represent a diverse set of names of politicians, countries, cities, political parties and software companies. For four conflated name pairs the data is balanced. For example, there are 3800 examples in total for the conflated name *Bill Clinton – Tony Blair* of which 1900 are for the underlying entity *Bill Clinton* and 1900 for *Tony Blair*. For the rest of the cases the data is imbalanced. For example, there are 3344 examples for the conflated name *Yaser Arafat – Bill Clinton* of which 1004 belong to *Yaser Arafat* and 2340 to *Bill Clinton*. The balanced and imbalanced data also lets us study whether LDA's performance if affected by the different sense distributions.

Next, we show in Table 2 the overall results from the disambiguation process. For each name, we first show the baseline score which is calculated as the percentage of instances belonging to the most frequent underlying entity over all instances of that conflated name pair. For example, for the *Bill Clinton – Tony Blair* conflated name pair, the baseline is 50% since both underlying entities have the same number of examples. This baseline is equivalent to a clustering method that would assign all of the contexts to exactly one cluster.

The second column corresponds to the results achieved by the second order co-occurrence clustering approach of (Pedersen et al., 2006). This approach is considered as state-of-the-art in name discrimination after numerous features like unigram, bigram, co-occurrence and multiple clustering algorithms were tested. We denote this approach in Table 2 as *Pedersen* and use it as a comparison. Note that in this experiment (Pedersen et al., 2006) predefine the exact number of clusters, therefore we also use the exact number of senses for the LDA topics. The third column shows the results obtained by our LDA approach. The final two columns represent the difference between our LDA approach and the baseline denoted as $\Delta_B$, as well as the difference between our LDA approach and those of *Pedersen* denoted as $\Delta_P$. We have highlighted in bold the improvements of LDA over these methods.

The obtained results show that for all experiments independent of whether the name sense data was balanced or imbalanced, LDA has a positive increase over the baseline. For some conflated tuples like the Spanish *NATO–ETZIN*, the improvement over the baseline is 47%. For seventeen out of the twenty name conflated pairs LDA has also improved upon *Pedersen*. The improvements range from +1.29 to +19.18.

Unfortunately, we are not deeply familiar with Romanian to provide a detailed analysis of the contexts and the errors that occurred. However, we noticed that for English, Spanish and Bulgarian often the same context containing two or three of the conflated names is used multiple times. Imagine that

| Category | Name | Distribution |
|---|---|---|
| **ENGLISH** | | |
| person/politician | Bill Cinton – Tony Blair | 1900+1900=3800 |
| person/politician | Bill Clinton – Tony Blair – Ehud Barak | 1900+1900+1900=5700 |
| organization | IBM – Microsoft | 2406+3401=5807 |
| location/country | Mexico – Uganda | 1256+1256=2512 |
| location/country&state | Mexico – India – California – Peru | 1500+1500+1500+1500=6000 |
| **SPANISH** | | |
| person/politician | Yaser Arafat – Bill Clinton | 1004+2340=3344 |
| person/politician | Juan Pablo II – Boris Yeltsin | 1447+1450=2897 |
| organization | OTAN (NATO) – EZLN | 1093+1093=2186 |
| location/city | New York – Washington | 1517+2418=3935 |
| location/city&country | New York – Brasil – Washington | 1517+1748+2418=5863 |
| **ROMANIAN** | | |
| person/politician | Traian Basescu – Adrian Nastase | 1804+1932=3736 |
| person/politician | Traian Basescu – Ion Illiescu – Adrian Nastase | 1948+1966+2301=6215 |
| organization | Romanian Democratic Party – Socialist Party | 2037+3264=5301 |
| location/city | Brasov – Bucarest | 2310+2559=4869 |
| location/country | France – USA – Romania | 1370+2396+3890=7656 |
| **BULGARIAN** | | |
| person/politician | Petar Stoyanov – Ivan Kostov – Georgi Parvanov | 318+524+811=1653 |
| person/politician | Nadejda Mihaylova – Nikolay Vasilev – Stoyan Stoyanov | 645+849+976=2470 |
| organization | Bulgarian Socialist Party – Union Democratic Forces | 2921+4680=7601 |
| location/country | France – Germany –Russia | 1726+2095+2645=6466 |
| location/city | Varna – Bulgaria | 1240+1261=2501 |

Table 1: *Data Set Characteristics of the Name Discrimination Task.*

| Name | Baseline | Pedersen | LDA | $\Delta_B$ | $\Delta_P$ |
|---|---|---|---|---|---|
| **ENGLISH** | | | | | |
| Bill Cinton – Tony Blair | 50.00% | 80.95% | 81.13% | **+31.13** | **+0.18** |
| Bill Clinton – Tony Blair – Ehud Barak | 33.33% | 47.93% | 67.19% | **+33.86** | **+19.26** |
| IBM – Microsoft | 58.57% | 63.70% | 65.44% | **+6.87** | **+1.74** |
| Mexico – Uganda | 50.00% | 59.16% | 78.34% | **+28.35** | **+19.18** |
| Mexico – India – California – Peru | 25.00% | 28.78% | 46.43% | **+21.43** | **+17.65** |
| **SPANISH** | | | | | |
| Yaser Arafat – Bill Clinton | 69.98% | 77.72% | 83.67% | **+13.69** | **+5.95** |
| Juan Pablo II – Boris Yeltsin | 50.05% | 87.75% | 52.36% | **+2.31** | -35.39 |
| OTAN (NATO) – EZLN | 50.00% | 69.81% | 96.89% | **+46.89** | **+27.08** |
| New York – Washington | 61.45% | 54.66% | 66.73% | **+5.28** | **+12.07** |
| New York – Brasil – Washington | 42.55% | 42.88% | 59.28% | **+16.73** | **+16.40** |
| **ROMANIAN** | | | | | |
| Traian Basescu – Adrian Nastase | 51.34% | 51.34% | 58.51% | **+7.17** | **+7.17** |
| Traian Basescu – Ion Illiescu – Adrian Nastase | 37.02% | 39.31% | 47.69% | **+10.67** | **+8.38** |
| Romanian Democratic Party – Socialist Party | 61.57% | 77.70% | 61.57% | 0.00 | -16.13 |
| Brasov – Bucarest | 52.56% | 63.67% | 64.96% | **+12.40** | **+1.29** |
| France – USA – Romania | 50.81% | 52.66% | 55.39% | **+4.58** | **+2.73** |
| **BULGARIAN** | | | | | |
| Petar Stoyanov – Ivan Kostov – Georgi Parvanov | 49.06% | 58.68% | 57.96% | **+8.90** | -0.72 |
| Nadejda Mihaylova – Nikolay Vasilev – Stoyan Stoyanov | 39.51% | 59.39% | 53.97% | **+14.46** | -5.42 |
| Bulgarian Socialist Party – Union Democratic Forces | 61.57% | 57.31% | 61.76% | **+0.19** | **+4.45** |
| France – Germany –Russia | 40.91% | 41.60% | 46.74% | **+5.83** | **+5.14** |
| Varna – Bulgaria | 50.42% | 50.38% | 51.78% | **+1.36** | **+1.40** |

Table 2: *Results on the Multilingual and Multi-category Name Discrimination Task.*

there is a single context in which both names *Nadejda Mihaylova* and *Stoyan Stoyanov* are mentioned. This context is used to create two name conflated examples. In the first case only the name *Nadejda Mihaylova* was hidden with the *Nadejda Mihaylova – Nikolay Vasilev – Stoyan Stoyanov* label while the name *Stoyan Stoyanov* was preserved as it is. In the second case, the name *Stoyan Stoyanov* was hidden with the label *Nadejda Mihaylova – Nikolay Vasilev – Stoyan Stoyanov* while the name *Nadejda Mihaylova* was preserved. Since the example contains two name conflations of the same context, it becomes very difficult for any algorithm to identify this phenomenon and discriminate the names correctly.

According to a study conducted by (Pedersen et al., 2006), the conflated entities in the automatically collected data sets can be ambiguous and can belong to multiple semantic categories. For example, they mention that the city *Varna* occurred in the collection as part of other named entities such as the *University of Varna, the Townhall of Varna*. Therefore, by conflating the name *Varna* in the organization named entity *University of Varna*, the context starts to deviate the meaning of *Varna* as a city into the meaning of university. Such cases transmit additional ambiguity to the conflated name pair and make the task even harder.

Finally, our current approach does not use stop-words except for English. According to Pedersen et al. (2006) the usage of stop-words is crucial for this task and leads to a substantial improvement.

### 4.2 Web People Search

Recently, Artiles et al. (2009b) introduced the *Web People Search* task (WebPS), where given the top 100 web search results produced for an ambiguous person name, the goal is to produce clusters that contain documents referring to the same individual.

We have randomly selected from the WebPS-2 test data three names from the Wikipedia, ACL'08 and Census categories. Unlike the previous data, WebPS has (1) names with higher ambiguity from 3 to 56 entities per name, (2) only person names and (3) unstructured and semi-structured texts from the Web and Wikipedia[1]. Table 3 shows the number of entities (senses) (#E) and the number of documents for each ambiguous name (#Doc).

In contrast to the previous task where the number of topics is equal to the exact number of senses, in this task the number of topics is approximate to the number of senses[2]. In our experiments we set the number of topics to 40. We embarked on this experimental set up in order to make our results comparable with the rest of the systems in WebPS. However, if we use the exact number of name senses then LDA achieves higher results.

To evaluate the performance of our approach, we use the official WebPS evaluation script. We report BCubed Precision, Recall and F-scores for our LDA approach, two baseline systems and the ECNU (Lan et al., 2009) system from the WebPS-2 challenge. We compare our results against ECNL, because they use similar word representation but instead of relying on LDA they use a clustering algorithm. We denote in Table 3 the difference between the F-score performances of LDA and the ECNU system as $\Delta_{F_1}$. We highlight the differences in bold.

Since a name disambiguation system must have good precision and recall results, we decided to compare our results against two baselines which represent the extreme case of a system that reaches 100% precision (called ONE-IN-ONE) or a system that reaches 100% recall (called ALL-IN-ONE). Practically ONE-IN-ONE corresponds to assigning each document to a different cluster (individual sense), while the ALL-IN-ONE baseline groups together all web pages into a single cluster corresponding to one name sense (the majority sense). A more detailed explanation about the evaluation measures and the intuition behind them can be found in (Artiles et al., 2007) and (Artiles et al., 2009b).

For six out of the nine names, LDA outperformed the two baselines and the ECNU system with 5 to 41% on F-score. Precision and recall scores for LDA are comparable except for *Tom Linton* and *Helen Thomas* where precision is much higher. The decrease in performance is due to the low number of senses (entities associated with a name) and the fact that LDA was tuned to produce 40 topics. To overcome this limitation, in the future we plan to work on estimating the number of topics automatically.

[1] We clean all *html* tags and remove stopwords.

[2] Researchers use from 15 to 50 number of clusters/senses.

| Name | #E | #Doc | ONE-IN-ONE | | | ALL-IN-ONE | | | ECNU | | | LDA | | | $\Delta_{F_1}$ |
|---|---|---|---|---|---|---|---|---|---|---|---|---|---|---|---|
| | | | BEP | BER | $F_1$ | BEP | BER | $F_1$ | BEP | BER | $F_1$ | BEP | BER | $F_1$ | |
| **Wikipedia Names** | | | | | | | | | | | | | | | |
| Louis Lowe | 24 | 100 | 1.00 | .32 | .48 | .23 | 1.00 | .37 | .39 | .78 | .52 | .63 | .52 | .57 | **+5** |
| Mike Robertson | 39 | 123 | 1.00 | .44 | .61 | .11 | 1.00 | .19 | .14 | .96 | .25 | .59 | .62 | .61 | **+36** |
| Tom Linton | 10 | 135 | 1.00 | .11 | .19 | .54 | 1.00 | .70 | .68 | .48 | .56 | .89 | .22 | .35 | -21 |
| **ACL '08 Names** | | | | | | | | | | | | | | | |
| Benjamin Snyder | 28 | 95 | 1.00 | .51 | .67 | .08 | 1.00 | .15 | .16 | .79 | .27 | .59 | .81 | .68 | **+41** |
| Emily Bender | 19 | 120 | 1.00 | .21 | .35 | .24 | 1.00 | .39 | .45 | .60 | .51 | .78 | .42 | .55 | **+4** |
| Hao Zhang | 24 | 100 | 1.00 | .26 | .41 | .21 | 1.00 | .35 | .45 | .78 | .57 | .72 | .36 | .48 | -9 |
| **Census Names** | | | | | | | | | | | | | | | |
| Helen Thomas | 3 | 127 | 1.00 | .03 | .06 | .96 | 1.00 | .98 | .96 | .24 | .39 | .97 | .08 | .15 | -24 |
| Jonathan Shaw | 26 | 126 | 1.00 | .32 | .49 | .10 | 1.00 | .18 | .18 | .60 | .34 | .66 | .51 | .58 | **+24** |
| Susan Jones | 56 | 110 | 1.00 | .70 | .82 | .03 | 1.00 | .06 | .13 | .81 | .22 | .51 | .79 | .62 | **+40** |

Table 3: *Results for Web People Search-2.*

## 5 Conclusion

We have shown how ambiguity in names can be modeled and resolved using a generative probabilistic model. Our LDA approach learns a distribution over topics which correspond to entities (senses) associated with an ambiguous name. We evaluate our novel approach on two tasks: *name discrimination* and *Web People Search*. We conduct a detailed evaluation on (1) Web, Wikipedia and news documents; (2) English, Spanish, Romanian and Bulgarian languages; (3) people, location and organization names. Our method achieves consistent performance and substantial improvements over baseline and existing state-of-the-art clustering methods.

In the future, we would like to model the biographical fact extraction approach of (Mann and Yarowsky, 2003) in our LDA model. We plan to estimate the number of topics automatically from the distributions. We want to explore variants of our current model. For example, currently all words are generated by multiple topics (senses), but ideally we want them to be generated by a single topic. Finally, we want to impose additional constraints within the topic models using hierarchical topic models.


## Acknowledgments

We acknowledge the support of DARPA contract FA8750-09-C-3705 and NSF grant IIS-0429360.


## References


Javier Artiles, Julio Gonzalo, and Satoshi Sekine. 2007. The semeval-2007 weps evaluation: Establishing a benchmark for the web people search task. In *Proceedings of the Fourth International Workshop on Semantic Evaluations (SemEval-2007*, pages 64–69.

Javier Artiles, Enrique Amigó, and Julio Gonzalo. 2009a. The role of named entities in Web People Search. In *Proceedings of the 2009 Conference on Empirical Methods in Natural Language Processing*, pages 534–542.

Javier Artiles, Julio Gonzalo, and Satoshi Sekine. 2009b. WePS 2 evaluation campaign: overview of the web people search clustering task. In *2nd Web People Search Evaluation Workshop (WePS 2009), 18th WWW Conference*.

Javier Artiles, Andrew Borthwick, Julio Gonzalo, Satoshi Sekine, and Enrique Amigó. 2010. WePS-3 evaluation campaign: Overview of the web people search clustering and attribute extraction ta. In *Conference on Multilingual and Multimodal Information Access Evaluation (CLEF)*.

Amit Bagga and Breck Baldwin. 1998. Entity-based cross-document coreferencing using the vector space model. In *Proceedings of the 36th Annual Meeting of the Association for Computational Linguistics and 17th International Conference on Computational Linguistics - Volume 1*, ACL '98, pages 79–85.

David M. Blei, Andrew Y. Ng, and Michael I. Jordan. 2003. Latent dirichlet allocation. *J. Mach. Learn. Res.*, 3:993–1022, March.

Razvan C. Bunescu and Marius Pasca. 2006. Using encyclopedic knowledge for named entity disambiguation. In *EACL 2006, 11st Conference of the European Chapter of the Association for Computational Linguistics, Proceedings of the Conference*.

Ying Chen and James H. Martin. 2007. Cu-comsem: Exploring rich features for unsupervised web personal name disambiguation. In *Proceedings of the Fourth International Workshop on Semantic Evaluations (SemEval-2007)*, pages 125–128, June.

Ying Chen, Sophia Yat Mei Lee, and Chu-Ren Huang. 2009. Polyuhk: A robust information extraction system for web personal names. In *2nd Web People Search Evaluation Workshop (WePS 2009), 18th WWW Conference.*

Silviu Cucerzan. 2007. Large-scale named entity disambiguation based on wikipedia data. In *EMNLP-CoNLL 2007, Proceedings of the 2007 Joint Conference on Empirical Methods in Natural Language Processing and Computational Natural Language Learning*, pages 708–716.

Hal Daumé III and Daniel Marcu. 2006. Bayesian query-focused summarization. In *Proceedings of the 21st International Conference on Computational Linguistics and 44th Annual Meeting of the Association for Computational Linguistics*, pages 305–312, Sydney, Australia, July. Association for Computational Linguistics.

Filip Ginter, Jorma Boberg, Jouni Järvinen, and Tapio Salakoski. 2004. New techniques for disambiguation in natural language and their application to biological text. *J. Mach. Learn. Res.*, 5:605–621, December.

Thomas L Griffiths and Mark Steyvers. 2002. A probabilistic approach to semantic representation. In *Proceedings of the Twenty-Fourth Annual Conference of Cognitive Science Society.*

Thomas L Griffiths and Mark Steyvers. 2004. Finding scientific topics. *Proceedings of the National Academy of Sciences of the United States of America*, 101 Suppl 1(Suppl 1):5228–5235.

Aria Haghighi and Dan Klein. 2010. Coreference resolution in a modular, entity-centered model. In *Human Language Technologies: The 2010 Annual Conference of the North American Chapter of the Association for Computational Linguistics*, pages 385–393.

Zellig Harris. 1954. Distributional structure. 10(23):146–162.

Vasileios Hatzivassiloglou, Pablo A. Duboue, and Andrey Rzhetsky. 2001. Disambiguating proteins, genes, and rna in text: A machine learning approach. In *Proceedings of the 9th International Conference on Intelligent Systems for Molecular Biology.*

Man Lan, Yu Zhe Zhang, Yue Lu, Jian Su, and Chew Lim Tan. 2009. Which who are they? people attribute extraction and disambiguation in web search results. In *2nd Web People Search Evaluation Workshop (WePS 2009), 18th WWW Conference.*

Gideon S. Mann and David Yarowsky. 2003. Unsupervised personal name disambiguation. In *Proceedings of the seventh conference on Natural language learning at HLT-NAACL 2003 - Volume 4*, CONLL '03, pages 33–40.

Matthias Blume Matthias. 2005. Automatic entity disambiguation: Benefits to ner, relation extraction, link analysis, and inference. In *International Conference on Intelligence Analysis.*

Andrew Kachites McCallum. 2002. Mallet: A machine learning for language toolkit. http://www.cs.umass.edu/ mccallum/mallet.

Hien T. Nguyen and Tru H. Cao. 2008. Named entity disambiguation: A hybrid statistical and rule-based incremental approach. In *Proceedings of the 3rd Asian Semantic Web Conference on The Semantic Web*, ASWC '08, pages 420–433.

Ted Pedersen and Anagha Kulkarni. 2007. Unsupervised discrimination of person names in web contexts. In *Computational Linguistics and Intelligent Text Processing, 8th International Conference, CICLing 2007*, pages 299–310.

Ted Pedersen, Amruta Purandare, and Anagha Kulkarni. 2005. Name discrimination by clustering similar contexts. In *Computational Linguistics and Intelligent Text Processing, 6th International Conference, CICLing 2005*, pages 226–237.

Ted Pedersen, Anagha Kulkarni, Roxana Angheluta, Zornitsa Kozareva, and Thamar Solorio. 2006. An unsupervised language independent method of name discrimination using second order co-occurrence features. In *Computational Linguistics and Intelligent Text Processing, 7th International Conference, CICLing 2006*, pages 208–222.

Octavian Popescu and Bernardo Magnini. 2007. Irst-bp: Web people search using name entities. In *Proceedings of the Fourth International Workshop on Semantic Evaluations (SemEval-2007*, pages 195–198. Association for Computational Linguistics.

Joseph Reisinger and Marius Pasca. 2009. Latent variable models of concept-attribute attachment. In *Proceedings of the Joint Conference of the 47th Annual Meeting of the ACL and the 4th International Joint Conference on Natural Language Processing of the AFNLP*, pages 620–628. Association for Computational Linguistics, August.

Alan Ritter, Mausam, and Oren Etzioni. 2010. A latent dirichlet allocation method for selectional preferences. In *Proceedings of the 48th Annual Meeting of the Association for Computational Linguistics*, pages 424–434. Association for Computational Linguistics, July.

Yang Song, Jian Huang, Isaac G. Councill, Jia Li, and C. Lee Giles. 2007. Efficient topic-based unsupervised name disambiguation. In *Proceedings of the 7th ACM/IEEE-CS Joint Conference on Digital libraries*, pages 342–351.

Xiaojun Wan, Jianfeng Gao, Mu Li, and Binggong Ding. 2005. Person resolution in person search results: Webhawk. In *Proceedings of the 14th ACM international conference on Information and knowledge management*, CIKM '05, pages 163–170.

# Measuring the Impact of Sense Similarity on Word Sense Induction

**David Jurgens**[1,2]
[1]HRL Laboratories, LLC
Malibu, California, USA
jurgens@cs.ucla.edu

**Keith Stevens**[2]
[2]University of California, Los Angeles
Los Angeles, California, USA
kstevens@cs.ucla.edu

## Abstract

Word Sense Induction (WSI) is an unsupervised learning approach to discovering the different senses of a word from its contextual uses. A core challenge to WSI approaches is distinguishing between related and possibly similar senses of a word. Current WSI evaluation techniques have yet to analyze the specific impact of similarity on accuracy. Therefore, we present a new WSI evaluation that quantifies the relationship between the relatedness of a word's senses and the ability of a WSI algorithm to distinguish between them. Furthermore, we perform an analysis on sense confusions in SemEval-2 WSI task according to sense similarity. Both analyses for a representative selection of clustering-based WSI approaches reveals that performance is most sensitive to the clustering algorithm and not the lexical features used.

## 1 Introduction

Many words in a language have several distinct meanings. For example, "earth" may refer to the planet Earth, dirt, or solid ground, depending on the context. The goal of Word Sense Induction (WSI) is to automatically discover the different senses by examining how a word is used. This unsupervised discovery process produces a sense inventory where the number of senses is corpus-driven and where senses may reflect additional usages not present in a predefined sense inventory, such as those for medicine or law (Dorow and Widdows, 2003). Furthermore, these discovered senses can be used to automatically expand lexical resources such as WordNet or FrameNet (Klapaftis and Manandhar, 2010).

Discovering the multiple senses is frequently confounded by the relationships between a word's senses. While homonyms such as "bass" or "bank" have unrelated senses, many polysemous words have interrelated senses, with lexicographers often in disagreement for the number of fine-grained senses (Palmer et al., 2007). For example, the most frequent four senses for "law" according to WordNet, shown in Table 1, are similar in several aspects and could be ascribed interchangeably in some contexts. The difficulty of automatically distinguishing two senses is proportional to their similarity because of the increasing likelihood of the two senses sharing similar contexts.

While the issue distinguishing between related senses is a recognized issue for Word Sense Disambiguation (Chugur et al., 2002; McCarthy, 2006), which uses supervised training to learn sense distinctions, measuring the impact of sense relatedness on the harder problem of WSI remains unaddressed. The recent SemEval WSI tasks (Agirre and Soroa, 2007; Manandhar and Klapaftis, 2009) have provided a standard framework for evaluating WSI systems, with a controlled training corpus designed to limit sense ambiguity in the example contexts. However, given the potential relatedness of a word's senses, we view it necessary to consider how WSI methods perform relative to the degree of contextual ambiguity. Our goal is therefore to quantify the similarity at which a WSI approach is unable to distinguish between two senses, which reflects the sense granularity at which the approach operates.

We propose two new evaluations. The first, described in Section 4, uses a similarity-based pseudoword discrimination task to measure the discrimination capability for related senses along a graded scale of similarity. As a second evaluation, in

*Proceedings of EMNLP 2011, Conference on Empirical Methods in Natural Language Processing*, pages 113–123,
Edinburgh, Scotland, UK, July 27–31, 2011. 

| | |
|---|---|
| 1 | the collection of rules imposed by authority |
| 2 | legal document setting forth rules governing a particular kind of activity |
| 3 | a rule or body of rules of conduct inherent in human nature and essential to or binding upon human society |
| 4 | a generalization that describes recurring facts or events in nature |

Table 1: Definitions for the top four senses of "law" according to WordNet

Section 5 we perform an error analysis using the SemEval-2010 WSI task, examining sense confusion relative to the sense similarities. For both evaluations, we examine twenty different WSI clustering-based models through combining five feature types and four clustering algorithms. These models were selected to be representative of a wide class of existing algorithms as a way of influence future algorithmic directions based on the current model's performance.

## 2 Clustering Contexts to Discover Senses

Frequently, WSI is treated as an unsupervised clustering problem: The contexts in which a word appears are clustered in order to discover its senses (Navigli, 2009). We selected four diverse clustering algorithms for evaluation based on three criteria: (1) the ability to automatically determine the final number of clusters given an upper bound or a set of parameters, (2) an efficient run time, and (3) high quality results in either WSI or other fields related to text analysis. The first criteria is essential for WSI; the final number of senses must be derived without supervision in order to reflect the true number of senses present in the corpus.

**K-Means** K-Means builds clusters based on the similarity between two data points. Clusters grow by assigning data points to the cluster with the most similar centroid. After every data point is assigned, each cluster's centroid is recalculated to be the average of all the data points assigned to the cluster. This process repeats until the centroids converge to a fixed point. We choose initial seeds at random and use the H2 criterion function (Zhao and Karypis, 2001). Although K-Means is efficient and widely used, it requires the number of clusters to be specified a priori. Therefore, we follow the WSI model of Pedersen and Kulkarni (2006) and use the Gap Statistic (Tibshirani et al., 2000) to automatically determine the number of clusters.

The Gap Statistic runs K-Means repeatedly with different values of $K$, ranging from 1 to some sensible maximum. The Gap Statistic first induces a data model from the feature distributions of the initial dataset and then for each $K$, creates a set of artificial datasets by sampling from the derived model. $K$ is increased until the "gap", i.e. the distance between the objective function of the original dataset and the average objective function of the artificial datasets, is larger then the gap for the previous $K$ value. We calculate the gap using 10 artificial data sets sampled from the model.

**Spectral Clustering** Spectral Clustering interprets a dataset's elements as vertices in graph with edges based on their similarity (Ng et al., 2001). Clusters are found by identifying the graph partition that produces the minimum conductance between every partition. This can be thought of as trying to find small islands that are connected by as few bridges as possible. We refer the reader to (von Luxburg, 2007) for further technical details. To our knowledge, only He et al. (2010) have applied spectral clustering to WSI, which was performed on a Chinese dataset. However, the algorithm used by He et al. requires the number of clusters to be specified.

We instead use a hybrid spectral clustering algorithm, first applied to information retrieval (Cheng et al., 2006), that automatically selects the number of clusters. This algorithm recursively partitions a dataset in half by finding the cut that produces the minimum conductance, which builds a tree of partitions. This split is done until either every data point is in its own partition or a maximum number of partitions is found. Partitions are then dynamically merged, starting at leaf partitions, based on a clustering criteria. We use the relaxed correlation criteria (Cheng et al., 2006), which tries to maximize both inter cluster similarity and intra cluster dissimilarity. The final cluttering generated is then the best tree-respecting partition of the original data set.

**Clustering By Committee** Pantel and Lin (2002) found that K-Means clustering folded all features found in a cluster into the centroid, many of which are not useful for identifying the desired word sense.

To overcome this, they proposed a novel clustering algorithm for WSI, Clustering by Committee (CBC), which includes only the most distinguishing features for a cluster into the centroid.

For each context, an initial set of "committees" is formed by clustering the most similar contexts to each context, with the resulting committees ranked to prefer larger, highly similar clusters. The final set of committees (sense clusters) are selected by recursively identifying the highest ranking committees that are dissimilar to each other and then repeating the process for any contexts not similar to existing committees. In essence, CBC aims to find the clusters that are similar to the largest set of contexts, while keeping clusters dissimilar from each other. CBC's recursion ensures that contexts dissimilar to the large committees are still grouped into their own smaller committees, which enables the discovery of infrequent senses with distinct contexts. We use a hard sense assignment for each context, i.e., a context is labeled with only one sense according to the most similar cluster.

**Streaming K-Means** As WSI moves into inducing senses from Web-scale amounts of data, existing clustering algorithms that keep all contexts in memory become impractical. Jurgens and Stevens (2010a) proposed an on-line hybrid clustering solution using on-line K-Means and Hierarchical Agglomerative Clustering, which automatically decided the number of clusters without retaining all the contexts. To the best of our knowledge, theirs is the only work using an on-line approach. We extend this work by applying a more theoretically sound online K-Means algorithm, called Streaming K-Means (Braverman et al., 2011), to WSI. We use Streaming K-Means to conduct a direct algorithmic comparison with K-Means in the hopes that online approaches can be made just as effective as off-line approaches.

Streaming K-Means processes each data point only once, thus reducing the memory overhead dramatically. Instead of recording each data point, it immediately assigns each data point to a cluster and maintains $K \cdot C$ clusters. $C$ varies as the algorithm runs, initially being set to 0. When assigning a data point, it is only assigned to an existing cluster when their similar is above some threshold, otherwise the data point becomes the centroid of a new cluster. Once $C$ reaches a threshold, based on an estimate of the number of data points, or the overall K-Means clustering cost reaches some limit, the centroids are treated as new data points and re-clustered, with the goal of merging some centroids. We follow (Jurgens and Stevens, 2010a) and cluster the final centroids with Hierarchical Agglomerative Clustering, with the average link criteria as suggested by (Pedersen and Bruce, 1997).

## 3 Modeling Context

For each clustering algorithm, we consider five context models that represent the types of lexical features used by the majority of WSI approaches.

**Co-Occurrence** Contexts formed from word co-occurrence are the most common in WSI algorithms. For each occurrence of a word, those words within a certain range are counted as features. Prior work has used a variety of context sizes, e.g. words in the same sentence (Bordag, 2006), in nearby lexical positions (Gauch and Futrelle, 1993), or within a paragraph-sized context window (Pedersen, 2010).

We consider two co-occurrence context models: a 5-word and a 25-word window. We note that in co-occurrence-based word space algorithms, smaller context sizes have shown to better capture paradagmatic similarity, while larger sizes capture semantic associativity (Peirsman et al., 2008; Utsumi, 2010).

**Dependency-Relations** Dependency parsing creates a syntax tree where words are directly linked according to their relation. These links refine co-occurrence based contexts by utilizing syntactic indications of how words are related. Dependency parsed features have proven highly effective for word representations in many NLP applications, e.g., (Padó and Lapata, 2007; Baroni et al., 2010). We follow Pantel and Lin (2002) and Dorow and Widdows (2003) using the sentence as contexts and all words with a dependency path of length 3 or less, with the last word and its relation as a feature. We note that recently Kern et al. (2010) achieved good WSI performance with only a small, manually-tuned subset of all relations as context.

**Word Ordering** Word ordering can provide a mild form of syntactic information (Jones et al., 2006; Sahlgren et al., 2008). While other syntactic features may provide significantly more information, word ordering is efficient to compute and provides an alternative source of syntactic information for knowledge-lean systems or for languages where NLP tools are not readily available.

Because we treat word ordering as a syntactic feature, we limit the context to words occurring in the same sentence. A feature is the combination of a co-occurring word and its relative position, i.e. the same word in different positions is treated as two separate features.

**Parts of Speech** Part of speech tagging can provide a preliminary coarse-grained sense disambiguation of a word's contextual features, where a word may have as many senses as it does parts of speech. For example, consider an occurrence of "house" in the context of "address" as a noun and verb: "I went to his house address," and "I heard the legislator address the house." Labeling "address" with its part of speech provides for more semantic information on its meaning, which further constrains the sense of "house." Prior work (Pedersen and Bruce, 1997) has suggested that this information can improve performance, but to our knowledge, the impact of POS features has not been evaluated in isolation.

Each context is formed from the containing sentence; a feature is a combination of each word and its part of speech, e.g., "board-NOUN" is distinct from "board-VERB."

## 4 WSI Performance on Related Senses

The proposed methodology measures the ability of a WSI approach to distinguish between related senses. However, generating a large corpus with manually labeled sense assignments and sense similarity judgements is prohibitively expensive. Therefore, we employ a pseudo-word discrimination task where a base word and a second word, its *confounder*, are replaced throughout the corpus with a pseudo-word. The objective is then to determine which of the words was originally present given the context of an occurrence of the pseudo-word. Due to not requiring manual annotation, this type of task was initially proposed as a substitute for word sense disambiguation (Schütze, 1992; Gale et al., 1992) and for selectional preferences (Clark and Weir, 2002).

Following the suggestions of Chambers and Jurafsky (2010) on designing pseudo-words, pseudo-words were created from words with the same part of speech and equal frequency in the training corpus. We selected nouns occurring more than 5,000 times in a 2009 Wikipedia snapshot and then drew 5,000 contexts for each. The snapshot was tagged with the Stanford Part of Speech Tagger (Toutanova et al., 2003) and parsed with the Malt Parser (Nivre et al., 2006).

| festival | | laws | |
|---|---|---|---|
| offices | 0.13660 | interests | 0.18289 |
| play | 0.13751 | politics | 0.20440 |
| convention | 0.20296 | governments | 0.29125 |
| tournament | 0.29007 | regulations | 0.40761 |
| concerts | 0.48348 | legislation | 0.56112 |

Table 2: Example confounders for "festival" and "laws" and their similarities

To evaluate the impact of sense similarity, pseudo-words were created from word pairs with a broad range of lexical similarities. We selected lexical similarity as an approximation of sense similarity in order to model the hypothesis that similar senses may appear in similar contexts. Similarity scores were calculated using cosine similarity on contextual distributions built from a sliding $\pm 2$ word window over the Wikipedia corpus. Table 2 highlights several example confounders and their similarities with the base term. In total, we generated 5000 term-confounder pairs from 98 base terms, with a mean of 51 confounders per term.

All clustering parameters were chosen using the default values provided in the original papers. K-means and Streaming K-Means were both set with a maximum of 15 clusters, with the final number of clusters being determined by the data itself.

### 4.1 Evaluation

The pseudo-word's senses are induced from a training segment using each feature and clustering combination. Given that both words making up the pseudo-word may be polysemous, more than two senses may be induced. Each sense cluster is labeled according to which of the original words was present in the majority of its contexts. For testing, each instance of the pseudo-word in a previously unseen context is assigned the label of the cluster

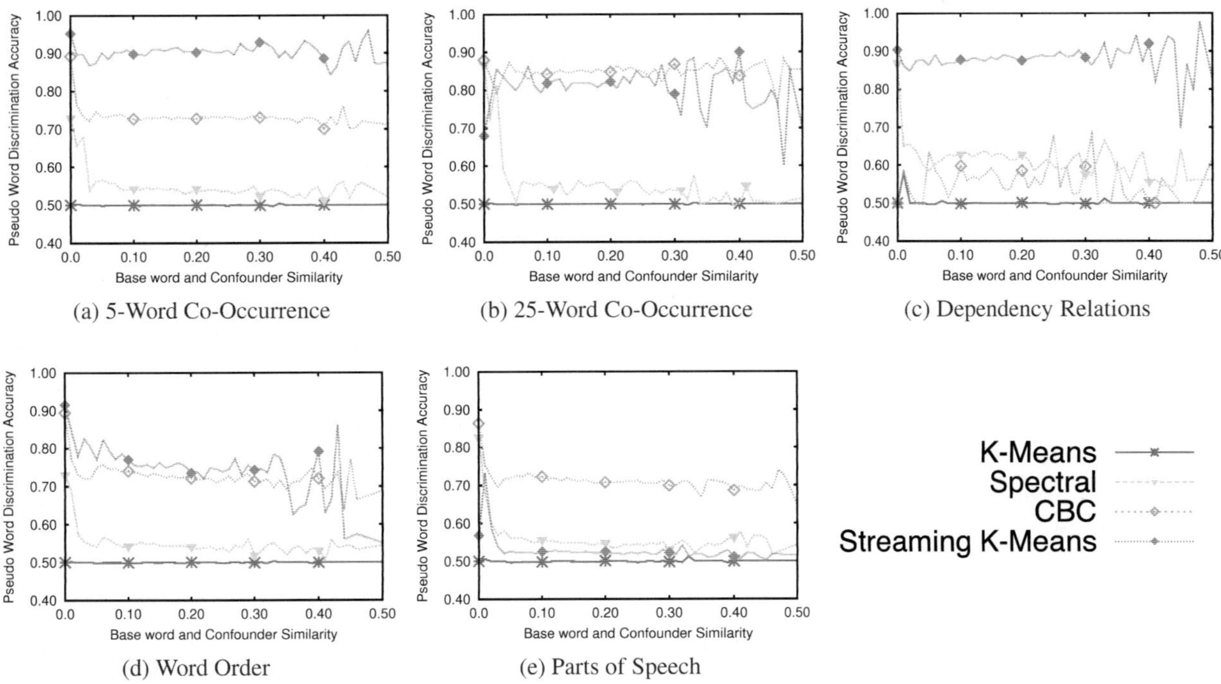


Figure 1: Pseudo-word discrimination performance

to which it is most similar. We perform five-fold cross-validation, using 4,000 contexts for training and 1,000 contexts for testing. Discrimination accuracy is reported as the average of all five runs. Since an equal number of contexts are used for each term, the base line accuracy of a most frequent sense model is 50% for each pseudo-word.

### 4.2 Results and Discussion

Figure 1 shows the discrimination accuracy relative to the similarity of a base pair and confounder, for each feature and clustering algorithm combination. Similarity values were binned at the 0.01 level with a mean of 39.0 scores per bin (median=11). Because most word pairs are not related, the distribution of similarity values is biased towards lower values. Therefore, we omit similarity ranges above 0.5, as too few confounders occurred in that range to draw reliable conclusions. The standard error (not shown) is $< 1$ for all measurements.

The general trends suggests that the clustering algorithm impacts the sense discriminatory ability far more than the lexical feature choice. Furthermore, sense similarity affects most clustering algorithms, with most systems seeing a noticeable performance drop when pseudo-word similarity is increased just beyond 0. Performance at high similarity becomes more variable for all algorithms and features.

For each clustering algorithm, we see dramatically different trends. Streaming K-Means performs well with co-occurrence based features and it does poorly when either contexts have too many features, as in the 25 Window Co-Occurrence feature space, or the feature space overall is too sparse, as in the Parts of Speech and Ordering feature spaces.

K-Means with the gap statistic converges to the most frequent sense baseline for nearly every confounder pair. We note that this behavior significantly differs from that seen in (Pedersen and Kulkarni, 2006), which clustered second-order co-occurrence vectors rather than the first-order features that we use. Our analysis showed that the H2 criterion was responsible for this behavior. A subsequent analysis revealed that K-Means still converged to MFS for the E1, E2, I1, and I2 criterion functions (Zhao and Karypis, 2001) as well as when the number of artificial datasets was increased up to 100. However, additional tests using the same features on the SemEval-1 WSI task did not converge to MFS. Further investigation is needed to identify the cause of convergence and what types of data are appropriate the Gap Statistic.

Clustering by Committee performs well on most models, but significantly worse on dependency relation features. A subsequent analysis showed that CBC generates significantly more clusters than all other models. For the POS, 5 word window, and 25 window Co-Occurrence feature spaces, CBC generated between 205 and 247 clusters on average, per word. With the order feature space, CBC generated 1087 clusters per word. However, when paired with dependency relation features, the number of clusters drops to only 78 per word.

Spectral Clustering is most affected by sense similarity, performing competitively for unrelated senses but dropping significantly when words become even slightly similar. This performance drop is seen across all features. Performance is therefore low, with the exception of dependency relations.

Overall, these results suggest that sense relatedness is a important factor in WSI performance and its impact should be considered in future WSI evaluations. A potential next step is to vary the proportion of contexts from the confounder. The current method intentionally uses a uniform distribution to avoid potential bias; however, word sense distributions are rarely equal, and a varied distribution would more closely model real world distributions. Similarly, the current method tested only two senses, whereas an n-way disambiguation between multiple confounders should also provide further insight into a WSI approach's discriminatory abilities.

## 5 Sense Confusion in SemEval-2 Task 14

As a second experiment, we analyze incorrect sense assignments on SemEval-2 Task 14 (Manandhar et al., 2010) to measure whether sense-relatedness biases which sense was incorrectly selected. For WSI systems, a similarity bias would indicate that similar senses are more likely to be incorrectly identified as a single sense.

We summarize Task 14 as follows. Systems are provided with an unlabeled training corpus consisting of 879,807 multi-sentence contexts for 100 polysemous words, comprised of 50 nouns and 50 verbs. Systems induce sense representations for target words from the training corpus and then use those representations to label the senses of the target words in unseen contexts from a test corpus.

The induced senses are then evaluated against the gold standard labels OntoNotes (Hovy et al., 2006) senses labels for the test corpus. For our evaluation, we use both the two contrasting unsupervised measures, the paired FScore (Artiles et al., 2009) and the V-Measure (Rosenberg and Hirschberg, 2007), and a supervised measure. For each metric, we use the evaluation framework provided by the organizers of SemEval-2 Task 14.[1]

The V-Measure rates the homogeneity and completeness of a clustering solution. Solutions that have word clusters formed from one gold-standard sense are homogeneous; completeness measures the degree to which a gold-standard sense's instances are assigned to a single cluster. The paired FScore measures two types of overlap of a solution and the gold standard in cluster assignments for all in pairwise combination of instances. This score tends to penalize solutions with many small clusters and highly heterogeneous clusters (Manandhar and Klapaftis, 2009).

The supervised evaluation measures the recall when building a Word Sense Disambiguation classifier from the induced senses. The WSI system labels the entire corpus, which is then divided into training and test portions. The sense labels in the training portion are used to construct a mapping from induced senses to the gold standard OntoNotes labels. This mapping is then evaluated for the induced labels in the test. We report the scores for the 80% training and 20% testing scenario.

### 5.1 Evaluation

We expect that if sense similarity is a factor in sense confusion, the probability of confusion will increase with sense similarity. Therefore, we measure the probability of labeling an instance with the incorrect OntoNotes sense relative to the sense similarity with the gold standard sense.

In order to calculate the incorrect assignments, the induced senses must be mapped to OntoNotes senses. Each induced sense, $s_i$, is mapped to the OntoNotes sense that occurs most frequently among the instances in the test corpus that are assigned induced sense $s_i$. We note that this labeling process is only an approximate solution to assigning gold standard labels to induced senses. A more robust

[1] http://www.cs.york.ac.uk/semeval2010_WSI/

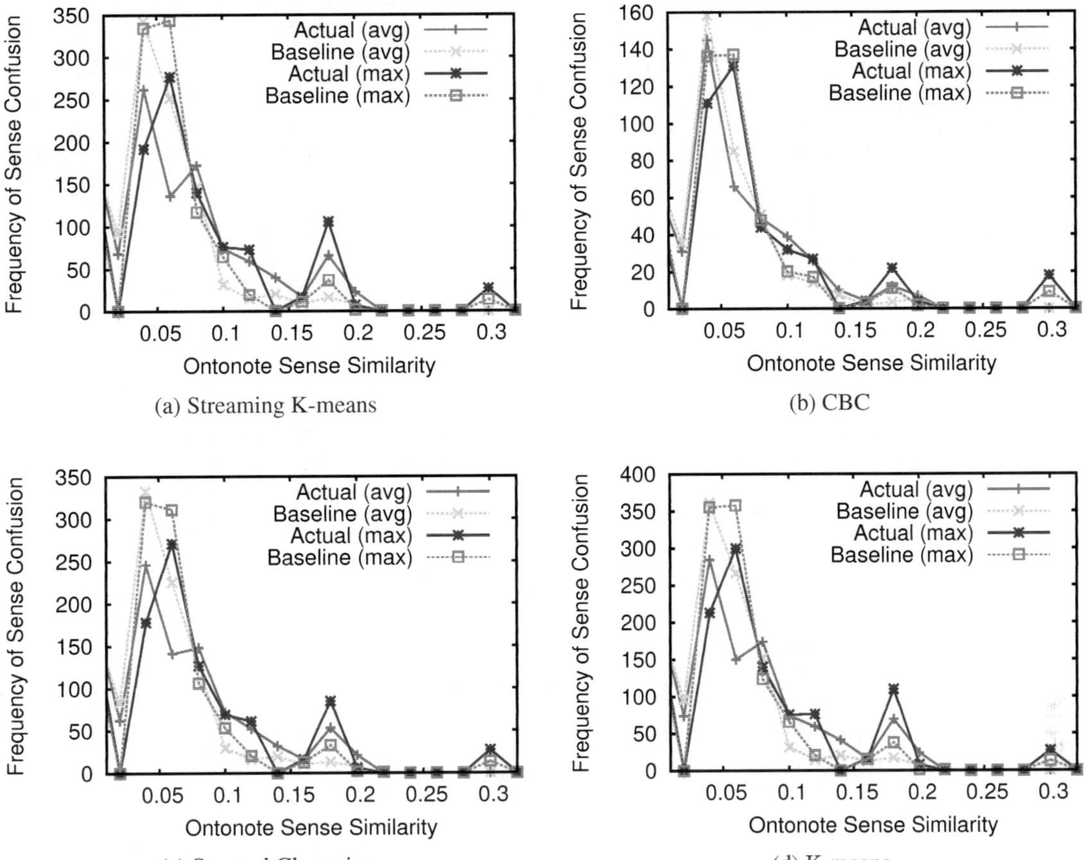


(a) Streaming K-means (b) CBC

(c) Spectral Clustering (d) K-means

Figure 2: The error frequency distributions for confusing the correct sense with another sense of the given similarity when using a 5-word co-occurrence window as context. Dashed lines indicate the null models.

labeling could take into account the distribution of gold standard senses labels in the corpus from which the senses are induced; however, such labels are not available in the Task 14 training corpus.

For each incorrect sense assignment, we measure the similarity of the confused sense to the correct sense. To our knowledge, no work has been done on calculating sense similarity within the OntoNotes sense hierarchy.[2] Therefore, we approximate OntoNotes sense similarity by using sense similarity in the WordNet ontology, on which has many similarity measures have been defined. Following Budanitsky and Hirst (2006), we estimate the WordNet sense similarity using the method proposed by Jiang and Conrath (1997).

Each OntoNotes sense $s^i$ is mapped to a set of WordNet 3.0 senses $S^i = \{wn_1, \ldots, wn_n\}$ using the sense mapping provided by the CoNLL shared task.[3] The sense similarity for two OntoNotes senses is computed using one of two methods:

$$sim = \frac{1}{|S^1||S^2|} \sum_{wn^i \in S^1, wn^j \in S^2} JCN(wn^i, wn^j), \quad (1)$$

or

$$sim = \operatorname*{argmax}_{wn^i \in S^1, wn^j \in S^2} JCN(wn^i, wn^j), \quad (2)$$

where $JCN$ indicates the Jiang-Conrath similarity of two WordNet senses, calculated using WordNet::Similarity (Pedersen et al., 2004). Eq. 1 computes similarity as the average similarity of all pairwise WordNet sense combinations, while Eq. 2 uses the highest similarity. The resulting OntoNote sense similarities range from 0 to 1, with 1 being maximally similar. We excluded 10 words from the test

[2] We suspect that this is in part because a word's OntoNotes senses have been designed to minimize sense confusion.

[3] http://conll.bbn.com/index.php/data.html

| Context Feature | Clustering | V-Measure | F-Score | Recall | # Clusters | Purity | GoF p-Value |
|---|---|---|---|---|---|---|---|
| 5-Word Co-Occurrence | Streaming | 6.7 | 55.5 | 54.8 | 4.74 | 0.103 | p < 2.07e-37 |
| | Spectral | 10.8 | 39.2 | 54.3 | 8.41 | 0.194 | p < 1.11e-25 |
| | CBC | 23.9 | 8.2 | 39.5 | 39.7 | 0.665 | p < 0.916 |
| | K-Means | 2.5 | **61.8** | **55.6** | 1.68 | 0.020 | p < 1.20e-37 |
| 25-Word Co-Occurrence | Streaming | 2.6 | 61.7 | 55.5 | 1.7 | 0.020 | p < 1.20e-37 |
| | Spectral | 5.0 | 48.6 | 55.9 | 3.3 | 0.083 | p < 4.36e-32 |
| | CBC | 21.3 | 11.6 | 45.0 | 32.2 | 0.561 | p < 0.011 |
| | K-Means | 2.5 | **61.8** | **55.6** | 1.68 | 0.020 | p < 1.20e-37 |
| Dependency Relations | Streaming | 3.0 | 61.5 | **55.6** | 1.9 | 0.022 | p < 7.33e-38 |
| | Spectral | 8.5 | 46.8 | 55.3 | 5.9 | 0.134 | p < 5.45e-14 |
| | CBC | 12.9 | 31.3 | 52.4 | 11.4 | 0.259 | p < 4.07e-12 |
| | K-Means | 2.5 | **61.8** | **55.6** | 1.6 | 0.020 | p < 1.20e-37 |
| Word Order | Streaming | 10.8 | 43.1 | 54.2 | 10.8 | 0.300 | p < 4.46e-24 |
| | Spectral | 12.2 | 32.4 | 53.7 | 10.0 | 0.26 | p < 3.27e-20 |
| | CBC | **27.2** | 11.8 | 30.3 | 54.9 | **0.857** | p < 0.999 |
| | K-Means | 2.5 | **61.8** | **55.6** | 1.6 | 0.020 | p < 1.20e-37 |
| Parts of Speech | Streaming | 6.6 | 53.0 | 54.5 | 4.7 | 0.117 | p < 1.06e-39 |
| | Spectral | 10.9 | 39.4 | 53.7 | 8.3 | 0.201 | p < 2.38e-13 |
| | CBC | 23.8 | 08.0 | 40.1 | 39.7 | 0.678 | p < 1.04e-2 |
| | K-Means | 2.5 | **61.8** | **55.6** | 1.6 | 0.020 | p < 1.20e-37 |
| SemEval-2 Most Frequent Sense | | 0.0 | 63.4 | 58.6 | 1.0 | 0.0 | p < 4.244e-23 |
| Best SemEval-2 FScore | | 0.0 | 63.3 | 58.6 | 1.0 | 0.0 | p < 2.893e-23 |
| Best SemEval-2 VMeasure | | 16.2 | 26.7 | 58.3 | 10.7 | 0.367 | p < 1.956e-14 |
| Best SemEval-2 Supervised Recall | | 15.7 | 49.7 | 62.4 | 11.5 | 0.187 | p < 8.910e-19 |

Table 3: Unsupervised and Supervised scores on the SemEval-2010 WSI Task for each feature and clustering models, with reference scores for the top performing systems for each evaluation shown below.

set that did not have mappings from OntoNotes to WordNet 3.0 senses, and additional 23 words that only had two senses, which prevented testing for a similarity bias. The remaining 67 words yielded 4,097 test instances for evaluation.

Each instance of the test corpus was tested for sense confusion, recording the similarity of the incorrectly assigned sense and the gold standard sense. The resulting incorrect assignments are transformed into an error distribution according by accumulating error counts into similarity bins where each bin has a range of 0.02. We analyze the WSI systems defined in section 4 as well as the results of three systems that participated in Task 14 and scored the highest on the paired FScore, V-measure, or Supervised Recall evaluations.

To quantify the impact, we compare each system's error distribution against a null model over the set of incorrect test instances missed by that system. In the null model, the incorrect sense for each instance is selected with uniform probability from the available senses. This behavior produces a distribution with no similarity bias. The cumulative error distribution for the null model is not uniform due to multiple sense pairings having the same similarity.[4] To quantify the difference between a system's error distribution and corresponding null model, we calculate the G-test as a measure of Goodness of Fit (GoF). The resulting p-values reflect the probability of observing the system's error distribution if there was no bias from sense-similarity.

### 5.2 Results and Discussion

We compare the error analysis against the evaluation measures of Task 14. Table 3 displays the eval-

[4]Verb senses often have a JCN similarity of 0 due to having no shared parent within the WordNet verb sense hierarchy, which results in high frequency distribution around 0.

uation measures. We also report the average number of clusters per word, the cluster purity, and the p-value when using Eq. 2 to measure sense similarity. Figure 2 visualizes the error distributions for the four clustering algorithms on 5-word co-occurrence features. The distributions in Figure 2 are representative of those of the other context models, which we omit due to space. Each plot reflects the frequency at which a sense with the specified similarity was confused for the correct sense.

The low p-values in Table 3 indicate a significant deviation from the null model. Examining the shape of the error distribution in Figure 2 reveals a noticeable skew towards higher similarity when an incorrect sense assignment is made. This distribution skew is also consistent for both similarity measures.

Comparing the Task 14 results in Table 3 to the sense confusion trends in in Figure 2 highlights an interesting pattern among the various models: as the number of induced sense clusters increases, the error distribution better approximates the null model. Specifically, the GoF for all models was well correlated with cluster purity ($\rho$=0.66), and the number of clusters ($\rho$=0.76). CBC generated the highest number of clusters and has a sense confusion distribution that closely matches the null model, indicating that it is less affected by sense similarity. In comparison, all of the Streaming K-Means models, which have the fewest clusters, differ noticeably from the null model. Spectral Clustering, which also generates fewer clusters than CBC, has an observed confusion rate that differs from the baseline. K-Means again reduces to the MFS baseline.

When comparing along the feature sets, we see that on average Word Order features generate the highest V-Measure scores, highest purity, and highest p-values for Streaming K-Means and CBC. This result correlates well with the average number of features seen per context: Word Order contexts used 0.03% of the feature space while contexts in other feature spaces used between 0.07% and 0.12% of the feature space, suggesting that the SemEval measures are determined in part by feature space density. Similarly, 25-word co-occurrence features had the highest percentage of features used per context, 0.12%, and generated the lowest V-Measure, purity score, and p-value for 3 clustering models.

These scores support another known trend in the SemEval-2 evaluation: the performance on the V-Measure is proportional to the number of induced sense clusters, while the paired FScore is inversely proportional. But what is surprising is that models which perform well against the V-Measure also exhibit a smaller sense similarity bias, suggesting that CBC and similar clustering methods are suitable for situations where competing senses of a word have a high degree of overlap.

As a final comparison, we also computed the sense bias for the top 3 SemEval systems under each measure. The best of these models are listed in Table 3. We did not find any consistent trends between the V-Measure, purity, and p-value among these models. The top F-Scoring models all used either a first or second order co-occurrence feature space similar to ours (Kern et al., 2010; Pedersen, 2010), whereas the top supervised score was achieved by a graph-based system (Klapaftis and Manandhar, 2008).

## 6 Future Work and Conclusion

We presented a two evaluation for WSI approaches and examined the performance of a wide range of algorithms. The results raise a potential issue for clustering-based WSI approaches: sense discrimination degrades notably as the sense relatedness increases. We highlight three potential avenues for future research. First, this methodology should be applied to additional WSI models, such as graph-based (Klapaftis and Manandhar, 2008; Navigli and Crisafulli, 2010) and probabilistic models (Dinu and Lapata, 2010; Elshamy et al., 2010). Second, we plan to extend the analysis to different sense distributions, varying number of senses, and for human annotated sense similarity data. Third, this evaluation makes the simplifying assumption of one sense per instance; however, Erk et al. (2009) note that the relations between senses may cause a single word instance to evoke multiple senses within the same context. Therefore, a future experiment should consider how WSI systems might address learning senses given the presence of multiple, similar senses for a single instance.

All models, associated data sets, testing framework, and scores have been released as a part of the open-source S-Space Package (Jurgens and Stevens, 2010b).[5]

[5] `http://code.google.com/p/airhead-research/`

## References


Eneko Agirre and Aitor Soroa. 2007. Semeval-2007 task 02: Evaluating word sense induction and discrimination systems. In *Proceedings of the Fourth International Workshop on Semantic Evaluations*, pages 7–12. ACL, June.

Javier Artiles, Enrique Amigó, and Julio Gonzalo. 2009. The role of named entities in web people search. In *Proceedings of EMNLP*, pages 534–542. ACL.

Marco Baroni, Brian Murphy, Eduard Barbu, and Massimo Poesio. 2010. Strudel: A corpus-based semantic model based on properties and types. *Cognitive Science*, 34(2):222–254.

Stefan Bordag. 2006. Word sense induction: Triplet-based clustering and automatic evaluation. In *Proceedings of the 11th EACL*, pages 137–144.

Vladimir Braverman, Adam Meyerson, Rafail Ostrovsky, Alan Roytman, Michael Shindler, and Brian Tagiku. 2011. Streaming k-means on Well-Clusterable Data. In *Proceedings of SODA 2011*.

Alexander Budanitsky and Graeme Hirst. 2006. Evaluating wordnet-based measures of semantic distance. *Computational Linguistics*, 32(1):13–47, March.

Nathanael Chambers and Dan Jurafsky. 2010. Improving the Use of Pseudo-Words for Evaluating Selectional Preferences. In *ACL 2010*.

David Cheng, Ravi Kannan, Santosh Vempala, and Grant Wang. 2006. A divide-and-merge methodology for clustering. *ACM Transactions on Database Systems (TODS)*, 31(4):1499–1525.

Irina Chugur, Julio Gonzalo, and Felisa Verdejo. 2002. Polysemy and sense proximity in the senseval-2 test suite. In *Proceedings of the ACL-02 workshop on Word sense disambiguation: recent successes and future directions - Volume 8*, WSD '02, pages 32–39, Stroudsburg, PA, USA. Association for Computational Linguistics.

Stephen Clark and David Weir. 2002. Class-based probability estimation using a semantic hierarchy. *Computational Linguistics*, 28(2):187–206.

Georgiana Dinu and Mirella Lapata. 2010. Measuring distributional similarity in context. In *Proceedings of the 2010 Conference on Empirical Methods in Natural Language Processing*, pages 1162–1172. Association for Computational Linguistics.

Beate Dorow and Dominic Widdows. 2003. Discovering corpus-specific word senses. In *Proceedings of the 10th EACL*, pages 79–82.

Wesam Elshamy, Doina Caragea, and William H. Hsu. 2010. KSU KDD: Word sense induction by clustering in topic space. In *Proceedings of the 5th International Workshop on Semantic Evaluation*, pages 367–370. Association for Computational Linguistics.

Katrin Erk, Diana McCarthy, and Nicholas Gaylord. 2009. Investigations on word senses and word usages. In *Proceedings of the Joint Conference of the 47th Annual Meeting of the ACL and the 4th International Joint Conference on Natural Language Processing of the AFNLP: Volume 1*, pages 10–18. Association for Computational Linguistics.

William A. Gale, Kenneth W. Church, and David Yarowsky. 1992. Work on statistical methods for word sense disambiguation. In *AAAI Fall Symposium on Probabilistic Approaches to Natural Language*, pages 54–60.

Susan Gauch and Robert P. Futrelle. 1993. Experiments in automatic word class and word sense identification for information retrieval. In *Proceedings of the 3rd Annual Symposium on Document Analysis and Information Retrieval*, pages 425–434.

Zhengyan He, Yang Song, and Houfeng Wang. 2010. Applying Spectral Clustering for Chinese Word Sense Induction. In *Proceedings of the CIPS-SIGHAN Joint Conference on Chinese Language Processing*.

Eduard Hovy, Mitchell Marcus, Martha Palmer, Lance Ramshaw, and Ralph Weischedel. 2006. OntoNotes: the 90% solution. In *Proceedings of the Human Language Technology Conference of the NAACL*, pages 57–60. Association for Computational Linguistics.

Jay J. Jiang and David W. Conrath. 1997. Semantic Similarity Based on Corpus Statistics and Lexical Taxonomy. In *Proceedings of International Conference on Research in Computational Linguistics*,.

Michael N. Jones, Walter Kintsch, and Doughlas J. K. Mewhort. 2006. High-dimensional semantic space accounts of priming. *Journal of Memory and Language*, 55:534–552.

David Jurgens and Keith Stevens. 2010a. HERMIT: Using word ordering applied to the Sense Induction task of SemEval-2. In *Proceedings of the 5th International Workshop on Semantic Evaluations*. Association for Computational Linguistics.

David Jurgens and Keith Stevens. 2010b. The S-Space Package: An Open Source Package for Word Space Models. In *Proceedings of the ACL 2010 System Demonstrations*.

Roman Kern, Markus Muhr, and Michael Granitzer. 2010. KCDC: Word sense induction by using grammatical dependencies and sentence phrase structure. In *Proceedings of the 5th International Workshop on Semantic Evaluation*, pages 351–354. Association for Computational Linguistics.

Ioannis P. Klapaftis and Suresh Manandhar. 2008. Word sense induction using graphs of collocations. In *Proceeding of the 2008 conference on ECAI 2008: 18th European Conference on Artificial Intelligence*, pages 298–302.

Ioannis P. Klapaftis and Suresh Manandhar. 2010. Taxonomy learning using word sense induction. In *Human Language Technologies: The 2010 Annual Conference of the North American Chapter of the Association for Computational Linguistics*, HLT '10, pages 82–90, Morristown, NJ, USA. Association for Computational Linguistics.

Suresh Manandhar and Ioannis P. Klapaftis. 2009. SemEval-2010 Task 14: Evaluation Setting for Word Sense Induction & Disambiguation Systems. In *NAACL-HLT 2009 Workshop on Semantic Evaluations: Recent Achievements and Future Directions*.

Suresh Manandhar, Ioannis P. Klapaftis, Dmitriy Dligach, and Sameer S. Pradhan. 2010. SemEval-2010 task 14: Word sense induction & disambiguation. In *Proceedings of the 5th International Workshop on Semantic Evaluation*, pages 63–68. Association for Computational Linguistics.

Diana McCarthy. 2006. Relating WordNet senses for word sense disambiguation. *Making Sense of Sense: Bringing Psycholinguistics and Computational Linguistics Together*, page 17.

Roberto Navigli and Giuseppe Crisafulli. 2010. Inducing word senses to improve web search result clustering. In *Proceedings of the 2010 Conference on Empirical Methods in Natural Language Processing*, pages 116–126. Association for Computational Linguistics.

Roberto Navigli. 2009. Word sense disambiguation: a survey. *ACM Computing Surveys*, 41(2):1–69.

Andrew Ng, Michael Jordan, and Yair Weiss. 2001. On spectral clustering: Analysis and an algorithm. In *Advances in Neural Information Processing Systems 14: Proceeding of the 2001 Conference*, pages 849–856.

Joakim Nivre, Johan Hall, and Jens Nilsson. 2006. MaltParser: A data-driven parser-generator for dependency parsing. In *Proceedings of LREC*, pages 2216–2219.

Sebastian Padó and Mirella Lapata. 2007. Dependency-Based Construction of Semantic Space Models. *Computational Linguistics*, 33(2):161–199.

Martha Palmer, Hoa Trang Dang, and Christiane Fellbaum. 2007. Making fine-grained and coarse-grained sense distinctions, both manually and automatically. *Natural Language Engineering*, 13(02):137–163.

Patrick Pantel and Dekang Lin. 2002. Discovering word senses from text. In *Proceedings of ACM Conference on Knowledge Discovery and Data Mining (KDD-02)*, pages 613–619.

Ted Pedersen and Rebecca Bruce. 1997. Distinguishing word senses in untagged text. In *Proceedings of the Second Conference on Empirical Methods in Natural Language Processing*, pages 197–207, August.

Ted Pedersen and Anagha Kulkarni. 2006. Automatic cluster stopping with criterion functions and the gap statistic. In *In Proceedings of the Demo Session of HLT/NAACL*, pages 276–279.

Ted Pedersen, Siddharth Patwardhan, and Jason Michelizzi. 2004. Wordnet:: Similarity: measuring the relatedness of concepts. In *Demonstration Papers at HLT-NAACL 2004 on XX*, pages 38–41. Association for Computational Linguistics.

Ted Pedersen. 2010. Duluth-WSI: SenseClusters Applied to the Sense Induction Task of SemEval-2. In *Proceedings of the SemEval 2010 Workshop : the 5th International Workshop on Semantic Evaluations*, pages 363–366, July.

Yves Peirsman, Kris Heylen, and Dirk Geeraerts. 2008. Size matters. Tight and loose context definitions in English word space models. In *ESSLLI Workshop on Distributional Lexical Semantics*, pages 34–41.

Andrew Rosenberg and Julia Hirschberg. 2007. V-measure: A conditional entropy-based external cluster evaluation measure. In *Proceedings of the 2007 Joint Conference on Empirical Methods in Natural Language Processing and Computational Natural Language Learning (EMNLP-CoNLL)*. ACL, June.

Magnus Sahlgren, Anders Holst, and Pentti Kanerva. 2008. Permutations as a means to encode order in word space. In *Proceedings of the 30th Annual Meeting of the Cognitive Science Society (CogSci'08)*.

Hinrich Schütze, 1992. *Context Space*, pages 113–120. AAAI Press, Menlo Park, CA.

Robert Tibshirani, Guenther Walther, and Trevor Hastie. 2000. Estimating the number of clusters in a dataset via the gap statistic. *Journal Royal Statistics Society B*, 63:411–423.

Kristina Toutanova, Dan Klein, Christopher Manning, and Yoram Singer. 2003. Feature-rich part-of-speech tagging with a cyclic dependency network. pages 252–259.

Akira Utsumi. 2010. Exploring the Relationship between Semantic Spaces and Semantic Relations. In *Proceedings of the 7th International Conference on Language Resources and Evaluation (LREC'2010)*, pages 257–262.

Ulrike von Luxburg. 2007. A tutorial on spectral clustering. *Statistics and Computing*, 17(4):395–416.

Ying Zhao and George Karypis. 2001. Criterion functions for document clustering: Experiments and analysis. Technical Report UMN CS 01-040, University of Minnesota.

# Author Index